Believed to be
ALIVE

Believed to be ALIVE

Captain John W. Thornton
with John W. Thornton Jr.

BLUEJACKET BOOKS

Naval Institute Press
Annapolis, Maryland

Naval Institute Press
291 Wood Road
Annapolis, MD 21402

Library of Congress Cataloging-in-Publication Data
Thornton, John W., 1922–
    Believed to be alive / by John W. Thornton with John W. Thornton, Jr.; introduction by Edwin P. Hoyt.
        p. cm. — (Bluejacket books)
        ISBN 1-59114-864-2 (alk. paper)
        1. Korean War, 1950–1953—Prisoners and prisons, American. 2. Prisoners of war—Korea (North) 3. Prisoners of war—United States. 4. Thornton, John W., 1922– I. Title. II. Series.
        DS921.6.T49 2004
        951.904'27—dc22

                                        2004049897

Printed in the United States of America on acid-free paper ∞

11 10 09 08 07 06 05 04   9 8 7 6 5 4 3 2 1

To my God, my family and the
P.O.W.-M.I.A.'s of Korea and Southeast Asia
who never came home

Preface

With the passage of time the Korean War has begun its retreat into obscurity, joining the ranks of western history's forgotten wars such as the Spanish-American, Boer, Crimean or Tripolitan. Probably because of the more widespread national traumas associated with the Second World War and Vietnam, my generation and its children are most mindful of the trials those two conflicts represent. Beside them, the Korean ordeal now stands in shadow. The record of the Korean War is a somewhat spotty one, perhaps for the same reason that "tie" ball games are always less interesting to hear about than the big wins or the major upsets described in Monday morning papers. This book then is an attempt to broaden the accounts of the Korean experience—the war we tied.

The events primarily surround my own activities during the war and those of my family. However, it is one of my hopes that these will serve to mirror a sadly common experience. We obviously did not pass through this crucible alone and my ordeals in Korea and those of my family at home were by no means unique to us. In some critical respects, we were far more fortunate than many—I lived where as other husbands, fathers and sons died. Likewise, my family emerged from its crisis intact while others were not so favored. Nevertheless, *Believed to Be Alive* may be viewed as a tale not of one man or one family but of many. In this larger sense, it is also the story of people swept up in the turmoil of war and captivity, people both living and dead, some of whose stories have never been told but should have been. At the same time, I have sought to interpret various events in terms of how these people survived them. For most, the keys to survival lay in four areas: faith, family, fraternity and fortitude.

The descriptions of various incidents and the language employed may offend sensitive tastes. Perhaps that is as it should be since the experience of combat, cruel captivity and violent death are by nature repugnant. Thus if a sense of revulsion is evoked by a particular event, it may well be that the intended point has been made. I would also note that the terms ''gook'' and ''chink'' should be recognized for the willful slurs that they were, cast at a despised enemy. They in no way apply to those free Asians by whose sides we fought and died.

The individuals who are named in these pages represent only a few of those with whom I proudly served both before and during my captivity. I have left out many other fine men whose legacies of courage and compassion are well known to me and my fellow P.O.W.'s. Those I have chosen to include represent a good cross-section of exploits, be they heroic, humorous or tragic. While some of these men may be less than flattered by the particular event or circumstances in which they appear, it is not my intent to embarrass or humiliate them. Quite to the contrary, it is my purpose to demonstrate the grave hazards, the mishaps and the challenges which men thrust into the harsh realities of warfare must face. There are other men whose stories appear here whom I have chosen to leave unnamed for a variety of reasons, not the least of which are the lapses in memory caused by the passage of thirty years. But more often their names have been omitted for the benefit of surviving relatives who deserve to be spared any reminders or revelations of the malevolent circumstances surrounding the demise of someone they loved. And while there were cowards and traitors among us in Korea, none of them will be found here, for it is a story of honorable men. Although they deserve notorious ignominy, I have chosen to exile them to anonymity.

Finally, I would like to pay special tribute to my wife Jinny for being with me, always, through wars and peace, and for giving me love and empathy during the 27 years it has taken me to get this story written; to daughter Joy for being here; and last but not least to our son Jay whose reading, revising, and rewriting of the manuscript contributed so much to my attainment of the impossible dream—this book.

And it is small repayment but a great pleasure to acknowledge the help of Bill Gordon who read and contributed to the manuscript, then led me to publisher Paul Eriksson. I am also in debt to many of my friends who responded generously by taking their time to read the manuscript and, liking it, encouraging me to go on.

For giving me love, guidance, and special understanding, my humble thanks to my family and to all.

J.W.T.

Pensacola, Florida

Contents

Introduction

Somehow, unpopular wars don't make for popular reading except in the debunking department, and as the years pass the tales of the men who fought these wars tend to be forgotten. Like the Viet Nam war, the Korean war of 1950-53 was a most unsatisfactory conflict in terms of military decision, and that negativism has been reflected in the literature dealing with that war.

Given that general attitude, the public has tended to shy away from such war stories. I hope they won't shy away from this one, because Captain Thornton has brought to life an aspect of the Korea war about which very little is known. Even in M*A*S*H* the helicopter opens the scene each week, but after that it is forgotten again. The Korean War brought to infantry tactics a whole new perspective that has not been discussed by many writers. Captain Thornton had many unique experiences in that war, starting with his service with the Thai frigate *Prasae*. Here was a grim reminder that in the Korea war the enemy was just as likely to be the elements as the North Koreans or the Chinese.

But Captain Thornton's most important contribution to the story of the Korean war is his personal account of captivity. That story began on March 31,

1951, when Thornton was assigned to a dangerous mission in connection with intelligence activities. He was to fly to a high ridge, 65 miles behind enemy lines and pick up and evacuate a team of 24 agents. He succeeded in getting only three out but vital military information went with them. In this sense the mission was a success. However, the remainder failed. Captain Thornton's helicopter was shot down while attempting a landing on a small clearing atop the ridge. The North Koreans surged forward and before the day was out, Captain Thornton found himself inside enemy territory, on the ground. He managed to elude the enemy for ten days, but was then captured. And the bulk of the story deals with his life in prison camp. Captain Thornton, however, has included an element seldom seen in military adventures. He has detailed for the reader the impact of his own capture on those dear to him, and in so doing has added something that makes his story poignant.

The remainder of the book deals with one man's struggle against his captors. The North Koreans offered him comfort in exchange for propaganda. He was to broadcast to the Americans in their behalf and help them write leaflets. He refused and he was abused for it, month after month. He was sent to school for "re-education." The school was actually a high-level interrogation center at Pyoktong. But by October 1951, the North Koreans seemed to have given up on their attempt to use Thornton, and he was transferred to a prisoner-of-war camp at Ping-chong-ni. Here he remained until September of 1953 when he was repatriated. The story of these years is a reminder of the quiet heroism of most of the men captured by the enemy during the Korean war. Captain Thornton has chosen to write about those who did not surrender mentally nor morally, and to say relatively little about "the cowards and traitors" whom he consigns to anonymity.

Throughout the account, Thornton has lent a sense of reality and urgency to his story by reporting what happened on the home front too, from the false report that he had died in prison camp to the joy of the homecoming. All in all, it is an inspiring story and a contribution of note to the writings about the Korean War.

Edwin P. Hoyt

Waimea, Hawaii

Believed to be ALIVE

PROLOGUE

And so the great democracies triumphed. And so were able to resume the follies that had nearly cost them their lives.

—Winston Churchill

It was only one day after the Japanese had signed the documents of surrender aboard the *USS Missouri,* in September, 1945. I was flying my heavily armed Navy Corsair fighter-bomber toward the peninsula of Korea which thrusts 600 miles south from the coast of eastern Asia, dividing the Sea of Japan from the Yellow Sea. My air group and two other air groups were policing this area, keeping it secure until our army of occupation made its amphibious landings that were scheduled to commence on September 8th and continue for three days. During these operations, we were to assure that the landings were unopposed.

As I approached this Asian "Land of the Morning Calm" from the sea, its mountainous countryside seemed suddenly to leap into view in a sort of bas-relief. I knew from our briefings that three-quarters of its area was hills, with mountains rising to an average height of over 1400 feet. Making landfall, it was like flying up an inclined ramp as we headed north where most of the higher mountains lay. There, situated on the Chinese-Korean border was the highest peak, Mount Paektu San (White Head) which reached over 8000 feet. This peak and everything north of the 38th parallel now belonged to the Communists. It was the day we allowed the

Bamboo Curtain to drop, trapping everyone north of it.

Ironically, the entire region was a tinderbox, despite the new peace that had just been won. Koreans opting for freedom in the American zone of occupation were fleeing south in droves. Russian troops were also moving south, penetrating as far as the 37th parallel, sixty miles into the soon-to-be-occupied American area. For four months since the collapse of the Third Reich, the Russians had been looting Germany and they now turned their well-developed skills on Korea. Russian troops began dismantling as much of the area's industrial base as possible. Our Russian ally had five days within this strip of U.S.-mandated territory to raze factories and gut manufacturing plants of their machinery. The task was accomplished with amazing speed. Utilizing the strong backs of southern-bound refugees, the Soviets turned them around northward to haul the spoils of war across the line to their own zone. Whole machine shops were denuded of lathes, presses and precision grinding machines, efficiently spirited away before we could get our troops ashore and into the area.

All the while, we flew overhead, impotently. We reported these gross violations of the post-war agreements, requested further instructions and were ordered to continue to observe and keep our weapons on safe. We did, and bit our tongues. The Japanese garrison's surrendered arms passed quickly into the hands of the North Korean Communists. The beaten soldiers of Imperial Japan then disappeared behind the Bamboo Curtain, prisoners of war never to be seen again. It was a power vacuum quickly filled by the Communists.

Despite this opening phase of Soviet and Asian communism's war against the West, American's embryonic policies of obsessive restraint and limited response became increasingly evident as Russian pilots flying in American-built lend-lease aircraft began putting bullet holes in some of our fighter aircrafts' tails. Again we could not return fire. We were shot at and hit over Port Arthur, Mukden and Dairen. But the order was *hold your fire, Americans must exercise restraint.* The most we could do was buzz the hell out of this new opponent and flat hat their asses off as they thumbed their noses at our military might. As a young, trained-to-win American fighter pilot, I swallowed hard and gulped down this bitter pill. It was difficult to observe and accept American diplomacy giving up what the American Armed Forces had so recently won. But as I see it now, giving up half a country was not nearly as shocking as seeing the beginning phases of a process of benign neglect that would ultimately result in the loss of nearly an entire continent. Free, Nationalist China would be Communist China by 1948.

With Korea partitioned and the safety of its southern half not in immediate jeopardy, we were soon deployed to the coast of China. It was a pleasure flying shows of strength over Shanghai, backing up Chiang Kai-shek's troops who had disarmed the Japanese and were enjoying their new-found freedom by exercising their power on the ground backed up by our power in the air. It helped to maintain a brief interlude of peace until our troops arrived and before civil war began in earnest. As we awaited the arrival of our own troops, others were on the move heading south. Our sorties were shifted to the far north to meet them—so far north we finally reached the Great Wall of China, the longest fortified defense line ever built. Now it was the demarcation line separating the Communists in Manchuria from free China below.

The Great Wall was a magnificent sight to behold, a true wonder of the world. From our cockpits flying at 10,000 feet, this "Wall of Ten Thousand Li" stretched before our eyes like a huge snake disappearing over the horizon. A remarkable engineering feat, it followed a winding course over the mountains and valleys, stretching the distance from New York to Omaha. Originally a crude, fence-like structure made mostly of clay in 200 B.C., the present wall was completed in the 1300's A.D. Standing twenty-five feet high with 35-foot watchtowers every two to three hundred yards, this wall of brick and granite blocks had been formidable enough to stop the northern Tartar tribes from moving south to invade China proper. With its top paved in brick set in lime, the Wall formed a roadway along which the emperor's military could move. While the Wall served at various times in history as a successful line of defense, these last days of September 1945 saw it being breached by a Red Tide.

From the isolated Mongolian north, bordered on the east by the Yellow Sea, to the area south of Shanghai to the China Sea; all of this would form the stage on which would be performed the dissection of the Nationalist regime, our World War II ally and the establishment of a Communist People's Republic. Employing a north-to-south strategy, the Communists sought to capture and consolidate Manchuria and north China, for possession of Manchuria has historically been the key to the whole of China. Mao Tse-tung's forces received "indirect" military aid in the form of Japanese war materiel captured by the Soviets in Manchuria who in turn passed it on, substantially building up Mao's strength. And so it went.

From aloft, we kept our guns on safe and watched the Trans-Siberian railroad running from Siberia to

Manchuria and down the east coast of China being taken mile by mile along with all the cities and towns adjacent to it. As was related to me years later by a communist Chinese officer named Chong, "The Peoples' Liberation Army moved into a town from its northern end. By the time they moved out of the south end, all Nationalist soldiers had "volunteered" to fight for the Liberation forces and all the Reactionary officers had been executed by these Volunteers." From fewer than 20,000 survivors of the Long March, Mao now had one million regular troops built mainly on these Nationalist surrenders. The days our friend and ally Chiang Kai-shek and his Kuomintang Army would enjoy on the mainland were numbered. They would get no help from us now and would eventually be forced to retreat to the island of Formosa.

In two short months, I saw a country-and-a-half set up to go down the drain. They were gelded by the Communists while the American government sat in perpetual standby position. Most of the junior officers and aviators who were there thought they were witnessing World War III's beginning in those early days, and were willing to carry this battle to the proper enemy's doorstep while we and America still possessed the greatest military power in the world. Then, as now, I asked myself why the mightiest and most benevolent nation on Earth chose to yield little by little for a short period of tranquility. If it was dictated by the tenets of some grander but unannounced plan of diplomacy, it was not made known to us. Worst of all, if there was such a plan, it didn't work, as it turns out. For in less than five years, we were at war again with these very people. On the other hand, if there was no plan, the consequences of this oversight were disastrous. As I flew over the Great Wall in the autumn of 1945, I wondered where it would all end, never suspecting that the great convulsions of history unfolding below me would draw me back to Asia twice more in my life—once again to Korea and two decades later, Vietnam.

PART ONE
KOREA
Winter 1950-1951

1

War is Hell.
—Gen. W. T. Sherman

It was now 1950. Armed with Soviet weapons, North Korean Communist forces invaded South Korea on June 25, 1950. Six days later, a battalion of the U.S. 24th Infantry Division was rushed in from Japan. The division was soon seeing action against the enemy on the outskirts of Seoul.

While the war was raging in Korea, I had switched from flying fighters to learning to pilot a helicopter, and completed the prescribed training syllabus on October 28. I was now a qualified helicopter pilot, the 298th in all the Navy and Marine Corps. I had great expectations of being deployed to the Mediterranean Sea.

By November 1950, the North Koreans had been completely beaten. Their capital, Pyongyang, was in Allied hands and their remnant forces were scattered and disorganized. The victory was almost at its climax when the Chinese avalanche crashed over the Yalu River. They opened a massive counter-offensive, hurling our forces into retreat. Early in December, American and United Nations forces were trapped at the Chang-Jin Reservoir. Surrounded by Chinese, 20,000 U.S. Marines and Army infantrymen began bloody withdrawal from this area in northeast Korea to reach the port of Hungnam.

At Lakehurst, New Jersey, on the morning of December 4, 1950, a priority-one Top Secret message was received by the commanding officer of my helicopter squadron. The Chief of Naval Operations requested that twelve pilots, twenty-five crewmen and eight helicopters be made ready for airlifting to the West Coast by 0800 hours the next morning. By one o'clock in the afternoon, I had received my own orders to move out along with the thirty-six others at 0800 the following morning just like the man said. Due to the secretiveness of this operation, I had to ask and was given permission to drive to my home in Philadelphia, tell my wife about the orders, pack my gear and as they say in the Navy, give her a bouquet of roses and kiss her good-bye. Since I commuted regularly between the Naval Air Station at Lakehurst and my residence in Philly, coming home a little earlier than usual would be no surprise to my wife Jinny. There would be no cause for alarm when we greeted each other with our usual hug and kiss. Certainly our two-year-old son Jay would be glad to see me home early and after a soft smooch he would ask, "Pay (play) toys Daddy?" This was one of those days, unfortunately, in which there would be little time to play.

The Jersey pine trees lining the sides of the highway were a blur in my peripheral vision as I sped homeward on Route 70. I wondered how my family would take all this. Would my young son understand? Would my wife be able to take it when I announced that I would be leaving so precipitously at the crack of dawn for a far-off Asian war? Thinking of myself I asked, How do I break the news to her? Right after I get inside the front door? Wait until after dinner? Can't wait too long because I have to pack. The radio was on and an up-and-coming singer whom I had told Jinny I thought would become very popular one day, was singing a beautiful new song, "Be My Love." To my ears, he had a voice like the famous Italian tenor Enrico Caruso. His name was Mario Lanza. The song reminded me of Jinny and our love for each other. I could hardly know that this new vocalist and his song were to be one of the mainstays of my survival. Years later I would learn that the song and Mario Lanza had indeed won wide notice in 1951, he especially for his title role in the motion picture "The Great Caruso."

The pine woods were giving way to houses and commercial buildings and as I approached Red Lion Circle, I estimated that I would arrive at home around 4:30 p.m. This would give me only twelve hours to say hello, eat, pack my gear and then—good-bye. Since both Jinny and I were always straightforward and open with each other, I decided to break the news to her soon after I arrived. I paid my toll to cross the Tacony-Palmyra Bridge into Philadelphia. The traffic was heavy since the Frankford factory workers were letting out. I wondered how much time would pass before I would come this way again. The sun was starting to set on this wintry December day as I drove my car to a stop in front of my row house. It was a pretty home and always cozy to come into.

I received my expected welcome and Jinny said we would eat around six. Since Christmas was only three weeks away, our conversation centered on this. It would be our son's third Christmas and we talked about the many things we had planned for his Santa Claus day. Jinny described all the tasks I needed to do, from setting up trains to buying presents, in the short time left. I knew the time had come to tell her that I would not be here then; that I would not be with my family in the celebrating of Christmas.

"Honey," I said, "I just got my orders to Korea."
She looked at me, not too upset.

"For when?"

"Tomorrow morning." She stared in disbelief.

"How long?" she asked.

"Four, maybe six months. I don't really know for sure."

"Well, it won't be as dangerous as World War II when you were flying fighters. You almost got killed then. Helicopters are safer." As always, Jinny had taken it like a trooper.

"Yeah. Well. I guess I ought to start getting some things together."

Hurried telephone calls were made to our folks, and I made arrangements with our neighbor to drive me back down to Lakehurst early next morning. We tried to make the most of our last few hours together. It was not our first experience at saying indefinite farewells, but at best it was always tough. Our son Jay and I played a little together until it was time to ready him for bed. I felt that even though he was only two-and-a-half years old, we should have a little man-to-man talk. I told him the reasons why I had to leave him and his mother alone, that he had to take over for me, be the man of the house and help his mother whenever he could. He was the man in charge. I kissed him and Jinny tucked him into bed. The long night had begun.

The alarm clock loudly proclaimed that it was 5:00 a.m. We didn't need much to rouse us since neither of us had slept well. We were finishing a quick breakfast when a knock on the door announced the arrival of our good friend and neighbor, Joe Miller, who would drive me down to Lakehurst. I took my last peek at Jay who was peacefully sleeping, leaned down, kissed him lightly on the cheek and told the new man of the house good-bye for awhile. As I came quietly down the stairs, Jinny was standing there silently. We embraced and I kissed her on the neck, cheek and lips. With a heavy case of the blues, I picked up my bags and headed down the cellar steps and out the back door where Joe was waiting with his car. As we drove out the long driveway behind the row houses on that dark December morning, I waved good-bye to all that I loved. My odyssey was beginning.

* * *

Joe got me to the air station in plenty of time, wished me *bon voyage* and departed. All hands were there. The eight helicopters had been disassembled and crated for transcontinental airlift and we stood by, waiting for five cargo planes to arrive. They came on schedule, we loaded, and ten hours later landed in San Diego, California. We off-loaded the planes, then boarded an aircraft carrier. Within two weeks, naval history's first mass take-off of helicopters from a carrier's decks occurred and we were in Asian waters. The entire operation, conducted in total secrecy, was a huge success and was reported this way in December 27 newspapers:

> The giant aircraft carrier Valley Forge, which has returned to action off Korea was completely reloaded with supplies, ammunition and planes in an around-the-clock operation in San Diego that took only three days, it was reported today. The 27,000 ton carrier, which arrived in San Diego on December 1 for an overhaul was ordered returned to duty immediately following the Chinese intervention in the Korean War. The carrier remained in port five days, one hour and eight minutes. The loading was accomplished in three days and included a record of 2,000 tons of supplies and ammunition. An entire air group was assigned to the carrier.

During her stay in port the Valley Forge received a complete paint job.

While *we* knew that helicopters, pilots and qualified crewmen were in extremely short supply, we did not want the enemy to know. Accordingly, no mention of rotary wing aircraft was mentioned in the news. Stripping our east-coast squadrons of men and equipment would have made useful and interesting intelligence reading for our opponents.

Once again I found myself flying over the Yellow Sea, heading for Korea. But instead of speeding along in the fastest fighter in the world as in 1945, I was cruising along at sixty miles per hour in the fastest helicopter then available, in 1950. Some things never change though. The Korean political scenario was as it was in 1945, the only exception being that a cold war had gone hot. The players were all the same and so were the stakes. The Chinese had attacked in strength, sending four armies against the U.N. The assault crumpled the U.N.'s right flank and tore a hold in the defenses to the west. We were withdrawing along the entire front. The wedge between Eighth Army troops in the west and the Tenth Corps in the east was ever widening. General MacArthur was at an extreme disadvantage because of his Commander-in-Chief's orders proscribing the use of air strikes against the Communist troops and supply dumps being massed north of the Yalu River in Manchuria.

But that was up north. Having departed Itazuke, Japan, I was making my approach to Pusan after a two-hour transit of the Yellow Sea. Once again the mountain ranges along the coast dominated my view as I landed in this battered city of South Korea. The chief port of Korea and the nearest to Japan, Pusan was now the temporary capital. Its normal population of one million was now swollen to over three million as white-clad refugees streamed in. The scars of heavy fighting were everywhere as the U.N. forces had broken out of the Pusan Perimeter only three months before after one of the most spectacular military defense efforts of all time. But now the U.N. was in retreat again.

The very next day found me heading north, refueling at Taegu, the western terminus of the Perimeter, and then going across the Naktong River. Maps were poor so I chose to follow, generally, a railroad running from Pusan to Seoul. Other terrain features were blanketed with snow. The extemely harsh winter became increasingly inclement as we flew north. The temperature kept dropping toward zero and below as the cold Mongolian winds blew down on us. These fierce north winds and the bitter cold had turned all rivers and lakes to stone. As I looked down on the whitened ground, Korea appeared to be a land of snow and lonely villages with little else visible. The houses were huddled together around a common well. Usually located where the plains met the hills, the village houses always seemed to face south to put their backs to the bitter winds. Even in this cold, I could see women at washing places, slapping their wet and freezing laundry against stones. As I flew into the rugged terrain, it was as I remembered it in 1945, flying up an inclined ramp, only this time I didn't have a powerful engine to pull me along.

As part of my mission was to locate bypassed enemy guerrilla forces, I had flown off the easily traversed railroad route to verify a sighting my crewman had made. We were flying at fifty feet, crawling at twenty miles an hour. A sudden eruption of ground fire quickly verified his sighting. It was, as he suspected, a pocket of approximately five hundred

geurrillas. I applied power and jinked the helicopter
up, down and sideways to get out of their small-arms
range. I succeeded, but in the process managed to
put us up a dead-end valley with too little airspeed to
lift us over the five-hundred-foot mountain ridges
lining our left, right and front. I came to a hover and
slowly turned on the spot to give myself time to
think. I had at least managed to put three miles
between us and the enemy down in the valley.
Would they have gone to cover to avoid further
detection or would they rather take a chance at
shooting me down? I decided, but really had no
choice but to turn around and make a downhill run
through them and the valley again if I were to pick
up enough airspeed and altitude to get over the
mountains. I nosed down and started my run, skimming over oak trees and pines, gaining airspeed
quickly, and some altitude. I ran through the guerrillas, apparently surprising them since they didn't
react quickly enough to open fire. I assumed I had
gained enough altitude and airspeed to turn around
and surmount the peaks. It was like taking a running
leap. My airspeed was over the red-line limit by
about ten to fifteen miles an hour but my rotor
blades felt, sounded and flapped good. I proceeded
to make a slow, easy and gradual turn to maintain
my lift, keep my blades away from a high-speed tip
stall and avoid sinking. It was working! I completed
my reversal, and with 105 miles per hour indicated
airspeed, headed toward the ridge. It loomed larger
and larger as we began, unnervingly, to notice more
details about it. We could see clearly the texture of
the denuded granite portions of its slopes as the steep
mountain beckoned to us like the Sirens of Ulysses.
Slowly I eased up the nose. As we closed in on the
mountain, we skimmed over the tree tops, as I had
sacrificed altitude for precious speed. I told my

trusty bird she could make it as my airspeed decayed. I was milking her for all the power I could get. There was a distance of a hundred feet to go as the forward airspeed dropped from forty to thirty miles per hour. Do I abort and go back down again or is she going to pull us over the top? I made a prayerful plea as she chugged up the hill, her blades whopping at the air. Sluggishly, like the Little Engine That Could, we floated over the crest and breathed a sigh of relief. Skimming along the top of the ridge now, I built up enough translational (forward) lift and sixty miles an hour worth of speed to nose her down and continue my movement north to the town of Suwon.

After reporting my encounter with the guerrillas, and their location, I began to fly parallel to the railroad again. I saw a twenty-car train coming south with black smoke belching out of the locomotive's stack. It was the whitest looking train I had ever seen. From a distance, even the engine showed mostly white instead of the normal black, sooty look of a train locomotive. I suddenly realized that it wasn't camouflage but people. Hundreds of them, clad in the traditional white garb of Korea, covered the train like maggots. Holding on to whatever they could, there were refugees clinging to the engine's cow-catcher, sides and top, back along the freight cars' tops and sides all the way to the caboose. Fleeing south, these half-frozen people were evading the Communist onslaught by every means available. Death by falling off this overloaded train was preferable to being caught by the Reds, and die they did. I saw them fall when their hands, freezing from the cold, lost their grip. Some who fell between the cars lay still on the tracks, mangled by the steel wheels as they were crushed to death. No one looked back, and the train roared south, never slowing.

They dared not stop for fear of being attacked by lurking bands of guerrillas such as we had just observed. It was a heart-rending scene of tragic desperation.

Enemy activity increased as I approached Suwon lying thirty miles south of Seoul. Through my open cabin I could hear the increased sniper fire coming up at me as I dropped in low to land. I touched down in an airfield surrounded by more North Korean guerrillas who were getting hyperactive on its perimeter. They were becoming braver and exposing themselves more in confident anticipation of soon joining forces with the massive body of Communist troops poised to attack just north of Seoul. The situation was deteriorating at the airfield and efforts were already underway in preparation of its abandonment. All heavy equipment had been evacuated and what little remained was to be burned or destroyed.

It snowed like hell that night. My crewman and I were wrapped up in blankets most of the time. We were allowed to have as many as we wanted and when we departed we would be permitted to take as many as we could carry since those left behind would have to be destroyed. We ate steak cooked on an Army field stove and enjoyed other unexpected goodies since all unconsumed foodstuffs, like the blankets, would also go up in smoke. After observing some of the destruct orders being executed, I had little doubt that our present circumstances were growing increasingly precarious. The horrible weather was the type that guerrillas were quite adept at exploiting. That night we slept, or more accurately catnapped, with our carbines and .45 automatics cuddled beside us. My Navy crewman and I never expected to be called upon to help the Army repulse boarders, but when one North Korean attack made a breakthrough and breeched the airfield's perimeter defenses, all hands were ordered on deck to repel the assault. The enemy besiegers paid heavily for their unsuccessful effort that snowy night.

Morning dawned bright at twenty degrees below zero. We took all the extra ammunition, grenades and blankets we could safely load, beyond our own gear, and prepared to depart. We were happy to be going, as the F-51 Mustangs based here at Suwon were taking off, carrying maximum loads of napalm, rockets and bombs toward their assigned targets. Within only five to ten minutes, they would be back on the ground again for a reload, immediate take-off, another close-in strike and return. Seeing this fast cycle of action, I didn't have to be hit in the head to realize the enemy was now getting dangerously near. As I flew off, I decided that Suwon looked best when you were leaving it. But it hardly made any difference, since I was heading into Seoul where 90,000 enemy troops were massing just north of the city across the Han River.

The United Nations forces had already withdrawn from Pyongyang and 205,000 Allied troops had been successfully evacuated from northeast Korea at Hungnam in an amphibious landing in reverse. In the west, the Communists had crossed south of the 38th parallel and Intelligence predicted that they would launch a major offensive on New Year's Day. Despite the drifted snows clogging mountain roads and passes, civilians were pushing and slogging away from the combat zone. Traffic was halted almost more by this human deluge than by the snow drifts. I always found it interesting that while reconnoitering enemy locations, I never had to rely on a map to know when I had crossed the battle lines. It was obvious because the flow of refugees suddenly ceased. And so since everyone else seemed to be headed south, it caused me some anxiety to be flying north toward Seoul. Always the non-conformist, I thought.

The snow which began falling in November would continue to be blown down from the same Manchurian and Siberian low-pressure areas that would also keep the temperatures well below zero through much of the winter. In that grueling environment, the Chinese and North Koreans launched their huge new attack against Seoul on New Year's Eve of 1950. The Intelligence boys had called it pretty close. By January 10, 1951, the U.N. forces had abandoned Seoul to the Communists for the second time in the war and dug in on a line twenty-five miles south of the capital. Briefly, I retreated south with them to a rendezvous with a Japanese-manned LST (Landing Ship—Tank) of World War II vintage, only to find myself heading north again to a fateful encounter with the Thai navy.

2

Calypso came up to him and said: "Poor old fellow! Please don't sit here lamenting anymore, don't let yourself pine away like this. I'm going to send you off at once, and glad to do it. . ." As she said this, the ever-patient man shivered, and said plainly: "I am sure there is something else in your mind goddess, and no kind send-off for me. . ."

—Homer
The Odyssey

The raging weather of winter 1950-51 was in keeping with the best traditions of North Korean winters—only worse. It was as if the season had gone out of its way to show us visiting U.N. troops just what it could do. Winter could have spared itself the effort without disappointing any of us newcomers in the slightest. But it chose to do otherwise.

January 8, 1951 emerged from the aftermath of another bad, but not unique, blizzard. Spawned somewhere deep in the Asian land mass by another one of the infamous Manchurian low-pressure areas, this storm had left for other parts providing us with some degree of relief. Relief was only a relative term, for on this day it meant that winds were down to twenty-five miles per hour with forty-mile gusts, seas eight to ten feet and temperatures sub-zero. Low clouds raced across a menacing sky through which no sun penetrated. For the moment, there was no snow falling.

It had not been so the day before. With heavier winds and driving, dense snow, operations at sea were limited but still underway. Weather of this kind produces a variety of problems which go beyond the more obvious of simple freezing or wind chill. There is snow blindness and white-out. One causes loss of vision, the other vertigo. The first term is well known to land travelers in snow-bound areas, the second to aviators caught flying in sudden, dense snow squalls. I was never sure if sailors had coined an expression for their own unique snow problems. A healthy mixture of blindness and seasickness in a bad storm would roughly approximate and embrace the problems of both land and air. It didn't matter though. Be it land, sea or air, the result was always the same—you got lost.

No one knew this better than the hapless crew of the Thailand frigate *HMTS Prasae.* More accustomed to the steamy monsoons of Southeast Asia than the bitter harshness of sub-arctic snowstorms, the crew was at an immediate disadvantage. Added to this was an unfamiliar coastline and an urgent mission to deliver an inland bombardment from just offshore. Sixty-five miles behind enemy lines, *Prasae* ran aground. No longer the attacker but now the attacked, she lay helplessly stranded on the beach within the sight of enemy troops and soon, it was feared, enemy artillery. A task force of friendly vessels was being hastily assembled to pull *Prasae* off the shore and out of harm's way.

Forty miles to the south of *Prasae's* postion at a coastal town named Bokuku Ko, I was observing the evacuation of Korean refugees. The commander of Carrier Task Element 95.66, now coordinating the rescue of *Prasae,* ordered me to proceed north to a small coastal village called Yang-yang. Here I would find the stricken vessel and lend all necessary assistance. I launched my helicopter and flew up the coast, deeper into enemy territory than I had been at Bokuku Ko. Upon arrival, I was to make radio contact with one of the friendly vessels, a destroyer mine sweeper, the *USS Endicott.*

As I headed north, I saw several ships moving toward the area, swelling the size of the Task Force steadily. Arriving at Yang-yang, I sighted *Prasae*. Even from a distance, I could see that her plight had already taken its toll as the battering of heavy surf so close to the beach had damaged or swept away much of her on-deck equipment, leaving her appearance one of disarray and desperation. There was a baleful aura about her, one that inspired pity and sorrow for a stricken comrade-in-arms and the seamen who manned her. Alone, isolated and paralyzed, here lay a dying ship, so near and yet so far from help. And nearer still was a determined enemy to whom the ship and her crew would be a prized trophy.

My brief reflection over, I turned to the task of raising *Endicott* by radio. I sent my signal. Nothing came back. Again. Silence. Another frequency and then the others. No response. I tried the other ships in the vicinity. My headset was quiet as a graveyard. There were few options available to get the show on the road and neither time nor personal inclination would permit me to abort. I left *Endicott* and headed for *Prasae*.

I circled her, taking a quick, closer look. She was a ship in a maelstrom, heaving and shuddering as the merciless shorebreak pounded her relentlessly. No vessel could withstand that kind of punishment for long, no matter how seaworthy. She still had internal power and appeared to be watertight for now but all that could change quickly in conditions like these. Worse, a well placed barrage from the North Koreans would suddenly consummate what the sea had not yet concluded. Thinking of this, I turned inland and quickly reconnoitered the surrounding hills. I had flown only five thousand yards when I encountered enemy troops. They were already entrenched behind a series of low-lying ridges. It was obvious they were doing more than just passing through the area. They were permanently established and had a specific mission in mind. So did our side. With a renewed sense of urgency, I returned to the beach.

Still without radio contact, I decided on a more basic approach to the communications problem. I landed my copter on the snow-covered sand close by *Prasae*. My crewman, a black-bearded sailor named Marciano, clambered out and ran over to the water's edge where *Prasae* was firmly dug in. Her bow towered overhead as he shouted up to a gaggle of frozen men standing along her side.

"Hey! *Prasae!* We're from Task Element 95.66. Is there an American communicator aboard named Havard? He's supposed to be our liaison man." There was some stiff shuffling among the group and one, a Black man, stepped forward.

"I'm Havard," he called back. "Welcome to Yangyang. What the hell are you doing on the beach?"

"We can't raise anybody by radio. No one's responding on any frequency. We tried them all and all of the ships too, but we're not getting anything. Our radio was working on the way up but it must have gone out." Marciano was numbing up quickly and he pressed his arms around his chest, hugging in body heat against the cold wind and the blowing salt spray. Frost was forming on his beard from his own moisture-laden breath. He went on.

"You know you got gooks only two, three miles from here? We spotted them when we flew inland. Christ, it's *cold* out here!" Havard was unimpressed with these stale pieces of intelligence.

"Yeah, yeah. Listen, what are your names anyway, you and your pilot?"

"Thornton and Marciano. I'm Marciano. what do you want us to do?"

Havard didn't answer right away. He was muttering something inaudible to a colleague and then
turned back to Marciano who was hopping up and
down to stay warm.

"Marciano?"

"Yeah! Hurry up will ya? I'm freezing my ass off!"

"All right! Tell your pilot to get back in the air on
the double and haul ass out to that salvage ship over
there," he said motioning to a grey silhouette offshore. "It's the *USS Bolster*. Tell him that he'll
receive further instructions from them."

"How the hell do we do that?! No radio,
remember?"

"We're in radio contact with them. We'll call ahead
and get them to use a chalkboard and nice big letters
to talk you through."

"Then what?! I'm *dying* out here, Havard!"

"What the *hell* you think I'm doin'?! You need to
pick up a Lieutenant Dudley and then drop him here
on deck. He's the salvage officer. You think you can
do it?"

"Not much choice is there?"

"Nope. You got it all straight, Marciano?"

"Yeah. Anything else?"

"That's it." Havard waved and turned back to his
weary-looking associates. Marciano ran stiffly back
to the helicopter and its inviting shelter from the
wind. We lifted off the frozen beach and headed for
the *Bolster*.

On the way out, everything around us looked
grey—the sea, the sky and the *Bolster*. She was an
average size auxillary ship and like most auxillaries
she lacked the smooth, sleek line of combat vessels.
Making slow headway, she wallowed and mushed
along with a kind of calm, unhurried dignity. As
men emerged from hatches here and there, I could
see the warm glow of the lights of her compartments

and they exuded a sense of warmth and security which was sadly absent on *Prasae*. But even for *Bolster*, all this could change for the worst. As the task of freeing *Prasae* would fall upon this salvor, she would be forced to draw perilously near to the treacherous shore, its swift currents and the converging North Koreans. Safety on this day was a temporal blessing guaranteed to no one.

The chalkboard was there waiting for us as Havard had promised and its messages directed us aft to a pick-up point. The large hand-written words confirmed that we would hoist up one man, Dudley, and deliver him to the rolling decks of *Prasae*. We dropped our cable and horsecollar sling which Dudley donned. Marciano then raised him upward with the winch through freezing winds made even more intense by the air currents stirred up by my beating rotor blades. Dudley climbed into the copter without complication and the three of us headed for shore.

"I'm John Thornton. That's my crewman Marciano who just brought you in."

"Nice to meet you. Sorry for the rotten circumstances."

"Don't mention it. what's the plan?"

"After you get me aboard *Prasae*, I'll supervise rigging her beaching gear. We'll use it to link up with *Bolster*. Running the lines across is gonna be pure hell in this kind of sea, though. We're gonna have to work this thing pretty fast or we're gonna have two beached ships on our hands instead of one. I hope like hell the gooks don't make things any worse. They're pretty close, aren't they?"

"Yeah, about three miles inland, behind those ridges. *Prasae's* crew is probably a lot more nervous about that than being beached."

"I don't blame them. So's everybody else. They'll

be happy to know there're more ships on the way. We just got word that *Manchester's* coming in. Already got a bunch of destroyers out there."

"The gooks must be getting pretty damn thick to draw that much fire power. There's *Prasae,* Dudley. I figure we'll put you down on the fantail. Let's go check it out."

As we approached the ship, we could see that the situation had not improved at all. She continued to be buffeted by rip-tide waves and her side-to-side roll was becoming more frequent and severe. I pulled up over the stern where I hoped I could drop Dudley but it looked bad. The deck was coming awash periodically as surf broke over it. Compounding this hazardous condition was a junk yard of tangled equipment and debris that was twisted among her depth charges and racks. As if this wasn't enough, her lay into the wind was driving the smoke from her funnels aft. The fantail was shrouded in a dense, black cloud. The warmth of the exhaust mixing with the sub-zero wind was creating dangerous and unpredictable turbulence. Still, it was worth a try if we could get some help on deck.

I tried to entice some men aft to grab for Dudley when he descended. There were no takers for sliding around on the wet, iced deck plates. I appealed for a brief shutdown of the stacks. Negative again came the response.

"The Thais don't seem to think a hell of a lot of my ideas, Dudley. It's probably just as well. The stern doesn't seem like a workable option. The place is a wreck."

"I gotta get down there somehow. I can't do a damn thing up here."

"Midships is out. There's no place to put you. Let's check out the bow."

"Suits me, I guess."

The bow was a less than desirable location. A 4.6-inch gun turret sat in its midst. The entire length of the area forward of the superstructure measured only forty feet. My rotor blades were thirty-eight feet in diameter. That left two feet for mistakes. The northwesterly winds blowing off the beach were still holding at twenty-five miles an hour with forty-mile gusts. The frigate was facing almost straight into them. To maintain a heading into the wind and make my drop would have placed my tail boom and its rotor virtually into the bridge. I would therefore have to maintain my hover at an angle about twenty-five degrees out of the wind direction to keep the boom clear. Another factor compelled me to draw in close to the ship—my hoist, located on the copter's left side. I had to pull in to center it over clear deck space. This, combined with my angle would have the effect of blinding my field of vision to the rear and to my right. In those two critical directions, I would not be able to see. I could only guess, apply a Jesus factor and hop to God I could pull this one off. I prepared to move in.

"Marciano! Up here!" I shouted with a growing sense of uneasiness. Marciano lurched toward the cockpit. His dark eyes were wide and shone white amid the blackness of his beard and headgear. He was tense, being fairly new as a crewman, and having dealt generally with hoisting conditions much better than these. I briefed him quickly on my problems and how we'd go in.

"Get Dudley in the sling and ready to go at the hatch. I want his butt *out a* there the minute we hit a hover. You make him *move*. I got *no* time to fool around. It's gotta go fast, Marciano. You know what I'm up against, right?"

He knew. With an unsmiling nod, he moved silently aft to ready Dudley. Under more auspicious circumstances, Marciano might relish the thought of hastily booting some lieutenant's ass out of the hatch. But as the copter bucked around in the turbulent winds, there was no sense of frivolity in him or me.

We moved in to *Prasae*. Where before she had seemed to me mournful and helpless, she now seemed menacing. Like the drowning swimmer who drags under the rescuing lifeguard, she seemed to harbor a potentially dangerous reserve of strength that, misdirected, would destroy us all.

My rotor blades slapped at the air as I gingerly approached the frigate. My own tension seemed to be flowing through the controls and into the whirlybird's soul, her engine sounding more strained to me than before. I often attributed the traits of the living to machines that shared the same hazards I confronted. I talked to them, encouraged them, worried over them and petted them as if they were live things. It always seemed to help for they appeared to respond as best they could under the worst of circumstances. This bird was reading my feelings and I felt close to her somehow. We would go at it together, me and my chopper, down to the bitter end.

We made our approach and I pulled to a hover over the bow. Marciano was at the hatch with Dudley in the sling. Their eyes were glued to the cockpit awaiting my signal to lower away. Ready . . .

Suddenly, the wind and sea erupted with a renewed ferocity, carrying the *Prasae* with them. She heeled over violently, a monstrous grey creature leaping toward us like that drowning victim grabbing at anything in panicked desperation. The ship's mass bore down on us, her bridge, electronics mast and its web-like rigging ominously closing in. It was like being trapped in a cave-in with the roof collapsing on you.

My maneuvering room evaporated in an instant. I attacked the controls and wrenched the copter back and away. The chopper roared in protest at this rough handling and the unprovoked assault from the vessel she sought to resurrect from the dead. Marciano and Dudley, thrown off balance, bounced around the inside of the compartment grabbing for a handhold. *Prasae,* as if sobered by the shrieking howl of the outraged flying machine, righted herself and backed off. We were out from under her.

It was no good. We were lucky to have gotten out intact. Another go-round would no doubt be a repeat performance but possibly with a worse ending. I looked aft toward Dudley.

"This is impossible! We can't get in! There's no *room* in there. Another bad lurch like that one and she's liable to shear off the blades down to the nubs. What about a launch from the beach? Can't you take a damn boat?" I asked. Dudley shook his head emphatically.

"No! No way! We already tried that one!" he shouted. "Before you got here we tried bringing in a landing craft this morning. It broached and the whole goddamn crew went under. They're all dead. This water's too shallow and the surf is impossible. A boat will never make it. You gotta get me *in* and *now* or the *Prasae* can kiss it good-bye. There's no other way." So that was it.

"Aye aye, Lieutenant," I called back, "but the odds are way against us."

I resigned my self to performing the impossible and prepared for another approach. We moved in cautiously, taking advantage of a momentary lull as wind and sea relented. I came to a hover over the bow and the drop was primed. The timing was right. Now was the opportunity we had been waiting for. Marciano and Dudley were ready at the hatch.

"Go! Hit it!" I called back.

"O.K. Lieutenant, this is it. Step out and I'll lower away," prodded Marciano.

Dudley looked out the hatch and down at *Prasae*. Although less violently than before, the deck was still rolling. A small group of Thai sailors peered upward with solemn Asian faces awaiting his arrival. The distance between him and them was disconcerting— it seemed like a long way down. The frothing sea looked sinister as it roiled around the ship and clawed at the nearby beach. It seemed to be waiting patiently for a misstep. *Prasae* rolled lazily, a moving target that might easily be missed. The helicopter was weaving back and forth in the air as if it and the pilot were slightly drunk. In sub-zero weather, Dudley began to sweat. It was such a long way down.

The seconds ticked by. A minuted passed and then another. What the hell was taking them so long?

"I'll be swinging out there like a yo-yo!" protested Dudley. The wind was starting to come up again and buffeted the copter. *Prasae* continued her restless bobbing. "What if I'm out there and the ship goes berserk again? What'll you do?" he implored of Marciano.

"You'll be all right, Lieutenant," replied Marciano, not fully believing his own reassurances. "Go now while you can. It's as good as it'll ever be. It'll all be over before you know it," said Marciano hoping he sounded convincing. Dudley was skeptical.

As their debate continued, my impatience grew. So did my wrestling match with the controls. Early helicopter models like this one were unstable at best. Unlike conventional aircraft, they would not fly themselves for even a moment if the controls were left unattended. Every limb of my body was totally engaged in the struggle to maintain flight: a rudder pedal for each foot, the stick for the right hand and the collective and throttle for the left. To let up on any one of them would topple the helicopter and the present conditions only made the effort more difficult.

Surely Dudley would be ready to go any second now, I thought. I mentally and physically braced myself for the renewed battle to fight off the instability that Dudley's unbalanced weight on the hoist would precipitate. But where was it? Dudley was still at the hatch looking down.

"C'mon, Lieutenant, *please!* You can make it but you gotta go now!" begged Marciano. Dudley was still thinking it over.

Three minutes had now elapsed. It was an eternity. Dudley would have gone up and down twice by now, I fumed to myself. If I could leave these controls, I'd throw them *both* out, I thought, smoldering and climbing the walls with frustration. Too much time was gone. Dudley was hesitating and Marciano, in deference to the Lieutenant's rank, was not being forceful enough. I had had it and started bellowing to them.

"Marciano, will you kick him out, godammit!? *Move* it! You're taking too long! I can't keep flying this thing in the same damn place forever! Now *lower* him! Do it! Do it!" I raged. My fists were crushing the controls with fury and I was half bouncing in my seat. Running through my mind was the old saying that he who hesitates is lost. We were hesitating and running the growing risk of losing.

The blades kept pounding at the air, the engine rhythmically booming in my ears. The wind was rising again dangerously and was doing its best to

push us every way but the right way. Despairing, I
called back to Marciano.

"If he won't go then *forget* it this time! Wave me
off and let's get the hell out of here, Marciano!
Marciano?"

And then—there is was! The weight! Dudley was
out! A quick glance over my shoulder confirmed that
he had done it at last.

Marciano ran out the cable and Dudley was now
at eye level with the copter's flight deck. The buf-
feting continued. I fought and held my position.
O.K. Dudley, you're gonna make it, I thought. She
was staying in there. Steady, steady . . .

Then, without warning and to my instant horror,
the Sea of Japan attacked with the ferocity of the
Great Flood. From out of nowhere, a monstrous
green comber rose up from the depths as if it had
been laying for us, a crouching beast that was
waiting for its quarry's weakest moment. The sea exploded with full fury against *Prasae's* hull, striking
crashing blows broadside to her, one after the other.
The ship seemed to crumble beneath the onslaught
like a worn-out prize fighter. She reeled under the
tempestuous impact of these watery haymakers.
Enormous geysers of spray erupted into the air and
the Thai crewmen were inundated. They slid across
the deck, clawing desperately for a holdfast,
anything tied down as *Prasae* rolled hard to port, her
now sloping decks fully awash with foaming sheets of
freezing seawater.

There was no time to react. As if suddenly struck
by a seizure, *Prasae* convulsed. Shuddering from the
impact of a sea gone mad, the frigate, her mast and
rigging careened over with the ship's roll. My
helicopter, like a bug that had flown too close to the
spider's web, was trapped. The rigging swooped
down on the furiously beating main rotor, entan-

gling the unsuspecting blades. They began to shatter, hurling splinters in every direction. Spattering across the deck, they raked the ship like exploding artillery shells. A wild melee broke out as men scrambled, fell and ran for their lives away from the destruction overhead.

The fanning action of the disintegrating rotor was violent and sucked the copter in toward the bridge. The chopper went completely out of control and I sat in the cockpit powerless, a bewildered spectator watching as we smashed into the superstructure. The helicopter, now working with its own will, seemed insane with fury and lashed back at the attacking ship. As if determined to maul, to kill the vessel that was its own destroyer, the copter threw itself full force into the battle. Its blades now sheared off completely, the rotor head churned with unrestrained ferocity, the engine raging in uncontrolled and mindless anger. Bouncing, punching and roaring in its dying wrath, the copter seemed hell-bent on revenge before it would finally give up the ghost.

Caught in a contest of behemoths, I was flung about in my seat like an egg in an egg beater. I reached out for the fuel control on the auxillary control panel between my legs, hoping to cut the engine as the clatter and violence of the crash went on. But my body, like the copter, seemed swept away, controlled by another force. The powerful strength of the moving aircraft held me at bay and rendered my efforts futile. I was hopelessly locked into my own imminent destruction.

My heart was sinking and my mind raced as the cacophony of shrieking, tearing metal and the bellowing engine consumed the whole world. The moments of the crash seemed to stretch unnaturally. My mind turned to God as my life seemed to be slipping away. I quickly prayed, having found no other way to help myself. I appealed to God for my deliverance from the lethal destruction that was all around me and which would momentarily destroy me.

And then my miracle occurred. The chopper, thrashing once more in its final death throes, smashed a gaping hole in the starboard plexiglass of the cockpit. In what must have been one motion, I released my harness and threw myself toward the beckoning hole. Hurtling through, my hands tore out at the air, grabbing for anything and finding dangling wreckage, masting, cables to cling to. I scrambled downward without thought toward the main deck, the copter and ship still locked in their struggle. Chunks of debris were plunging down, accompanying me on my descent. I reached the bottom of my makeshift ladder ten feet above the deck. There was nothing left to grab and I plummeted the remaining distance.

As I rose to my feet, I basked for a moment in the pleasure of the blessing I had just enjoyed. My reverie was shattered as the helicopter, now a gasping hulk, cataclysmically blew itself to pieces. With a momentous boom, its two fuel tanks ruptured, exploding in a ball of brilliant orange light. The blazing fuel cascaded down toward me in a fiery waterfall. Pouring onto the deck, it surrounded me in a curtain of flame that blotted out everything in view. I recoiled as the heat blazed in my face. An eerie glow was roundabout. Before turning away to escape, I peered into the fire as if I had forgotten something. Perhaps I was looking for another miracle, a sign to lead me through the flames to safety.

And strangely enough, it appeared. There, amid the raging inferno that danced in front of me, appeared the face of Christ Himself. It was Him,

sure enough. He looked at me, bearded, serene, surrounded by a bright and unearthly light. It was Him!
For a brief instant, I registered shock, surprise and a
giddy sense of confusion. Squinting into the light, I
spoke to him aloud, perplexed.

"Jesus Christ, what are you doing here?!" He didn't
respond. My attention riveted on that face, I paused
a split-second more rather than turning and fleeing
the flames. The face changed as I watched it. It took
on a different, yet familiar appearance. Who *was*
that?

"Jesus Christ!" I shouted again as the light of
understanding and recognition illuminated my
groggy brain. The face was Marciano's! He was
sprawled in the flaming wreckage unconscious. If
ever there was a miracle, surely this was one. Were it
not for the face of God's Son, I might not have
lingered for that brief moment or looked closer into
the flames. I might not have had the sudden
knowledge I now had that I was not alone in this
burning hell. I might not have been able to draw up
the fortitude I now needed to come to Marciano's
aid—the kind of fortitude that faith inspires.

I ran into the flames to Marciano, hoping to pull
him free. But as I reached for him, my right arm did
nothing. It hung there limp and useless. Already the
heat was growing unbearable. My flight jacket began
to smolder and then burn. I looked nearby to two
Thai sailors and screamed at them to come help.
Their fear was profound. They were frozen in terror,
completely immobilized by the scene before them.
They stood unmoving, unseeing, riveted to the deck
like statues. They could do nothing for themselves
and less for Marciano and me.

My newly found courage shaken loose, I turned
once more to God as I struggled with the dead weight
of Marciano's body. He wouldn't budge. I prayed

to God for the superhuman strength that would extricate us from this inferno. Again, I cried out for help and *again* another miracle!

Seemingly from nowhere, an American sailor named Kuykendall charged from behind the wall of flame and leaped through it like a comic strip superhero. His two good arms were the superhuman strength I prayed for and his presence the help Marciano and I so desperately needed. Together we pulled Marciano's limp body out of the fire, beat out his burning flight suit and carried him aft. Although burned, lacerated and in shock, Marciano regained consciousness, and lived—his life snatched from the flames by a caring God.

It was a day of miracles for Lieutenant Dudley too. Dangling outside the helicopter in the horsecollar sling, more vulnerable and exposed than any of us, he had somehow been thrown by some inexplicable quirk of force and motion completely over the crashing copter. Hurtling downward, he landed on the bridge's catwalk. As the chopper began to disintegrate, a Thai sailor saw him lying there dazed. In the instant before the helicopter's wreckage would have fallen on them both, the intrepid Thai rushed over to Dudley, shoved him out of the way and off the catwalk. Dudley plummeted to the main deck where incredibly he landed cat-like on both feet. Bounding forward, he struck the ship's guardrails, ricocheted backward and onto his feet again. Had he continued forward, he would have plunged overboard into the sea and almost certain death. Instead, he survived the day with only broken ribs.

The fires ignited by the exploding copter were spreading through the bridge, superstructure and across the main deck. Uncovered ammunition which had been readied for action in the ship's guns was being torched off by the flaming heat. Fifty calibre and twenty millimeter rounds were exploding, skyrocketing into the air like Fourth of July fireworks. Recovering from its initial shock, the crew raced about the ship in an organized frenzy pulling fire hoses forward to the leaping flames that now threatened to engulf the entire ship. Amid the din of exploding ordnance, officers and chiefs bellowed commands and an ordered effort emerged. Some men moved the injured away from the burning bow aft. Still others clambered among the tangle of rubble and hoses toward the hedgehog racks, whose anti-submarine explosives would detonate at the least provocation—and provocation was all around. Cradling the touchy weapons in their arms like babes, these courageous sailors stumbled their way out and to the stern saving their ship and themselves from the swift and fatal chain reaction that would occur if the hedgehogs blew.

The fire-fighting efforts were going badly and slowly. The water pressure for the hoses was woefully inadequate due to damage inflicted on the pumps when *Prasae* ran aground. The unbeaten flames hung on, seeking to maximize their damage. They advanced on isolated pockets of men whose escape routes had been cut. Choosing to take their chances with the sea, where their odds were only slightly better, they leaped overboard into the swirling, seething froth. They could be seen crawling up on the hostile shore where they would now take their chances with the enemy and exposure. They sat there on the snow-covered beach, soaked through to the bone, shivering uncontrollably in the sub-zero cold.

Surely the North Koreans had witnessed our crisis, no doubt with grim satisfaction. At any moment, we expected our weakened condition to invite a coup-de-grâce from them if we didn't succeed in blowing ourself up first. Despite the total wreck-age of her mast and a huge portion of her bridge, *Prasae* remained in radio contact with the offshore fleet. She appealed for help but despite her urgent pleas, there could be no aid from any ship, including *Bolster*. The conditions were no better and without Dudley, no progress could be made on rigging the beaching gear. The fleet could only stand by and watch us burn—and perhaps explode.

As the morning hours drew to a close, *Prasae's* flames were finally quenched. We stood by, help-lessly waiting for some word on our next move. It would come in early afternoon as more ships and the broader options they offered arrived on the scene.

Among the new arrivals was the *USS Comstock,* an LSD (Landing Ship—Dock), bearing with it a large, heavy landing craft known as the LCVP. Its large size and weight, which was increased by a heavy load of minesweeping equipment, would have served Dudley, Marciano and me well several hours ago. Its presence then might have allowed us to forego our calamitous aerial delivery.

Belated as it may have been, its value to us now was far greater than before. The LCVP was dis-patched to our aid and carried with it emergency equipment, two doctors, three boat crewman and another salvage officer, a Lieutenant Taylor. All were volunteers on a hazardous trip to the beach that could very possibly end in broaching, capsizing and drowning as it had for the first crew.

The LCVP labored shoreward, battling, pitching and rolling its way toward the smoldering *Prasae.* The frigid sea broke over its blunt bow, showering the occupants with icy spray. Despite the stability enhanced by her heavier weight, the maneuvera-bility of the LCVP was limited. As she reached the fast-running waters near shore, her sluggishness seemed to be magnified. The helmsman struggled to maintain a position perpendicular to the waves, a task which was increasingly difficult in the tumultuous swirl of surf near the beach. The craft lurched, bobbed and then got punched sideways, its full length now dangerously exposed broadside to the assault of the incoming waves. One and then another crashed against the LCVP's seaward bulkhead, driving down the other side perilously close to the waiting sea. The helmsman wrenched the tiller and attacked the throttle to right the vessel and stabilize her course. Fountains of brine shot overhead and the passengers were thrown across the LCVP's cargo bay as her huge engine bellowed with determined fervor. Her bow swung around avoiding the threat of capsize. The sea, almost with intelligent malignancy, seemed to sense the LCVP's shift in direction and, capitalizing on her redirected momentum, locked onto her stern, spinning the vessel farther around than the helmsman had intended. Another onslaught of waves fell upon the LCVP. Her seaward side raised up, almost half her belly exposed to full view. Running surf cascaded into the cargo bay as her shoreward side dug into the sea. Freezing water swirled around the feet of her battered and agonized crew. She was broaching and near capsizing.

The LCVP shook violently from the cavitation produced by her prop in the tightness of the turn. The engine roared louder as its burden lightened from the lack of water resistance below. The helmsman would not yeild. Cursing, he threw the tiller back again and eased off on the throttle long enough for the prop to regain its bite into the water. The LCVP's bow rotated once more and hit the surf squarely. Careening up and then down, smashing into a concrete sea, she righted herself and was back on course, her near-capsize averted. For the moment, the sea relented. The LCVP had run the gauntlet.

She pulled along *Prasae*'s port side which, being near the shore, afforded some protection from the surf. Quickly, the injured were taken off *Prasae* and transferred to the beach to be evacuated later by helicopter. I went with them to try to lend what assistance I could. Time was becoming increasingly precious. There were thirty-four Thais and Americans on the beach now, eighteen of which had to be evacuated as quickly as possible. Several of the water-soaked sailors were so stiff and cold they could barely move. Two Thais who had evaded *Prasae*'s flames by jumping overboard had been severely injured and were in shock. Already suffering from exposure, they would be the first to die with the others following quickly as the day wore on and the temperature began to drop. They were freezing to death.

The remainder of the crew stayed aboard *Prasae,* some taking up positions as lookouts and spotters. They gazed inland toward the enemy-held hills. Ominous activity was appearing amid the North Korean positions and there was little doubt that they were now fully aware of our extreme vulnerability. Reacting to our exposed position and the slow impotency of the rescue effort, somewhere within the North Korean command structure, the decision was made to attack.

As the North Koreans emerged from their positions, the frozen statues of the lookouts in *Prasae*'s mangled superstructure sprang to life, the rising heat of impending battle thawing their preoccupation with the cold. The terrain and its coordinates already implanted firmly in their minds, the spotters lost no time in quickly relaying troops positions to the destroyers standing to seaward. Five-inch guns spun on their mounts, the barrels adjusting themselves to the correct ranges inland. Almost in unison, a great chorus of gunfire erupted. The sea glowed red as it reflected flames belching outward from the firing ships. Smoke poured out in billowing clouds creating smoke out to sea. Seconds later, the baritone rhythm of a dozen exploding guns accompanied by the rippling shriek of the projectiles passing overhead, carried across the water to *Prasae*'s shipwrecked crew. In a few moments more, like an echo of the firing guns, came the rumbling thunder of the shells' detonation three miles inland. The cruiser *USS Manchester* had arrived on the scene and, seemingly intent on convincing everyone that it was the meanest kid on the block, turned its nine eight-inch guns toward the advancing North Koreans. Her long, finger-like barrels looked askew as each sought its own range and target. And then, like a prima donna stealing the show, *Manchester* showed her stuff. She looked like a volcanic eruption and we could feel the shock waves as they arrived on the beach. Her shells sounded like empty boxcars rolling by as they rifled through the air above us. Their inland explosions had a distinctly resonant boom as they opened huge craters in the frozen earth.

The bombardment continued in deadly earnest as we huddled close to the snowy beach watching in anxiety as the North Koreans pressed on. Their casualties were heavy and their dead littered the scorched and smoldering earth behind them. Still they charged on, knowing that as soon as they closed on us, the offshore barrage would have to lift, lest friendly be destroyed with enemy. Despite their dwindling numbers, the lead platoons charged forward. The fleet's fire was relentless and devastating. The sound of the wind was overpowered by the back and forth argument between firing gun and exploding ordnance. Still the North Koreans came on. Anticipating their arrival within small-arms range, the few able-bodied crewmen ashore began shifting about, preparing some semblance of a defensive perimeter. With our paltry numbers and limited weapons, there was little doubt in anyone's mind that we would be quickly overrun if the assault succeeded.

The tenacity of the North Koreans was as incredible as the barrage they were running through. They came on and on, three thousand yards away, now only two thousand. *Prasae*'s spotters were frantic, barking out coordinates for relay to the offshore fleet. As the connonade continued unabated, the stench of burnt explosives wafted over us from the impact area. The carnage mounted as every gun at sea was brought into play. It didn't seem to be enough as the gooks bore down on us. *Prasae*'s spotters begged for maximum close-in suppressive fire as the lead element drew closer.

The nearest destroyer had every battery in action and a full load of urgent targets. Rather than divert his heaviest weapons, the gunnery officer called up an anti-aircraft gun which lay quiet until now. Its twin forty-millimeter gunmount came alive and jerked landward, its two barrels almost parallel to the surface of the sea. With the deadly efficiency that is unique to rapid-fire weapons, the twin guns alternately spat out a withering fusillade of armor-piercing rounds. The shells, designed to punch holes in metal and shear off the wings of aircraft, now flew headlong toward flesh and bone. In a savage display of concentrated destruction, the earth around the North Koreans came to pieces as if pounded by some huge fist. The ground trembled as the shells slammed home exploding in a shower of sparks, shrapnel and dense smoke. The detonation of each round was almost indistinguishable from the next and a rumble somewhat akin to an earthquake was emitted. The target area was totally obscured in roiling clouds of smoke that folded on themselves, hovering about as if to make sure nothing had been overlooked. The forty-millimeter guns ceased fire. Almost as if nothing else mattered, our eyes focused exclusively on the smoldering area where the North Koreans had been. It was desolate and empty. Where were they? Perhaps they had concealed themselves, lying low. But where? Confused, the beached sailors began drawing hasty, nervous conclusions.

"They missed! The stupid bastards missed!" grumbled one sailor, fully expecting the tenacious gooks to rise up from the ashes like a flock of phoenixes.

"How could they miss?! They hit them square, they *had* to hit them!" pleaded another nearby.

There was no movement, no renewal of the attack by the lead element that had been struck. An anxious silence gripped the sailors in tortured expectation. Incredulous, another crewman murmured to himself.

"They're gone. They're just . . . *gone.* They blew them to pieces." The others looked toward the blackened patch of sand, nodding their heads, barely able to believe what was now indisputable. There wasn't even a shoelace left to show where the gooks had been only a moment before.

The annihilation of the lead element broke the resolve of the remaining attackers and they fell back rapidly to the inland hills. The attack had failed, to our undying glee. As the offshore barrage wound down, we breathed a collective sigh of relief. We had gained precious time to continue our efforts at rescuing *Prasae.*

The *Manchester* dispatched its helicopter bearing another doctor and blankets. The pilot, AMC D. W. Thorin, landed on the snowy beach and took on the two badly suffering Thai sailors. Thorin continued his shuttle flights, gradually reducing the number of wounded on shore. As his fuel supply was consumed, the helicopter's weight was reduced, allowing him to take out three at a time instead of only two. Finally, all the injured members of our beach party had been safely evacuated to the *Manchester* when Thorin's fuel and daylight ran out.

Those of us who stayed behind had to get back to the *Prasae* for the night. The tide had receded, making it difficult for the LCVP to back off the beach. To be sure she would make it, it was necessary to keep her light and hold off the extra weight our own bodies represented. As she cleared the sand and regained flotation, we waded into the frigid water. Our heavy, fleece-lined winter clothing and boots were soaked through and doubled in weight. We struggled to climb up and into her, the first to succeed helping the others out of the foam. We got underway and lurched the short distance to *Prasae.*

Back on board, my wounds were dressed and the doctor pronounced my arm to be unbroken. It had suffered nerve damage and had turned blue from capillary ruptures. Feeling and movement were beginning to return though and by morning I would be able to fire a weapon and perform other useful tasks.

The *Prasae*'s officers and crew broke out all the available dry clothing and shoes they had. The frigate was still producing internal heat and as we warmed up, our spirits climbed. Expectations were high that the next day, with Lieutenant Taylor's salvage expertise, we would be successful in rigging the beaching gear and freeing *Prasae* at last. Even if we failed, we were certain that our own evacuation would be quickly effected, as it had been for the wounded.

Throughout the night, sporadic interdiction bombardments continued at fifteen- to twenty-minute intervals. the destroyers had moved in extremely close and the concussion of their guns sounded like mallets on kettledrums to us below deck. Sleep was nearly impossible as the projectiles scissored the air overhead.

Bedraggled but dry, we emerged at dawn on the second day to renew our labor of freeing the ship. The *Bolster* drew in close. By the use of small explosive charges, messenger lines of thin cords were fired over to us but repeatedly fell short or went astray in the wind. One finally got to us but then snapped. *Bolster* tried again. And again. More failures. The wind became menacing and blustery as the sky darkened and the ceiling dropped. Snow began to fall and the surf picked up with growing intensity. It began to batter *Prasae*'s fantail again, spraying the crew standing by, and they quickly withdrew. As the sea's strength increased, it began lifting and pushing *Prasae* further into the shore. Like a beached whale, she was being slowly driven up onto the sand.

The weather rapidly deteriorated into a blizzard worse than the one that had run the frigate aground. Visibility dropped to zero. *Bolster* was forced to pull out to the safety of deeper water. There was no chance of resupply from the air. Operations came to a standstill. We retreated below and as the light faded, another day was lost.

Night descended as did the temperature and morale of the Thais. Being accustomed to the hundred-degree climate of the tropics, the sub-zero temperatures of the frozen north chilled their spirits and sapped their will to get their ship off the beach. The night wore on. As it did, the LCVP which was tied up beside *Prasae* was bucked and battered about by the high seas. Torn loose from some of her moorings, she was shoved up on the beach and rammed into the sand. She would never sail again.

At first light, there was hardly any light to be seen as the blizzard continued to howl. *Prasae*'s angular surfaces were softened by a deep coating of snow and frozen salt spray. Her trek up the beach continued unabated as the relentless sea pounded her stern. Our own survival was now becoming precarious. Totally isolated, we had no provisions except what remained aboard. The first to be exhausted was water. We would have to replenish our supply with snow.

While the ship was nearly buried in it, the snow was dirty and that which was clean was inadequate to meet our needs. A snow brigade was organized for the beach, the men passed the drums along, up to the LCVP and aboard *Prasae*. On deck, I and a chief from the ship into the knee-deep water. Over the side clambered crewmen carrying empty fifty-five gallon drums. Filling these with the abundant clean snow of the beach, the men passed the drums along, up the the LCVP and aboard *Prasae*. On deck, I and chief petty officer tended a smoky charcoal fire melting the contents of the drums. As it melted, we strained the water through gauze and dropped in halizone tablets from the C-ration packs we had. It became apparent that the drum-filling operation would move much more quickly than the melting operation. After consuming a vast amount of charcoal fuel and fourteen hours' time, we had our precious distillate—one pitiful drum of water from more than fifty drums of snow.

As darkness fell, exhaustion was epidemic and the soaked men who had served on the snow brigade were ready to drop. And then the worst that could have occurred finally happened. After three days on the beach, having endured incredible weather, a helicopter crash, a major fire and a near-successful enemy attack, *Prasae's* overtaxed heart stopped beating. Quietly and in the company of her faithful crew, she died. Her boilers exhausted, they could give no more. And with their failure went the last of our steam, our heat and our electricity. There was no way to dry our soaked clothing or warm our frozen bodies. We were plunged into total darkness except for a few candles. *Prasae* had died but her crew clung to life and prayed for this hellish storm to lift.

On the fourth day, the weather finally cleared. Again our hopes climbed, with the thought that today would surely reward our suffering with success. Perhaps, after all we had been through, fate would smile on us and permit us to raise our inert ship from the dead. The *Manchester's* helicopter came in and dropped dry clothes and water. This good omen was followed by the return of the *Bolster* and the successful firing of a messenger line to *Prasae*.

Jubilant, Lieutenant Taylor set to work himself on this line and the others that would follow. He and a sizeable contingent from the crew pulled and tugged—for six hours. In time, each thin cord brought in a heavier two-inch line and then a three-inch. The crew strained and battled with the ropes and I recalled the first day when Dudley had prophesied that we would play hell getting the lines across. It was like a gigantic tug-of-war. The men fought against the resistance posed by the line's growing weight and the running sea which pushed *Bolster* to and fro, first slackening, then tightening the rope. Blisters rose and broke on the men's numb fingers and hands, exposing raw tender flesh to the coarse line.

As the hours dragged on, each seemed to yield only a few painful feet of rope at a time. To maximize the failing energy of the crew, the men were rotated off the lines and onto walkie-talkies and lookout positions, or to manning *Prasae*'s guns. Fourteen hours passed, but even with several lines now successfully across, we had still not completed tying up to the *Bolster*. Rigging the beaching gear could not be accomplished until then. We would have to try again tomorrow.

But as the fourth day ended, the crew was near total collapse. We returned to our refrigerated compartments below for another freezing night. There was virtually no protection from the cold, but at least we were out of the wind and away from the sea.

During the night, the mercury dipped to twenty below zero. It was deathly freezing, even inside the ship. The condition of the men deteriorated that night as one came down with pneumonia and another, whose compartment was not adequately ventilated for the charcoal stove inside, was nearly asphyxiated. As the morning of the fifth day broke, it was now alarmingly evident that many of the Thais were also coming down with pneumonia and suffering badly from exposure. Today had to be the day to move the ship.

The few men who were able made their way aft to check the lines we had struggled to secure for fourteen grueling hours. Their hearts sank as they viewed the stern. The ship and lines were covered with ice. Its weight and freezing brittleness had snapped our hold on the outside world. Every line had broken and dropped into the sea. Crestfallen, the beleaguered group trudged below to announce the dreary news to the rest of us.

It was finished. *Prasae* would never put to sea again. She was dead and her crew lay dying. To work healthy men under these conditions would have been difficult but for these sick and exhausted Thais and Americans, it was simply out of the question. Our water was almost gone again, the C-rations we had been eating were turning the Thais' stomachs and there was little in abundance except charcoal. There were no other choices. We had to be evacuated. *Prasae* would be destroyed.

On January 12, as detonating charges were placed through the frigate, the crew dragged off *Prasae* and down to the LCVP. From there, instead of into knee-deep water, they stepped onto snow and sand. The *Prasae* had washed high and dry. We were all flown out to the *Manchester* by her hard-working helicopter and from the warmth and protection of this sanctuary, we watched *Prasae*'s final moments remorsefully.

A small, lonely and far-off victim of war, she looked lost and forsaken on the broad, rugged beach that would be her final resting place. As her slender form was shattered from within, black clouds covered her in a proper funeral shroud. There was a certain poignancy to the scene as the fleet seemed to salute her with a final bombardment that pounded her remains into rubble. Somehow her burning wreckage was an inadequate testimony to the struggle her crew had mounted to save her or to the men who died in that cause. And yet there was a grim justice in her destruction, for as a result of it neither the military value nor the spiritual value she held for us would be stolen or corrupted by her enemies. She had died and would be remembered honorably with her human dead. In memory of them all, I imagined a brief epitaph for the gravemarker the ship would never have:

HIS MAJESTY'S THAI SHIP *PRASAE*
KILLED IN ACTION BEHIND ENEMY LINES
12 JANUARY 1951
FAIR WINDS AND FOLLOWING SEAS

In the coming months, I would reflect often on the events surrounding the wreck of the *Prasae*. It had been a great trial of men and machines as only war and nature can concoct. And yet, for me it was far more than that. In time I would come to know that I had uniquely benefited from the misfortunes that had occurred here. The tragedy had helped prepare me for still greater tests that would come later. The burning flames and bitter cold of *Prasae* had served to temper my soul, hardening my ability to cope with the unbearable and to suffer the insufferable. I had learned a valuable lesson on how much I and others could physically endure. But more importantly, it had refreshed in my mind a sense of God's nearness, a feeling I had strongly sensed on one desperate occassion before but whose edge time had blunted. In the aftermath of my passage through this spiritual furnace, my soul had begun to anneal with a greater sense of confident faith.

It would have been easy for me to think that it was good fortune alone that had smashed open my cockpit, dragged Marciano from the flames and saved Dudley's life. It would have been easy to credit solely the fleet's big guns with holding the enemy at bay for five days. It would have been easy to write off a lot of things as just lucky. But to do so would have been to oversimplify wrongly and ignore the totality of what had happened to me. It wasn't only good fortune and big guns that had pulled us through, although, to be sure, they played their part. There was more at work here than that. A hand had moved amid the chaos, creating brief opportunities for deliverance and providing the strength for humans to perform beyond limits which none had ever dreamed they could surpass. Perhaps no one sensed this but me. It didn't really matter, though, for as time and events unfolded, it would become clear that no one here would need such beliefs as much as I.

When David was delivered from Saul, he was moved to write Psalm Eighteen wherein he described his peril and salvation:

> The sorrows of death compassed me and the floods of ungodly men made me afraid. The sorrows of hell compassed me about: the snares of death prevented me. In my distress I called upon the Lord, and cried unto my God: he heard my voice . . .

David closed his hymn with a humble note:

> Therefore will I give thanks unto thee, O Lord, among the heathen, and sing praises unto thy name.

For now, I would give my thanks among the godly. My chance to do it among the heathen was yet to come.

PART TWO

CAPTIVITY

1951-1953

3

This advance of the enemy seemed to the youth like a ruthless hunting. He began to fume with rage and exasperation. He beat his foot upon the ground, and scowled with hate at the swirling smoke that was approaching like a phantom flood.

—Stephen Crane
The Red Badge of Courage

Two months had passed since the death of *Prasae*. It was now late March and we impatiently awaited the end of a miserable winter. Spring, we hoped, was not far off. Tens of thousands of men from more temperate climes would welcome the melting away of winter's immense accumulation of snow, the milder days and nights and a return of green in place of deathly frozen white. It would be a return of life to the Korean peninsula. Yet even so, the war would remain very much with us as would the prospect of sudden death. It was that prospect that made life far more precious and dear now than in normal times. The atmosphere of war compelled one to savor life in whatever brief respites came along and from time to time assess it. I reflected on my own now and then and while not applying too keen an intellectual edge to the question, I always concluded that despite the adversities and the suffering, life was essentially a good thing, a worthwhile enterprise. It was of course something to be preserved and protected although not so much out of fear of dying. Rather it was for the sake of continuing to experience the fundamental goodness it held. Life was a gift and it was good to be alive. By the grace of God, I still was. Unlike others far less fortunate, I could savor such simple pleasures as breathing in the crisp winter air, seeing a sunset and wiggling my toes. I was not wounded. Neither was I dead. I was intact, alive and surviving. I had a wife whom I loved and who loved me. I had a child. I had a home. I was lucky.

I guessed for all that, I was pretty rich, and besides, it was Easter. This high Christian holiday fell on March 25th in 1951. Someone had mentioned that it was one of the earliest Easters of the twentieth century and that it would never come this early again until the year 2008. I wondered if I'd live to see that one. I was delighted to have lived to see *this* one. No matter, I thought. Happy Easter, everyone.

On this slate-grey morning, I flew low, just above the blowing whitecaps of the Sea of Japan in the helicopter that had replaced the one whose life *Prasae* had claimed. The water zipped beneath me and the whitecaps nearby were indistinct blurs. I was alone for the moment and with neither friend nor foe nearby, I felt calm and unthreatened here, far out to sea. This sense of safety, along with the monotony of the grey world surrounding me, combined with the chopper's droning engine to create a kind of placid spiritual calm. It was one of those fleeting moments of solitude that are rare enough in normal life and virtually extinct in war, aboard ship and in the ceaseless company of a vessel's cramped inhabitants. Farther off in the distance lay the carrier *USS Valley Forge*. Valley Forge. The name and the place carried my thoughts home to nearby Philadelphia. It would be Easter Eve there now. Easter Day was yet to come for my two little people—the grown one and the baby one. Jay would no doubt be going to bed by now. Being almost three this year, he would enjoy his Easter baskets and goodies tomorrow morning. We had always set it up pretty for him. Jelly beans, chocolate rabbits and dyed eggs. I wondered if Jinny had taken him downtown to see the Easter Bunny. Jay liked him almost as much as Santa Claus. In two more months would come Jay's third birthday. Remorsefully, I realized that I had missed much of his young life already. They change so fast at that age, I thought. I missed Jinny, too. But we'd been this route before, during the last war. We'd made it all right then. She'd make it all right now, I knew. All of us would make it.

Reluctantly, I pried myself loose from my reverie and, leaving home, returned to Valley Forge Far East. I radioed in for clearance to set down on the flight deck. This copter and I were sharing our last flight together. We had fought long and hard together and made a good team. She bore the scars of a warrior. None of her many wounds had been given very meticulous or aesthetically pleasing attention. Her rotor blades had been riddled time and again with bullets, patched with only paper and paste made from the fruit of the Orient—rice. Yet she flew on. Three rotor-gear-box mounts had been shot away. Still she flew. Her herniated engine was long overdue for major maintenance but continued to power me through the air. She deserved a rest and a good overhaul. Her having had that, I hoped we would team up again to challenge the skies and our enemies once more.

I laid her down gently on the flight deck of *Valley Forge*, cut the engine and sat with her until her blades came to a full stop. Sentimentally, I took one more look around her cockpit and then reluctantly departed. As I walked across the flight deck I stopped to glance at her one last time. Her blades drooped with fatigue and oil dripped from her belly as if she were bleeding from an open wound. Her fuselage was rent with bullet holes. But somehow she seemed proud sitting there. Almost defiantly, she wore the combat-mission insignia painted on her side. She had a right to be proud. We'd been to hell and back again. In spite of all her troubles, she had even landed me safely aboard ship under her own power. She was a good bird. In respect for what we had endured together, I gave her, my faithful comrade-in-arms, a parting salute.

Feeling like a man walking out on a devoted wife, I headed over to a shiny new helicopter. We lifted off *Valley Forge* and returned to the deck of my mother ship, LST 799. With a little luck, my association with this new copter would be brief and without incident. Our ship was due for rotation out of the line and back to Japan for resupply. After four hectic months of combat duty, all of us could use a short respite. In less than a week, we would weigh anchor and head south and away from Korea, at least for a while.

Five days passed. It was late afternoon on March 30th as I returned from a three-hour reconnaisance and gunfire-spotting mission near Wonsan, North Korea. The sun was setting over the snow-covered mountains behind me as another day of heavy naval bombardment concluded. It was always good to get home aboard ship to safety, warmth, chow, maybe some mail from home, a rack to stretch out and sleep on. Silhouetted on the calm waters of Wonsan's outer harbor was the heavy cruiser *USS St. Paul.* Nestled among the protective guns of this imposing vessel and a large collection of destroyers and minesweepers lay home-sweet-home, LST 799. She looked especially inviting, for she was a vessel soon to depart. Early tomorrow morning, under cover of darkness, LST 799 would silently slip away for Japan. At least that's what everybody was saying.

A sense of anticipation was already rampant on board. I could see it in the uplifted face of my LSO,

Chief Petty Officer George Young—"Nine-Fingered George" they called him, since that's all he had. George guided me in, a mischievous smile smeared across his face. After bringing me in, he held up all nine fingers. What kind of a signal was that, I wondered as I waved back, grinning stupidly. Maybe George just needed some rest, I thought. I hopped out of the copter and headed below deck. I traveled to the wardroom, hoping to find there my close friend and fellow copter pilot Lieutenant "Dad" Whittaker. Dad was our officer-in-charge.

In the past, he and I had operated together in Wonsan on a wide variety of missions. One in particular involved identifying the disposition of Wonsan harbor's extensive minefields and helping to clear pathways through them. Over a period of weeks, we had managed to clear out some hard-to-reach mines ourselves with rifle fire while minesweepers dealt with most of the others. But our primary specialty was the free-floating mines that continued to plague our ships. In an effort to determine where the Communists were storing and launching these illegal unanchored mines, Dad, an Army intelligence officer, and I set off for Wonsan to investigate. We suspected they were coming from a point along the inner harbor's shore near Wonsan's airfield. We went into the snow-covered strip to check but on arriving found it deserted. There was no one visible and nothing around except some destroyed gun emplacements and a few decoys. We hovered but drew no ground fire. An eerie silence hung over the area. We could see tracks, footprints and other markings in the snow which showed that something heavy had been recently dragged along here toward the beach. This had to be a launching site but it seemed vacant now. We decided to land, allowing Dad and the intelligence officer to look around on foot to confirm whether or not the place was still operational. I put the copter down on the airstrip but kept the rotor engaged in case a trap or sudden attack made a quick departure necessary. I then released my two passengers. They disappeared from sight as they began nosing around. Thirty minutes later, they were back, very frustrated. They had found nothing. The intelligence officer climbed into the copter but Dad was fuming. He turned away and walked back a few yards from the helicopter.

"Where're you going, Dad?" I yelled.

"I gotta piss!"

"Piss?! Why the hell do you have to do it here?!" We were eighty-five miles behind the lines sitting on an enemy-held airfield.

"I want these bastards to know I was here!" He unzipped his fly and began, then started moving sideways.

"What the hell are you doing?" I shouted over the roar of the copter.

"Shaddap! I'm writing my goddamn name in the snow!"

I pondered the logistics of this. We'd been up for over three hours and it *was* cold but Dad's full name was D. L. A. Whittaker. He'd never make it. He finally finished the job and turned back toward the copter. Climbing inside, he still looked dour, cursing under his breath.

"What's the matter with you?" I asked.

"I didn't have enough to cross the t's and dot the *i*," he said pouting. Then he brightened. "Piss on 'em," he chuckled. "I *still* claim the whole damn airfield as U.S. territory."

That was Dad Whittaker. He always gave a lift to my day and now my eyes searched the faces in the wardroom looking for him. He spotted me first.

"This time tomorrow it's *Sasebo,* John!" he shouted

across the room. I went over and threw my tired self down next to him.

"I'll believe it when I see it, Dad," I replied cynically. "What's that old saying about the plans of men and mice? You ever heard that one?" I asked.

"Mice and men. They go astray," he replied, somewhat put off by my pessimism.

"The mice and men go astray?"

"The plans, ass," he said, unamused at my feigned stupidity.

"Ass, mice, men, plans. It's too complicated. Tomorrow we'll still be in Wonsan," I replied.

"Party pooper. Listen, John," he said, trying to rekindle his doused enthusiasm. "They should be passing the word over the horn any time now. We oughta be clearing the harbor in a few hours. Probably not long after midnight."

"Maybe that's what Nine-Fingered George meant when he was bringing me in. He held up all nine fingers."

"For you he should've held up just one, John—the *middle* one," scowled Dad, slouching back in his chair. "Is this going to be another bad joke?" he asked suspiciously.

"No, I'm serious." Nine-Fingered George held up all nine fingers when I came in at around 1700. So if he was telling me how much longer we had to go before leaving, that'd put us out of here in nine hours—around 0200. That ties in with what you said doesn't it?" Whittaker's spirits soared.

"There! You see? That's right! Sasebo, John! I can't wait!" he proclaimed jubilantly.

My dour outlook relented and we settled into a giddy discussion of what we would do and where we would go during liberty in Japan. We were laughing over something when I caught sight of Captain Williams, the commanding officer of our task group, coming into the wardroom. He didn't look happy.

"Hey Dad," I said nodding toward Captain Williams.

"Huh?" said Whittaker, turning in the direction of my nod. "Uh-oh. . . ," he mumbled, covering his mouth with his hand. We awaited Williams's approach in wary silence. "Evening gentlemen," Williams said, joining us. We grunted some salutation back. "There's been a change of itinerary. We just got orders to stand by. Looks like Sasebo's off, at least for a while anyway." Our hearts sank. Whittaker was crestfallen and my own spirits, having been inflated by my friend's contagious enthusiasm, popped. What the hell, I thought. It wasn't as if I hadn't expected it.

"What have you heard, sir? Nothing particularly bad, is there?" asked Whittaker.

"No, nothing *particularly* bad as things go," replied Williams. "They haven't told us much yet other than to stand by . . . and that all available helicopters are urgently needed," he said. A grim but mischievous smile was on his face as he looked at us both. "Pilots too, of course. Seems as though we've got an immediate operation tomorrow morning. They're calling it Operation Virginia."

"That's nice," I said. "My wife's name is Virginia."

"Well, that's a good omen then," smiled Williams, rising from his chair. "Things should go swell. I gotta get topside. See you both at zero-dark-hundred. There'll be an early-morning briefing on the *St. Paul*. I'll fill you in on the details soon as I find out." As Williams departed, Whittaker and I pondered our plight. So much for Sasebo. It would be business as usual tomorrow.

Friday morning, March 31st, found two pilots from the Japanese-manned LST Q-007, Whittaker and me boarding a small landing craft bound for the *USS St. Paul* for a meeting with the admiral, of all people, and the cruiser's two pilots. There we would receive weather, operational and intelligence briefings. We already knew the weather was generally favorable with the ceiling and visibility unlimited, temperatures at or just below freezing and plenty of snow still on the ground inland. Operationally, the situation would be less than upbeat. The task force's appeal for all available helicopters had yielded only three. In these early days of rotary-wing flight, that was understandable since both copters and pilots were scarcer than hen's teeth. At the war's beginning there were 386 qualified Navy and Marine helicopter pilots, total. Of these, some had been killed testing this embryonic aircraft and many more had died in Korea flying this new-to-combat machine. Fewer than three hundred of us were left. We would be in HO3S-1's, early Sikorsky models that could carry a maximum load of only three passengers or 450 pounds in addition to the pilot. Normally a typical mission would include the pilot, a backseat crewman and two passengers but this operation would demand flying without crewmen.

After arriving at the *St. Paul,* we went to Flag Plot and sat down. The Admiral gave a few welcoming remarks and immediately turned the briefing over to his operations officer. He began somberly.

"Gentlemen, we've got a sensitive and extremely important mission to run here. Two and a half weeks ago, we dropped a twenty-four-man intelligence team by parachute behind the lines. The team consists of four American agents and twenty ROK (Republic of Korea) agents who've been posing as North Korean Army officers. They've picked up some excellent intelligence that we believe will be of critical importance to future U.N. operations here on the coast." He paused, furrowing his brow as he sorted facts hastily crammed into a crowded brain, then continued. "O.K. There's an old saying about the best-laid plans of mice and men going astray. . ." Whittaker cast a jaundiced look my way and hacked offensively. I returned his gaze with a look of puzzled confusion as if it still wasn't clear to me who or what often went astray. The operations officer went on. ". . . and unfortunately, this has been one of those occasions. The retrieval of this team was to be done covertly but there's no secret anymore. Their cover's been blown and they're running like hell. We got their first S.O.S. last night." No wonder Sasebo got canned, I thought. "The team has been on the move ever since they got flushed out of their last safe base of operations a day or so ago. They've linked up with seventy or eighty friendly guerrillas and are headed in this direction up this ridge line here," he said turning to a topographic map clipped to a chart-board. "It's rugged, saw-tooth terrain with two-thousand-foot peaks. That should make for some very unusual flying conditions, don't you think?" Stoney silence ensued. Forsaking the map, the operations officer returned to his notes. "Yes. Well. The North Koreans are close behind but they may not yet know specifically where our people are right now. We can't imagine them not spotting a trail of two hundred footprints through the snow come daylight today though and we know they have a fully complimented division in the area to do the looking. We and the team are assuming it's a matter of hot pursuit so they've got to get out now before they're trapped. With all of this, I'm sure you can appreciate the need for a quick evacuation." He paused a moment and rummaged through some more notes. "We're calling this action . . . Operation Virginia," he added distractedly, his voice trailing off. Finding the notes he wanted, he continued. "Here's how we want you to go in. The three copters will rendezvous over the *St. Paul.* Our radar will vector you in a southeasterly direction to this point here on the coast," he said jabbing his pointer at the map. "From here, you're to proceed south along the coast for thirty miles. And that would put you . . . right about here," he said as we rubbernecked, comparing his map to our own. "This is where you'll join up with air cover from the carrier *Philippine Sea,* then head due west inland for another thirty miles. And 'X' marks the spot. Here's where you'll make your pick-up." It was brutal terrain. The contour lines on the map were so close together they were almost indistinguishable in places. That meant steep, steep slopes and abysmal valleys. The up-and-down thermal drafts would be horrendous even with moderate atmospheric conditions.

The operations officer began wrapping up his briefing. "We know your copters are slow—what is it, about sixty miles an hour?" We nodded back. "That means about two hours round trip plus time over the pick-up point. That's maybe three trips maximum for each copter, three passengers each trip, or nine team members per helicopter before sun-down. Makes it kind of tight with twenty-four bodies to pull out, doesn't it? And you have no night-flying capability. You'll have a busy day. Let's get it started, gentlemen." We left Flag Plot and the *St. Paul* to return to the LST 799. There we readied for take-off and cranked up our choppers.

We got airborne and all went smoothly. As planned, we met our combat air patrol at the rendezvous point. It was reassuring to look up and see twelve fighter and attack planes there for our protection. They would be particularly reassuring over the pick-up point when we would be hovering like sitting ducks. We turned inland and halfway to our destination picked up another escort, this one a twin-engine Air Force transport. It was to be our communications link with the intelligence team. He would lead us to the specific site.

Having spotted the Air Force plane first, I took over as flight leader. I increased my airspeed and, not realizing the other helicopters were having trouble keeping up, I pulled ahead. This put me first on the scene. High on top of a ridge, I spotted colored panel markers laid out on the ground. That was the intelligence team, I thought—or was it? My instincts cautioned me that this might be a trap, the likes of which we had run into before. The gooks would lay out markers in the manner prescribed for downed U.N. airmen. Sometimes they would even go to the trouble of staking down a captured pilot, camouflaging the stakes and ties to give him the appearance of being injured or unconscious. They would then surround the spot and, when the rescue copter came in to touch down, cut loose with a hail of small-arms fire. With this in mind, I circled once, then circled again. It looked good and as I closed in at low altitude, I spotted the friendlies. They were clearly visible now, perched on the ridge line and, as the intelligence analysis had warned, they were very nearly surrounded. The slopes seemed to be crawling with North Koreans. I was close enough to see the little puffs of gunsmoke being exchanged up and down the hillside. And going into a close encounter such as this, I always flew with both doors open in order to hear and determine the volume of ground fire and to pinpoint its origin. It was clear that a vicious firefight was in progress. Our escort cover went into immediate action strafing, rocketing and napalming the North Koreans to give us a chance to fly in and to allow the ground team to take a breather of sorts.

The clearing at the top of the hill was roughly half the size of a football field and served, appropriately enough, as a Korean burial ground. The slopes below fell off at a thirty-five-degree angle, extremely steep, and the up- and down-drafts were as severe as expected. I went in to try a hoist pickup first rather than try to land on so precarious a point as the hilltop with its swirling air currents. I came in, but try as I might, I couldn't maintain my position well enough to begin a hoist. After repeated, futile efforts, I radioed my problems to the other copters and told them I would try one other option before they arrived. If it didn't work, we'd simply have to try something else. Rather than fight the thermals, I decided to try using them to my advantage.

I dropped down into a quiet sector of the valley. I planned to ride a thermal up the hill like an escalator. At such time as I reached the hilltop, I would slide into the clearing, rest a wheel on one slope rather than attempt a near-impossible full landing and get three men to scramble inside. Clever thinking, I said to myself as I descended. Things below looked clear and I flew on, confident that I would be back uphill in a jiffy. After reaching a satisfactory point of departure, I turned to seek out a thermal and flit up the mountain. Gingerly but confidently, I mounted the escalator and took off. It was working nicely and I happily shot up the slope.

But then I spotted something. There was movement up ahead of me. My eyes bugged out of my head as I gaped at what loomed in the near distance. Gooks! They were only five hundred yards from the summit. Despite the horrendous pounding from the airstrikes, the North Koreans had succeeded in moving up and around the mountain. Without warning, I found myself flying into a cloud of them. The world suddenly became engulfed in a loud, clattering noise. The hull of my copter sounded as if it were in a mammoth hailstorm, pelted by gigantic stones of ice. Caught totally by surprise, I realized that I was flying through a murderous crossfire. Sounding like ball peen hammers pounding on an empty boiler, the bullets tore through the copter, ripping holes in her thin flesh and tearing away entire chunks of sheet metal. The racket was deafening as she vibrated, bucked and trembled with the shock of deadly injury, but there was no turning back. I had no choice but to fly through it and continue up the hill. Finally I broke through to the friendlies, breathing rapidly but relieved that I had run the gauntlet.

I applied power, pulled up on the collective to hover, and prepared to descend. It was as if my copter had known its end was near, for in that knowledge she did as much as she could—she delivered me to the care of friends. Hanging twenty-five feet above the clearing, she sputtered, choked and then died. Her battle damage was too severe and at the bitter end, her body gave out. We had known each other only five days. We dropped like a stone. As she hit the slope, she slowly began to roll over to her left. The *Prasae* was still vivid in my memory and I had no desire to get caught again in another crashing helicopter that was ready to explode. I had to get out, but like always, the question was where. The right side was best but the roll was against me—I would be thrown over with the copter and possibly into the still-turning blades. The left side was only a little better so long as I could avoid being crushed. I dove left and out. Digging my fingers into the frozen earth, I bunched up like a hedgehog hoping I would be a tiny microdot, fixed in one place where I wouldn't be smashed or slide downhill only to be hit by the blades anyway in spite of my intentions. The agonizing copter reared up, rolled and plummeted over. Her left wheel plunged down and with a dull thump, pounded into my right side, breaking a rib. She overturned completely, rolled again and crashed into a stand of trees and brush, upside down. To my amazement, she didn't explode and burn, despite the fact that the fuel pump was still pushing fuel up and out of her upside-down belly.

As I collected my senses, I concluded that I was pretty much intact. Lying here, I assessed what I should do next. A man knowledgeable in helicopter landings and operations would have saved my ass. Deciding to turn misfortune into some semblance of benefit, I resolved to apply my hard-gained insight toward completing the rescue. My own knowledge of helicopters and their limitations in this environment would be useful here on the ground side of the action. I realized now that the hoists would be the only way to get anyone out, bad air currents or not. The thermals would simply have to be overcome. A landing was impossible and the escalator route was foreclosed at every potential avenue of approach. I knew the agents would fumble with the hoist and horsecollar sling at the end of it, wasting time and risking a deadly fall. But with my help, I could hasten their departure and properly prepare them for the lift skyward. I crawled down to my wrecked copter, the gunfire cracking through the trees overhead, and retrieved the horsecollar from my hoist. I scrambled up the hill and found the group's leader, Sergeant Martin Watson, who was operating a portable radio. He had witnessed my humiliating crash.

"How bad are you hurt?" Watson asked as I joined him.

"Not much. Just a broken rib, I think, but it's not bad. I told the other copters before I went in to forget trying to slide in here like I did. They'll have to try it by hoist. I think I can give them some good directions on how to approach. I can also rig you guys up. I'll put this horsecollar around one man, unsnap the one that comes down on the hoist and hook his up to the line. They can reel him up on the way out, in flight if they have to, especially after the last man is in. Pick out your first guy and we'll get him outa here." Watson accepted this proposal and waved over another American.

As the first evacuee came over, I slipped him into the horsecollar and explained how he should hold on. I made it abundantly clear that once he was on the cable, he would have to hold on tightly for a slip would mean a long final plunge. The winds relented briefly as I directed in the first copter. The pilot successfully hovered and lowered his hoist. I unsnapped the horsecollar and replaced it with the other, the agent already in it. Up he went. The pilot was able to hold his position long enough to bring up a second man but the added weight and the renewed gusts of treacherous thermals prevented him from trying for a third. He sped away in a hail of ground fire. The second copter approached. With a third man ready and waiting, I quickly snapped him on to the cable. He stood there waiting, looking up at the hovering copter. Nothing was happening. The seconds ticked by.

"Why the hell isn't he reeling him up, for Christ's sake?" demanded Watson impatiently.

Shooting erupted again in a withering, unannounced barrage and we cringed reflexively. The waiting agent's head snapped back grotesquely as a bullet smashed into his face. The helicopter's dark skin sprouted white blotches as bullets tore through her, ripping away metal and paint. Suddenly, the pilot jerked her away, wrenching the injured but still conscious agent off the ground as he clung to the sling. Blood streamed down his face as the copter shot skyward. With the wounded man dangling on a string already five hundred feet up in the blowing, freezing air, the copter sped away over the hills. The agent trailed behind like the tail of a kite. We were horror struck by the pilot's precipitous departure. Watson exploded and turned on me venomously.

"What the hell do you call that?! Your goddamn pilot got *his* ass out O.K. but the hell with my guy hanging there with his face shot off. *Bull*-shit!" he roared. He stalked off. If was a poor showing all right. I had no explanation to offer. Why hadn't the pilot activated the hoist? Did he freeze up? Go chicken when the gunfire erupted? It sure looked that way. I became sullen and angry. The bastard bailed out with a gravely wounded man dangling below him on seventy-five feet of cable.

I would fume over this apparent act of cowardice for years before learning that it was not cowardice but good judgment first and later bravery that were at work here. As it turned out, the copter's winch had failed. Knowing that he could delay no longer and believing he could still get this third man out alive, the pilot pulled away while he could still maintain flight. He flew only a few miles, the wounded agent clinging to the hoist. They then landed— deep in enemy territory. The pilot touched down, completely disengaged his rotors, left his engine on idle and locked down the controls. An attack would have caught him completely flatfooted. Jumping from the cockpit, he ran toward the frozen agent who was lying on the ground in shock from his facial wound and cold. The pilot had to pry the man's freezing, clenched hands loose from the sling.

Having done so, he carried him back to the copter and then home. He had saved a life and precious intelligence. He had done the right thing.

With both helicopters now heading out to sea, we were left to ourselves on the hilltop. Our objective had been to evacuate twenty-four men and while we had succeeded in getting out only three, the vital information we needed went with them. In that sense, the mission had been a success. The North Koreans seemed well aware of this and the departure of the last chopper appeared to incite them. Their determination to take those of us remaining behind was heightened and they pressed their attacks. They may have allowed key intelligence to slip through their fingers, but they could yet destroy a thorny guerrilla force, capture twenty trained South Korean agents and most interestingly of all, pick up their first helicopter pilot. It would be a big first. None had ever been captured before. They could still come away from this operation with three feathers in their cap and only one black eye.

As the ring of fire closed around us, our casualties began to climb. The ROK's and guerrillas were getting picked off and overrun as the noose tightened around our neck. Their still forms lay slumped here and there. It was noontime and the Air Force communications plane, which was running low on fuel now, was forced to leave the area. It had been up there all morning and had been our only radio link. When it departed, so did our communication with the outside world. Happily, the combat air patrol contiued to stay with us by constantly replenishing itself with fresh planes. The air attacks had been merciless but despite fierce casualties, the North Koreans edged through this rain of destruction closer and closer to the clearing. They were edging in to the point that it would be only a matter of time before we would risk being struck by our own planes. Both helicopters would be gone at least an hour before we could expect their return. An hour was a long time at the rate the gooks were advancing. We had to buy time if we were going to pull through this one.

They were on the move now, hundreds of them in what seemed every direction. The air was buzzing with bullets. They splattered and ricocheted everywhere, whining and whistling as they split rocks and hurled splinters throughout our little fortress. We needed more ammunition if there was to be any hope of holding them off.

"If my people are lucky enough to get aboard ship the way you've been flying today, they know they're supposed to get ammo and weapons loaded on the copters for the return flight," Watson informed me, still fuming over the last pilot's dismal performance. I tried to respond positively.

"I've got a few things in my copter. They should still be O.K. I've got a carbine, some ammo, a bunch of grenades. It'll help. Lemme go get it," I said, turning to crawl back down the slope.

"I'll go with you. You'll need the extra hands and some cover," volunteered Watson.

We slithered down the hill under the sporadic popping of rifle fire and reached the junk heap that had been a brand new helicopter only a short time ago. We clammored inside and began rummaging around the scattered equipment and debris that was strewn about the cabin. Inside the crinkled fuselage, we muttered around like two characters at a rummage sale. The sounds of our stumbling and clattering did not go unnoticed. Silently, a squad of North Korean soldiers edged forward. Intent Asian eyes trained their gunsights on my dead chopper.

Instantly, a whole sector of the North Korean front seemed to erupt as they riddled the copter with gunfire. The ball peen hammering started again as the bullets slashed through one side of the copter and out the other. An automatic weapon opened up and the inside of the fuselage was like a beehive as slugs and metal flew and bounced around everywhere. Our bodies convulsed as we tried to duck invisible, supersonic bullets.

"Let's go! Get the hell outa here!" screamed Watson, bounding out of the wreckage. Needing no encouragement, I was on his heels. From the corner of my eye, I saw a North Korean appear then disappear. An object was in mid-air. Screeching to a halt, I prepared to jump anywhere away from the hurtling missile.

"Grenade!" I shrieked and hurled myself backward behind the rock with Watson cartwheeling in on top of me. The explosion was immense as the ground shook beneath us. Shrapnel flew overhead, ripping apart whatever stood in its way. Stray gunfire thwacked into the trees overhead, snapping off twigs and whole branches. Better placed shots drilled into the ground nearby, kicking up evil little geysers of dirt.

"Up the hill, move it!" demanded Watson in one continuous word. We scurried into the beleaguered perimeter, clutching our meager supplies to our bodies.

The air strikes were nearly on top of us. The rocket attacks were so close, their impacts were vibrating the ground with the same intensity as the near-miss grenade. They boomed rapidly, one after the other, inflicting wearying casualties on the North Koreans. Like strings of firecrackers going off, the cannons of the attack planes blitzed the earth, carving trenches in the ground and peppering the creeping ranks of this resolute enemy. The planes poured in napalm and scorched them. They machine gunned them, strafed them, rocketed them, and still hundreds survived to crawl upward, nearer and nearer. The valleys echoed with a thunderous roar but incredibly, maddeningly, the gooks were punching through the outer reaches of our perimeter. They were virtually upon us. Watson lost no time in organizing the last-ditch defense.

"O.K. this is gonna be it. We're gonna have to start unloading on them ourselves. They're here," he said with a note of desperation in his voice. He rushed about, coaching the ROK's and guerrillas in Korean, preparing them for a full-blown gun battle. Our ammunition would be quickly exhausted once we were engaged. There could be no air cover for us at these close quarters.

The gooks rose up in a frontal assault. My stomach was in a knot and all of my being seemed intent and focused on the onslaught that was now bearing down on us. Only a stone's throw away, the gooks poured in gunfire, one fire team covering for another as they leap-frogged forward. Bullets and men screamed as the ROK's to our front were being shattered. Their bodies catapulted uphill as they caught automatic fire square in their heads and chests. Their mangled, dead forms bounded downhill, catching on bushes and undergrowth. They took on horrible contorted postures, sprawled with their arms and legs tangled unnaturally around themselves. We threw fire back downhill, hitting the North Koreans almost point blank in the open. they spun and leaped backwards as if punched by some unseen hand and then, dead, tumbled downward. Their comrades were jumping out of their way, crawling and hopping over them as the assault pressed forward. The gooks seemed almost superhuman as they walked through our barrage.

Our casualties were becoming catastrophic. Of

our original ninety, only twenty were still functioning. The rest were dead or overrun. Watson had
some white phosphorous grenades which were
grotesquely effective against the North Koreans in
their heavy winter uniforms. He hurled one grenade
and then another. They detonated in brilliant
showers of glowing white streamers. The cascading,
white-hot embers slammed into the hapless troops
beneath them and ignited their quilted cotton
uniforms. Screaming in agony, they ran like
madmen as their bodies were engulfed by their own
flaming clothing. They writhed on the ground as
they were quickly immolated. The assault seemed to
falter in the face of this carnage. Boosted by the
momentary victory the phosphorous grenades had
produced, Watson hastily grabbed for another with
his ham-like paw. With the full weight of his hulking
six-foot-three-inch frame, he exuberantly flung the
incendiary downhill. His powerful follow-through
traveled full circle, blind-siding me as I watched the
bomb's flight. It sounded like glass breaking inside
my head as he inadvertently smashed me in the skull.

"Sonofabitch!" Watson roared, wincing as he
drew back his bruised hand.

"Who the hell are you trying to kill, asshole?!" I
bellowed as I refocused my vision.

"Keep your head down! You nearly broke my goddamn knuckles!" he groused, flexing his sore hand.

The grenades had taken an inhuman toll. For a
brief moment, the stunned attackers relented,
regrouping the mauled remains of their fire teams
into fuller squads. Our ammunition was three-
fourths depleted. We couldn't repulse another attack
and there were no more grenades. Another dozen
friendlies had been blown away or overrun. It was
hopeless. Down to only eight bedraggled survivors,
we were confronting what was clearly a big chunk of

the enemy division mentioned in the briefing aboard the *St. Paul.*

"Let's get the hell outa here while we can," muttered Watson. He directed the remaining ROK's away from the clearing to its wooded fringe. We scrambled away quickly as the gooks prepared for their final attack. As we reached the woods, Watson's face turned ashen. His head snapped around toward the clearing.

"Shit! Shit!" he roared. "We left the goddamn radio! Goddammit!" It was a grievous mistake as the radio was the only way we could reestablish contact with the Air Force communication plane when it returned. The contingency plan was that they would come up on the air every day to seek us out and arrange another evacuation effort. In our haste to withdraw, the radio had been abandoned and sat alone in the clearing. Watson was seething, cursing under his breath and blaming himself.

"I'm going after it. Take this," he said, handing over his rifle. I grabbed his arm.

"No, wait! Let me do it, Watson," I proposed. "If you buy the farm, nobody else can run the thing. We'll never get on the air without you." Watson considered this for a moment despondently. I could tell he wanted to do it himself to prevent any more mistakes. There had been too many today already.

"No. No, it's not your job, Thornton." He pondered the issue once more. "No, I'll send a ROK. Not a damn one of them knows how to run it but they should've picked it up anyway."

Watson called one over. They immediately started bickering and Watson began to steam. He angrily ordered the ROK to go, threatening to do him bodily harm if he refused. The ROK reluctantly complied, preferring angry North Koreans to the wrath of the giant Watson. Cursing in Korean, the ROK hugged the ground as bullets whizzed overhead. Reaching the radio, he grabbed a strap and, turning himself around, crawled toward us trailing the radio behind. He crawled faster and faster in his desperation to retreat and yanked the radio along callously. It bounced, rolled and smashed over the rocks. Watson was having a fit as he watched his precious radio disintegrate piece by piece, leaving a trail of broken knobs, handles and antenna sections behind it in the rocky terrain. We couldn't believe what was happening.

"He should have the damn thing on his back!" I said uselessly, wanting to pull my hair out.

"Well why the hell didn't *he* think of that?! Bastard's got his brains in his ass!" hissed Watson, totally disgusted.

The angry ROK arrived half pleased, it seemed, to present Watson with the wreckage that had been his prized wireless. The radio was a total loss, completely inoperable. We would pay for this costly mistake that very day as our planes returned and flew directly over our heads.

The Communists now rejoined their attack, opening fire in full force. It was coming from every direction. Or was it? The battle-wise Watson had earlier noted a gap in their field of fire, directly behind us, deeper into the trees. The fire was only coming from an arc spanning our flanks and front. There was none to our rear—yet.

The gooks broke into the clearing and swept the area with automatic fire. It was definitely time to go. Turning, we careened down the hill in a wild melee, stumbling, rising, running and falling again as the bullets hissed overhead from behind us and from either side. We were literally being shot off the ridge and our major fear now was that the enemy on each flank would converge, catching us in a pincers and crossfire. We continued our bruising, headlong plunge downward for a half mile and descended into a wooded ravine expecting an ambush at any time. But none came. For the present, we had slipped free of the closing noose up on the hill. Exhausted, we collapsed on the ground for a short breather and to plan our next steps. Sitting there, we heard engines overhead. We rose to our feet scouring the sky.

The helicopters had completed their one-hour circuit and were arriving back on the scene. Laden with fresh supplies, weapons and ammunition, they headed for the hilltop, unaware we had been knocked off only moments before. Later, I learned that my friend Dad Whittaker was piloting the first copter to arrive. He charged into the clearing and immediately began lowering a goodie bag of supplies. Peering out the side, he saw to his instant horror a score of hostile faces with raised rifles. They opened fire inhospitably, sending Dad into a hasty withdrawal. Word got around quickly that the situation had turned for the worse and the copters began searching for us as did the other aircraft. If only we had had that damned radio! Dropping into our ravine, the two copters flew just five hundred feet above us. They were so close, I could see the pilots sitting in the cockpits. I had never felt as helplessly cut off as I did then. So near and yet so far. Frantically, we tried to attract visual attention without revealing ourselves to the marauding North Koreans. For thirty minutes, the aircraft flew up and down the ravine searching for us fruitlessly. They never found us. As they flew off and the sounds of their engines diminished, so did our hopes. Soon they were gone. The sky was empty.

Quiet settled over the ravine. Except for the blowing wind and the rustle of the leafless trees, there was silence—lonely, empty silence. Two Americans and six ROK's found themselves alone, sixty-five miles behind enemy lines without water or food. We had no radio, almost no ammunition and a pitiful collection of weapons—one M-1 rifle and my carbine. The rest carried only pistols. It would be a long way home.

On this day, March 31, 1951, I had taken the first steps of a long and perilous odyssey. During the odyssey, my body would plunge into the worst depths of human misery. But it would also come to pass that at the nadir of my physical existence, my spirit would find broader horizons of faith and understanding. I would be buoyed up by two main pillars of strength. I had been drawn nearer to the first in the flames of the burning *Prasae*. There, God had reminded me of His presence beside me and shown me that I could always be confident in the knowledge that He would never abandon me. He had prepared me. The second pillar had ironically been the namesake of the mission which would launch me into a journey that would leave me forever changed, just as she herself had changed my life by becoming a part of it. Jinny would sustain me. As I sat amid the forbidding and heartless peaks of North Korea, I trusted that God would stay with me again and prayed that I would live to see Jinny once more.

My body was bruised and battered. I was winded and with every inhalation, my broken rib reminded me of its presence. As the shadows of afternoon lengthened, the first breath of the evening chill stirred in the ravine. A long night was approaching. It would last nearly three years.

4

Through Me The Way Is To The City Of Woe:
Through Me The Way Into The Eternal Pain;
Through Me The Way Among The Lost Below . . .
Relinquish All Hope, Ye Who Enter Here.

—Dante
The Inferno

"Time we got outa here," grunted Watson as he
rose to his feet. Knowing that the gooks would fan
out quickly to mop up any survivors, I and the six
ROK's needed no coaxing. We cautiously departed
and, after crossing a road, climbed the next ridge
where we holed up until sundown.

Perched at the peak of the ridge, we observed a
small town. Faintly in the distance we again heard
the sound of approaching aircraft but as they came
into view, it was clear that they were interested not in
us but in the town. It was a flight of F-51 Mustangs.
Piecing the planes and town together, I quickly
understood that there was the headquarters of the
North Korean division that had been reported in the
area and attacked us. Perhaps some of the intelligence carried back by Watson's evacuated team-
mates was already paying dividends. The F-51's
peeled off and began their runs, attacking with efficient malice. Their strikes were well placed as the
town was methodically pounded to ruin. Secondary
explosions erupted in the wake of the strikes as the
innocent-looking houses disgorged their caches of
burning fuel and ammunition. The baritone detona-
tions echoed off the hills and as the sun began to sink
below the peaks, a hellish glow began to illuminate

the valley as the gutted village was consumed in flame.

The planes departed and as the explosions died out, the same deathly silence that had fallen after we were thrown off the hilltop now gripped us once again. Our loneliness was offset only by the grim satisfaction we derived from watching the complete immolation of the enemy's headquarters and stores below us.

Watson's mind had been clicking throughout the climb up the ridge and during the airstrike as he assessed our options and various plans of action. He was an old hand at this sort of thing and knew most of the evasion tricks in the book. He, more than anything else, would sustain us and insure our survival. Added to this was his own personal determination not to be captured. He had been there already, having spent two years behind barbed wire in Germany. He announced his plan.

"First thing we do is travel by night only. There's no moon for at least a week which makes it that much the better. You and me being white doesn't exactly help us fit into the local population by daylight. Neither does my size," Watson advised.

"How long would it take us to make the coast? It's thirty-five miles as the crow flies from here," I observed.

"Five, maybe six days. We could go there or south to the front lines. They're both lousy options. The coast is a lot closer but getting through will be damn tough. I don't think we should try it," said Watson resolutely.

"Why not?" I asked, not fully comprehending his decision.

"You know the Navy's making feints up and down the coast, right? Phoney amphibious landings, massing ships, two- and three-day bombardments?

You've even put landing craft in the water, all empty of course, and faking a charge to the beach," he said like a patient tutor instructing a slow student.

"That's right. The gooks always beef up their defenses. Then we lay a smoke screen and duck out, lock, stock and barrel. Big surprise, no attack. Two days later we pull the same stunt further up the coast, like a shell game. They bite every time. Scared to death they're gonna get hit with another Inchon invasion," I recounted.

"Yeah, it's worked pretty well. They've pulled off loads of people from the front to cover about sixty-five miles of coast. Their lines are three deep, thousands of them just sitting there on their thumbs. Besides that, they're right there on the coast where you guys can pound the shit out of them with the big Navy guns like those sixteen-inchers from the Mighty Mo. Now you know why they need monkeys like me scrambling around in the weeds blowing the whistle on gook positions. So anyway, as thick as it is at the front and even considering the extra distance, I think we stand a better chance of slicing through enemy lines at an angle." This option had been relayed to us the night before in the event we did end up in a pickle like this. "Any survivors should strike out on a general compass-heading of 140 degrees, southeast toward the town of Yang-gu. Keeping to this route will give searching aircraft a navigational baseline of search. Plus we don't have to worry about a sea pick-up and all that. We just walk across. Simple, huh?" he asked sardonically. "Simple?" I retorted. "Shit, I suppose the southeast angle is better strategy than going due south or east and hittin' 'em head on. The shorter routes won't be the safest, but our longer route ain't gonna be simple."

The darkness was now complete. We set out for our goal, the little town called Yang-gu, which was sixty-five miles southeast of us across endless, three-thousand-foot mountain peaks. As the evening progressed, the exhaustion of a long day, its events, and night-time mountain climbing were taking their toll on me. We took a break and I immediately fell asleep. Watson waked me after what seemed to be only a moment but which in fact had been a half-hour. I pleaded with Watson to go on and assured him that I would catch up after I had properly slept. He knew better and gave me a benzedrine tablet. Sleep was no longer a problem for the remainder of the night, although being without water made thirst a new difficulty to contend with. As dawn approached, we assessed our progress. A full night's work had yielded only five miles. If the vertical distances we had covered climbing the mountains were added in, it was probably more than three times that amount. Leaving one ROK on watch, the rest of us quickly fell asleep.

DAY ONE

After two hours, I awoke to find everyone else already up. Watson had dispatched two ROK's to scout the valley. There was movement below us.

"They're in white, Watson. Civilians?"

"Yeah. Probably on the way to their fields. They terrace these hillsides and plant all the way up, just about. Some are so high they have to climb two hours before they can even start to work."

"You don't think they've been alerted to look for us do you?" I asked fearfully.

"Mmm. Possibly. Even if they haven't, I'm sure they'll pass the word if they see us. We'll stay put like I said. Keep a lookout, clean our weapons and lay low." Watson concluded the discussion and went to sit by himself.

A little past noon we were startled by shots and the

drone of airplane engines. Our eyes groped across the sky and then spotted them. They were the same type of planes that coordinated our rescue mission the day before. They were still searching for us. If only we had the radio, thought eight minds simultaneously. The search aircraft flew a square pattern overhead, the sides of the square ever expanding. As each leg became longer, the plane went farther and farther away from us. Finally, she and the rest were gone.

"Close, but no cigar," grumbled Watson, probably more aggravated at being reminded of the smashed radio than at being missed again by friendly searchers. But after all, it was April Fool's Day.

Watson pulled out his one and only map and showed me our game plan for the night. To continue moving southeast, we would have to cross a river swollen from the spring thaw, a large highway, and then a railroad.

"It's a main supply route," observed Watson, "and come sundown it'll be choked with gooks, supplies and equipment. Only way they can avoid air strikes. We have a contact here locally who might be able to show us a good way across all this if he's still in business. I'll see what I can do," he said, talking to himself almost as much as me. He summoned a ROK and sent him to seek out the contact.

Two hours passed and the sun was beginning to touch the mountain tops. Activity would be picking up as the nocturnal gooks emerged for their nightly movements. A lot of time had passed since the ROK had left and we were getting anxious. Had he been caught? Would he be followed back to our position? Was the contact still operative?

Darkness had almost completely enveloped us as two figures made their way toward us up the slope.

One was in white civilian dress with a Korean "A" frame pack on his back. The other, much to our relief, was the ROK. The civilian, Watson's contact, told us he would get us across the three obstacles but would have to leave at once to avoid leaving his own zone of operation and risking undesired attention.

It was now pitch-black night. We began down the mountain side single file and soon reached the river. Across it, the scene on the nearby road was almost unearthly. The bat-like North Koreans were now out in the thousands, a long sinuous stream of humanity moving along the highway. It looked like a procession of the dead as every tenth person or so carried a torch of burning sticks bound together. The flickering lights created an eerie glow that cast long grotesque shadows roundabout. As a torch failed and burned out, a new one would be lighted and blaze up. It was nightmarish to behold this mass of people moving through the gloomy night as if a huge funeral were in progress. Loaded trucks appeared and added their own spooky contribution as their lights blinked on and off, acknowledging signals to move, stop or wait. Next came the train, farther over, on the tracks parallel to the road. It too had a flickering light which blinked on and off as orders were given to slow up or proceed. My skin crawled with a creepy anxiety. A disconcerting chorus of sound joined this macabre scene as the off-key Asian singing of the troops combined with the occasional sounding of a truck horn and the train's whistle. Blending it all together was the rolling murmur of the flowing river. It was like approaching the mythical River Styx encircling the Lower World and across which Charon the Boatman ferried the dead souls.

Our guide led us cautiously to the river bank where we turned west and walked for a mile. Stopping, the guide told us to remove our shoes, socks, all clothing below the waist and our weapons. After doing so, each of us rolled his belongings into a compact ball. We tied our boots together and hung them around our necks. Holding our gear above our heads with one hand and grasping the man ahead of us with the other, we waded into the frigid water naked from the waist down.

We were crossing, strangely enough, on a submerged man-made foot bridge of stone rubble. Air strikes had knocked out most normal bridges so the North Koreans responded by building new ones just below the water surface where they would be more difficult to spot from the air. Some, like this one, were built by laying large stones from bank to bank for troop crossings. The stones were slippery and the swiftness of the current, combined with the increased depth caused by the melting snow, made the crossing a difficult one. We stumbled and fell but our human chain never broke. Our only loss was one set of boots belonging to a ROK. I replaced these by giving him the winter overshoes that I had been wearing over my flight boots. Shivering and cold, we rested on the opposite river bank collecting our strength for the next step—the highway crossing. We dressed and prepared to move out toward the road. Crossing the flow of people would be a greater challenge than the flow of the river.

Suddenly, we heard shots. Our stomachs leaped as the torches of the procession were quickly extinguished, plunging the area into complete darkness. It soon became apparent that it wasn't us they had spotted but a U.N. night-intruder aircraft. But it was too late for the gooks. The pilot had seen the column from afar. Like an apparition appearing out of nothingness, the shrieking night fighter swooped down, launching rockets, its cannons blazing.

Violent explosions shattered the night calm as the plane roared overhead. As the fighter shot up the enemy column, the gooks scattered in terror, screaming and running for their lives. It was a marvelous opportunity for us to make a run for it. Amid the chaos of rushing humanity diving for cover, we would scarcely be noticed. We scrambled across the road, then the railroad tracks, and flopped down on the far side. It worked! We had made it across unseen.

A short time later, we managed to slip away and bade our surreptitious guide farewell. We pressed on for the remainder of the night and settled in for the next day on top of another mountain.

Day Two

We sat out the next day overlooking a tiny village, watching carefully for signs of enemy activity. We were ravenously hungry, for with the exception of acorns, little green shoots of grass peeping out of the ground and two dried ears of corn we had found, we'd had no food. We picked out one small house on the outskirts of the village where we felt we could safely pilfer some provisions.

At dusk, Watson picked two of his most capable ROK's and sent them to forage in the village. The orders were that we would wait one hour and if they didn't return we would depart. They headed down the mountain and we stood by. Forty-five minutes later, they were back with food and an enemy patrol on their tails. There was no time to waste and without pausing to eat, we hastily took off.

We stayed on the move for an hour and a half, hoping to ditch the patrol. Normally the North Koreans were unwilling to chase around in the wilderness at night but this group was unusually persistent. We were tiring out quickly as we reached a trail between two hills. Halfway down the path, we saw another village ahead. That probably meant more enemy. We were boxed in.

"Get off the path and up the hillside about two hundred feet. We'll let them pass by," Watson whispered.

We had only climbed about fifty feet when we heard the patrol clambering down the trail making enough noise to raise the dead. We lay down in the brush, still as mice. The patrol stumbled along the rock-strewn trail in front of us. There were twenty of them. They kept moving and disappeared around a bend headed toward the village.

"It worked, Watson. We gave them the slip," I hissed, elated at our elusiveness.

"Wait and see," he cautioned me. Ten minutes passed.

More racket betrayed the return of the patrol. They were backtracking. The climb back up the trail had tired them and as they approached, we could see that the men were strung out too much. An idea flashed through Watson's brain.

"Stay put and don't make a sound," he whispered and silently motioned to a ROK to join him. The two of them slithered away into the gloom, down toward the trail.

The patrol moved up the path, looking tired. I counted the soldiers as they passed by. Fifteen . . . sixteen . . . seventeen . . . eighteen . . . nineteen. Twenty was lagging behind, a dangerous mistake for him to make. The rest of the patrol was pulling far ahead. He was alone and unprotected.

Like a demon popping out of the ground, Watson leaped silently at the Korean from behind. His massive hand swung around like a boomerang, smashing the Korean's throat to stifle any scream. In the same motion, he plunged his bayonet into the small of the Korean's back and jerked it upwards, slicing his entrails. Soundlessly, the Korean slumped in Watson's grasp and was dead. Watson and the ROK dragged the corpse off the trail and hid it among the brush.

Farther up the trail, the Korean platoon leader halted his patrol and initiated another periodic head-count. He found he was one short—number twenty was missing. The patrol looked back down the trail, listening for his approach. They heard nothing. They waited with growing apprehension. The dark, moonless night was quiet as a graveyard except for the haunting whisper of a light wind. A creepy sensation must have come over the isolated patrol as its members assessed their position. It was both dangerous and tenuous. Far from help and not certain of what they were up against, they decided they didn't want to find out. Fearfully, the patrol withdrew and headed home. They would search for their lost man and those who took him come daylight. But by then there would be miles between us.

DAYS THREE, FOUR AND FIVE

"We got a good-sized town coming up soon," Watson informed me. "Can't go around it without adding on too many damn miles and I don't think we're up to that."

"How many more miles?" I asked, not relishing the prospect of a trip downtown.

"We'd have to go out of this mountain range and into another. Could cost us three, maybe four days," he answered. He sounded dejected. "I think we can fake our way through the town tonight. Be best if we walked right through the middle of it rather than skulk around the outskirts. They probably have it guarded out there thick anyway."

"How are we gonna handle this, Watson?" I asked, a sense of impending doom sweeping over me.

"With the ROK's in those North Korean uniforms, we can pose as a patrol from someplace else just passing through on a sweep. Like that bunch last night. You're short enough where you won't stand out if you stay in the middle of the crowd. Me, I guess I'll just have to slouch a lot."

I shook my head, hoping Watson knew what he was doing. We lined up with four ROK's in front, then Watson, me and two more ROK's behind. We headed toward the town. As we approached, sentries spotted us and ordered us to halt. My heart leaped into my mouth. Thank God they didn't have flashlights and the darkness was inky. My adrenalin began flowing as a loud discussion commenced in Korean between the disguised ROK's and the sentries. I was dying inside. Surely the sentries would check out the line of crap the ROK's must be feeding them, I thought. The conversation concluded abruptly. To my stunned disbelief, we were allowed to pass through. We then headed toward the heart of the town. My mouth was dry as dust and my stomach was in knots as we casually ambled along the town's dark streets, brushing shoulders with enemy troops the entire way. After what could have been an eternity, we emerged on the other side of the town, unmolested and unnoticed. Reaching the outskirts, I died a little more as we were challenged by yet another guard post. The same animated and furious discussions in Korean ensued, more baloney being foisted off on the sentries and then, unbelievably, we were granted safe passage again. It was incredulous as our group receded into the dark countryside. I felt as if I had just lost twenty pounds.

We pulled this stunt twice more the following two

nights, and with much luck and anxiety, completed three more days of our perilous journey south.

DAY SIX

Our ordeal was taking its toll on the group. We were weakening rapidly. The stress of endless walking, the constant threat of being discovered and the absence of any meaningful food was deteriorating our cohesiveness. This and a growing sense of frustration resulted in flare-ups of temper and arguments over what to do next. By now, I was exhausted. My broken rib was killing me and my feet were getting frostbitten from being constantly wet and cold. The skin on the balls of my feet was literally peeling away. I was at the point where I was unable to maintain an adequate pace and was holding up the rest, which only served as another source of friction. I told Watson that the group could move no faster than its slowest man and that I was that man. I appealed to him to go on with the others and allow me to proceed alone as best I could. I simply couldn't keep up anymore. Watson was indignant and violently opposed this. Not only was I one more element of centrifugal force spinning apart the group for which he was responsible. He felt obliged to get me out since I had crashed trying to extricate him. I refused his demands to go. He had been out in the sticks far longer than I had and his condition was deteriorating at a dangerous pace too. We argued. I refused to move. Finally, we parted company on a badly strained basis, he thinking me insubordinate for ignoring his demands as the man in charge, I thinking him crazy to risk capture over someone who was only a damper on his chances at escaping. Angrily, Watson bequeathed me two of his least reliable ROK's as a going-away gift. I would have preferred that he keep them for it was to be an alliance that would not endure. As Watson left that night, I wondered if we would ever see each other again.

DAY SEVEN AND EIGHT

If Watson had been strenuously opposed to leaving me, the two ROK's were equally in favor of taking me up on the offer. I was a dual liability to them, first for being increasingly disabled and secondly for being an Occidental. On their own, they could move rapidly, but with me growing ever weaker, they were carrying dead weight. Further, an American in their midst would restrict them to night travel. Without me, they would have little trouble blending into the local background day or night, especially in their North Korean uniforms. An American tagging along would only draw undesired attention and raise all kinds of troublesome questions. I began to fear that they might even go so far as to switch their allegiance altogether, betray me and turn me in to save their own skins. At the minimum, I knew I was a risk they were no longer willing to bear. The tensions between us grew dangerously until finally, in no uncertain terms, they made their positions clear. After angry exchanges in broken English and Korean, we split up—at gunpoint. I was now totally alone. In my possession were my .45 pistol, one clip of ammunition, a pocketful of soybeans for sustenance and a wrist compass for navigation. These things, my broken body and the whole of North Korea were mine.

By dawn on the morning of the eighth day, my route had taken me down the side of another mountain to a point where I would move into the next set of ridges. Ahead, out in the open, lay a creek which paralleled a road. My attempt at passage would be exposed as there was little vegetation and a few trees along the fringes. I limped downhill and reached the creek. The sound of a large truck convoy suddenly reached me, catching me out in the open. I had spotted a ford across the creek which appeared to have been constructed by the locals. It consisted of four carefully placed boulders and a large tree trunk. I clambered over the boulders and stepped onto the tree. It was coated with ice. My feet splayed out from under me and I tumbled headlong into the frigid mountain stream. Completely drenched, I stood up in waist-deep water and hastily waded across the rest of the way. In desperate flight, I scrambled up the bank, across the road and up the hillside as the trucks rumbled by. Did they see me? I lay low and covered myself with leaves. The trucks never slowed their pace. I stayed down, waiting for thirty minutes to see if they would send someone back to look. No one ever came.

I emerged from my leafy cover sopping wet. I was wickedly cold in the brisk dawn air. My soaked clothes were freezing on my body and my boots were filled with icy water. I was freezing to death like this and decided I couldn't be much worse off if I was completely naked, so after climbing to the top of the ridge, I stripped. After removing all my clothes, I wrung them out and then slapped them against a tree to purge the freezing water. I couldn't hang the clothes up to dry for fear of betraying myself with a semaphore-like display of laundry so I laid them on the ground. It would be three hours before the sun was high enough to begin doing anything helpful. I sat naked and shivering with my wet flight jacket draped over my back—and waited.

As the day dragged by, I contemplated the condition of my wretched, naked body. I had received some shrapnel wounds on the first day when the grenade went off near my wrecked helicopter. Under normal circumstances and with proper treatment, they would have been considered minor but now they were infected and festering. My feet were in horrifying condition. My frostbitten toes were turning black. The skin was virtually non-existent on the heels and the balls of my feet. My broken ribs continued to ache. I was miserably weak from lack of food. I was certain that I could not carry on much longer.

The front lines were now about twenty miles away. One last supreme effort would do it. I had to stay on the move, I believed, because I was certain if I sat down again, I would never get back up. The snow was still deep up in the hills and this would not help my speed. I had to fight this and the limits of my flagging endurance if I was to survive. A sense of desperation swept over me and I decided to throw my main protection, the cover of darkness, to the winds and press on day and night. That was a grievous mistake.

The day turned out to be a beautiful, sunny spring day. The sun warmed me and eventually made my clothes dry and wearable for the cold night ahead. As the sun dipped below the jagged North Korean peaks, I dressed and embarked on my final, all-out effort.

DAY NINE

It was daytime on April 9th, the first of my diurnal treks. I was covering ground well, much to my satisfaction. In late afternoon, I came to a fork in the ridge line I was traveling on. The right fork appeared to run generally more to the south, the direction I was heading in, while the left fork seemed to go due east. I took the one on the right but as I went along it began to veer more and more to the west. I decided the other fork would probably suit my needs better and rather than retrace my steps, I thought I would short-cut through the ravine dividing the two ridges. Moving down the slope and reaching the ravine, I started up the other side. About halfway up, there was a startling shot and my right heel was stung as a bullet grazed my foot. I dropped reflexively to the ground and lay still.

I could hear movement, the crackling of tree branches and the rustling of dead leaves. It sounded like only one man. The careless racket being made and the absence of further shots led me to conclude that this joker thought he'd killed me. The sounds seemed to be coming from the area I'd just left, the right fork. It turned out that the fork was connected triangularly by a third ridge. The Korean was coming around by way of that third ridge rather than climbing down into the ravine and up. He was taking the lazy route. He could have kept his eye on me by going the hard way but chose to do otherwise. I knew he couldn't see me the full distance around. I was now certain he believed I was dead. I would take advantage of his overconfidence.

As he disappeared into the thicket of the third ridge and angled around, I bolted up the slope with a sudden burst of energy that shocked me. I settled in at the top of the ridge facing where I thought he would pop out of the woods. It was an easy enough guess to make as I tracked his noisy progress. Sounding like an elephant crashing through the jungle, he slowly, unwittingly approached. I reached down for my .45 automatic and lay down quietly, awaiting his arrival.

He was close now, very close. My eyes scoured the thick brush and my ears pricked up like a dog's, audibly focusing and refocusing his position. A few more steps and he'd be in sight. I raised the .45, gripping it firmly in both hands. There were no second thoughts, no hesitation, no moral conflicts running through my mind as I prepared to carry out an act in which there were no choices to be made. With grim resolve, I determined not to miss as I bore-sighted the spot where somehow I knew he would emerge. Unwittingly, he stepped into my arms. Without remorse, I pulled the trigger.

The gun went off like a bomb, hurling its massive slug forward in an attacking cloud of smoke. The Korean leaped backward as the bullet smashed into him. The gore seemed to explode as pieces of his body sprayed into the brush behind. Mercifully, he never knew what hit him. He was dead before he struck the ground.

Staring at the Korean's dead form, I took a deep breath and paused for a moment. I pondered the ugly mess I had made of him. I had not enjoyed what I had done. Even so, there was a morbid sense of gratification in knowing that it was he, and not I, who was dead. I had no regrets. Callously, I dismissed from my mind all further thought of what had just occurred and immediately began assessing what I should do next.

I knew he couldn't have been in the area completely by himself and even if our two shots had not been heard, he would surely be missed before long. It was imperative that I move out quickly and put as much distance as I could between him, me and this place, so I did. I was close to the lines now, perhaps less than fifteen miles. I knew I would get through only if I could avoid more bloody, noisy encounters like this one. I also knew that as I approached the lines this would be increasingly difficult, but I believed I could do it. With a growing sense of optimism, I pressed on. To my relief, I was not followed.

That night, it began to rain and as the temperature dropped, rain turned to snow. Night travel was at best a dangerous endeavor in steep, unfamiliar terrain and in a storm it was that much worse. I couldn't see a thing and rather than risk plunging off a cliff I decided to stop under the shelter of a small ledge. I spent the night there as the snow and cold closed in on me.

The day's bloody events did nothing to deter my rampaging hunger. I was obsessed with the thought of food. As I stared out from under my little rock haven at the falling snow, my mind left Korea, for, of all places, Atlantic City, New Jersey where I had spent many a summer's day. I was on Pacific Avenue near the boardwalk at a favorite eatery, the Gem Restaurant. The Gem served the sandwiches of your dreams with turkey, roast beef, swiss cheese, kosher dill pickles, the works. I assembled a monstrous sandwich in my mind and greedily gulped it down, savoring the flavor. I made another and ate it. And then another. My mouth watered as I consumed food that existed only in a starving man's fantasy of a place half a world away. I vowed to gorge myself at the Gem as soon as I escaped from this God-forsaken wilderness.

As dawn approached I swallowed the remains of a tall glass of milk, wiped my mouth clean and relaxed at my special table at the Gem. I contemplated the warmth of the Jersey coast's summer sands and thought I might go lie in the sun awhile.

DAY TEN

The storm lifted and I emerged from my shelter with high hopes. I traveled for three hours and estimated that I was perhaps ten miles from the front. Another day to get out and I'd be with Americans again, in a warm bed with clean sheets, maybe even on my way home. Driven by my optimism, I tried to ignore my physical condition.

I came upon a high ridge with lots of snow on it. It looked deep so I chose to travel along a ledge circling a lower part of it and proceed from there. I began walking. But then a strange sensation came over me. Something was wrong. Instinctively I sensed that I was in danger. Some unknown receiver within me was registering a warning signal. The hair on the back of my neck stood on end like the hackles of a dog. I looked behind me to my right and then upward. An electric shock jolted me when I saw him. A gook, wearing a gauze face mask like a doctor in surgery, was peering down at me. Taking careful aim, he drove the rifle's bolt home.

I leaped away before he could shoot, if in fact he intended to. I was taking no chances as I scrambled behind a vertical slab of outcropping. My mind raced as I tried to assess my chances, escape routes, vantage points. I was so close to the lines. I still had ammunition and could shoot it out with him but if I killed him, I'd have to make up a lot of distance in a very short time. A week ago I might have been able to but I was in no shape to do so now. Should I try?

I mulled it over. I was so weak and tired, I couldn't do it, I decided. I was whipped and I knew it. It was finished. Dejectedly and with great reluctance, I tossed out my .45 and emerged with my hands up. The Korean stood there stupidly and then yelled something—to whom? I looked behind me and was shocked to see a second gook only a few feet away. Had I opened fire on the first, I surely would have been killed by the second.

I was shattered, spiritually and physically. Even my sixth sense had proven itself to be only fifty percent accurate. It's all over, I thought, standing there miserably. Rationalizing, I decided I probably wouldn't have made it anyway. As it turned out, I learned that I was more right than wrong.

As we traveled about a thousand feet down the mountain, I wondered in deep anxiety what would happen to me next. I reflected on the consensus on imprisonment that I had picked up from Watson and others over the past few months.

"Koreans don't take prisoners," many had said. "If you're gonna get picked up and have a choice, go with the Chinese. You'll live longer. Maybe two, three days," advised others. Watson had sworn they'd never take him alive and I wondered if he'd gotten through or, at worst, been killed. A Ranger who'd been captured in Italy, he'd had rough treatment in the hands of the Germans for two years and he vowed it would never happen again. His special status now as an intelligence agent would insure vicious torture and probably death if he was caught. The Germans had classified him as an incorrigible and if the Communists caught him, they would soon do likewise and make him pay for it. "They'll never get me," he had said, and I believed him.

Upon reaching their encampment in the valley, my captors ordered me to strip down. They took my dog tags, wallet, clothes, boots and heavy flight jacket. Having been fully pillaged, I looked like a fool as I stood there helplessly in my long underwear. I was advised by an English-speaking Korean officer who had arrived on the scene that I had nothing to fear.

"You must not worry, Thorn-ton. We have the Lenient Policy for all prisoners. We are peace-loving peoples. We will give you the good treatment. We only ask you to give the cooperation," said the nameless officer.

"How about the flight jacket? Can I have that back?" I asked, taking him up on his Lenient Policy.

"Why you want that? What will you give us?"
he asked, bargaining with me like a Chinese tea
merchant. He eyed my long underwear. "You give
the shirt, I give you the coat," he offered. I removed
my long underwear top now looking like a complete
ass and getting chillier by the minute. He made good
on the deal, though, and returned my jacket. I then
angled for the return of my boots to protect my
ruined feet again under the auspices of the Lenient
Policy.

"No shoes allowed! You walk barefoot and consider
your crimes. You must do this until you learn the
truth!" the officer retorted.

"These are capitalist boots. You don't want
capitalist boots, do you? Aren't yours better?" I
asked, grasping desperately at one last straw. The
Korean was untouched by this reasoning.

"We can use these boots," he replied simply, eying
them with satisfaction.

He left the area and I remained with my two captors. They ordered me to sit and then joined me, a
guard on either side. One had my .45 automatic and
was examining it with a mystified expression on his
face. The other, bored, paid no attention. The guard
with my weapon succeeded in removing the clip, and
looked it over. He didn't know I always carried one
extra round in the chamber. Its presence required
that the hammer be back in the firing position, which
was acceptable as long as the safety was on. The
guard kept fiddling with the pistol, trying to release
the hammer by pulling the trigger. I hoped he would
inadvertently release the thumb safety while pointing
the gun at his distracted friend. They'd both get the
surprise of their lives.

The guard was getting frustrated. He couldn't
figure out the mechanism to release the hammer.
Stupidly, he returned the weapon to me, thinking it

was empty. It wasn't. This was my chance. Should I take it? One quick flick of the thumb would release the safety and I'd send this gook's brains all the way south to Pusan. I could smash the other guy in the face with the pistol since he was doping off. I had to decide as I looked at the gun. The guard poked me impatiently, wanting his first lesson in the operation of the .45 calibre pistol. I could make it his first and last lesson very easily. I looked up at him.

I couldn't do it. I was just too exhausted. I'd be lucky to give the second guard a cut lip as weak as I was. I released the safety and pulled back the slide. As the bullet popped out, I gazed intently at the Korean. A look of stunned surprise swept across his Asian features. He was bewildered that I had passed up a golden opportunity. I let go the slide and pulled the trigger. The hammer clicked quietly. He snatched the gun away hastily.

A short time later, I was taken to a town—Yang-gu, surprisingly enough. It was the very town Watson and I were aiming for ten days ago. Ironically, the same day of my capture, Yang-gu was retaken by the Communists. Had I still been free, I'd have walked into town dumb and happy in a day or so expecting a fast flight home. Instead, I'd have stumbled into a North Korean stronghold and been captured anyway. Escape was simply not in the cards for me it seemed.

I was told that I had been picked up eighteen kilometers (twelve miles) from the lines. I had traveled fifty miles in ten days. I had almost made it, but almost doesn't win ball games. Twelve miles. They would prove to be the longest twelve miles of my life. Sick and starving, I had covered five miles a day. It would take almost three more years to cover the remaining distance.

5

So huge, so hopeless to conceive,
As these that twice befell.
Parting is all we know of heaven,
And all we need of hell.

—Emily Dickinson
My Life Closed Twice

"Jinny, you need to take a break, now. I *know* you should," counseled my wife's mother, Ethel Kauffman, over the phone.

"I don't know, Mother. I just don't feel right about leaving the house while Johnny's in all this. What if something happened? I'd be gone and not there to find out. I just don't feel right about it," she replied uneasily.

"Well, you haven't been anywhere but down here to our place since last summer. I think you should go down to Avalon and stay with Aunt Doll, since she has asked you, just for the weekend, maybe. It'd do you good," said Effie, persisting.

"I don't know," Jinny replied.

"The weather's getting nice and you'd enjoy it. April's pretty at the shore. Besides, George or Dan will come up and get you."

"All right. Come to think of it it'll be Friday the Thirteenth. Now I *am* worried," she joked.

Friday, April 13th came and after packing enough to last her and Jay for a couple of days, she left for New Jersey with Cousin Danny. It was a nice ride, getting out of the city into the atmosphere of the South Jersey shore. The wind carried the smell of salt spray into the car as they neared the coast. Even the fishy aroma of the marshes was refreshing, somehow. Grouchy gulls wheeled overhead as they pulled in front of Aunt Doll's drugstore. Jinny had spent many summers of her childhood here and it had almost been a second home to her then, leaving many happy memories. It might be a nice break after all. Besides, she thought, two letters had just come from Johnny. He seemed in great spirits. He even mentioned that he expected to get his "railroad tracks" for his collar soon. *Lieutenant* Thornton. No more of this Junior Grade stuff. He always hated being called junior when he was a kid anyway, she recalled. Reassured, she greeted her aunt and went back to the house to get settled. Friday the Thirteenth passed happily without incident.

Nat Winokur puttered around his Philadelphia gas station near the intersection of Oxford and Summerdale Avenues, not far from our house. Saturday, April 14 had been a mild, sunny day and spring was happily in place. In addition to his regular business, Nat worked with Western Union, taking and delivering telegrams as an adjunct source of income. He began examining the latest batch and noticed one to Virginia Thornton, a friend over on Van Kirk Street. A surge of anxiety hit him. It was from the Department of the Navy. Not John, he thought breaking into a sweat. It couldn't be. He hurried out of the gas station and into his car.

Turning one corner and then another, he made his way down Van Kirk to the middle of the block and parked. Climbing the high steps up the row house's terrace, he knocked on the door with a nervous rapidity and waited. No answer. Of course she couldn't hear him, he thought. She's probably upstairs with the kid. Ring the bell. Still no answer. He stepped back to peer inside the window. It crossed his mind that she might be out back hanging laundry but he decided to save himself the steps and

check with the neighbors. He went next door to the
Millers' residence and rang the bell. The door
opened.

"Hey, Nat. What's up?" asked Joe Miller, warmly.
Joe and his wife Peg were among our closest friends.
They had a little girl, Christine, the same age as Jay.
"Joe, I'm sick. I think I have some awful bad news
for Jinny. It's a telegram from the Navy," said
Winokur, distraught. "Do you know where she is? I
need to deliver this to her personally. And quick."
Suddenly alert and now upset himself, Joe
remembered.

"She left for the weekend. Avalon, I think, to see her
Aunt. I don't know where the hell she lives but I can
reach Jinny's parents. C'mon in a minute."

Joe quickly rang up Effie and related the grim
news. Aghast, she gave Joe her husband Herman's
phone number at Gimbel's Department Store where
he was working that day. Joe succeeded in reaching
Herman, who in turn immediately called Avalon.

"Keen's Pharmacy," answered one of Jinny's
cousins.

"This is Herman. Is Jinny there?" he asked. His
manner was quick.

"Yeah, sure. Back in the house with mom, why?"

"Who am I talkin' to, Dan or George?" Herman
inquired.

Dan identified himself and Jinny's dad continued.

"Telegram came for her from the Navy up here.
Sounds like bad news. The delivery guy has to give it
to Jin. Can you get her and Jay up here real quick?"
Dan was speechless. Things like this just weren't
supposed to happen.

"Well . . . yeah, sure we can, right away, Herm. Let
me go and we'll get started. Christ, I don't know
what to say, Herman. Poor Jinny, what the hell is
she gonna do?"

"I don't know, Dan. Bring her by our place first, will you? I think Eff and I will pack a few things and spend the night at her house. I'll take us over there in my car."

"Yeah, O.K. Herm." He hesitated a moment. "Jesus, how am I gonna tell her this? I guess . . . I guess I better go do it though," he stammered. "Thanks for the call."

"Bye, Dan."

Jinny was with her Cousin George when Dan entered the house. George sensed trouble in his brother's face.

"Something wrong, Dan?"

"Yeah. Herman just called. It's about Johnny. A telegram from the Navy up in Philly. That's all I know about it. We need to get you home, Jin. They gotta deliver it to you." He looked away feeling weak.

Jinny's stomach knotted like a tightly twisted rope and she was suddenly swept with nausea. Her eyes blurred with tears as she automatically assumed the worst. I was dead and she knew it. Crumpling against George, she wept grievously.

"He's gone, I know he's gone," she sobbed.

"You don't know, Jin. We haven't even seen the telegram yet. Maybe he just crashed or something."

"He's dead, I just feel like he's dead," she said, coughing out in a renewed surge of grief. The two brothers felt helpless as they watched her anguish mount.

"Don't cry, sweetheart," said George, trying to console her.

As she would learn to do so well in the coming years, Jinny forced calm on herself quickly. She had to get ready to go. She had a son to care for. Taking a deep breath and wiping her eyes, she went to pack her things.

It was 10:00 p.m. before Jinny completed the circuit from Avalon to her parents' home and then to her own. Herman pulled up to the curb and discharged his family. He was not parked as he wished and returned to the car to turn it around so it would face the traffic. Perhaps he was just fidgity. What a night this would be, he thought, feeling very fatigued. He pulled into the silent street. There was no traffic. He pondered how his daughter's whole life had collapsed in a day. It wasn't right, he thought bitterly. She never deserved this and God knows John didn't either. He'd already fought one war and narrowly survived a crash into the sea making a carrier approach in a Corsair. It was a lousy world, he thought, just a lousy goddamn world. He was angry. But then his throat tightened and he broke down like a small child in the privacy of his car. Wiping his eyes under his glasses, he pulled over to the opposite corner. As he put the car into reverse for a three-point turn, he tried to compose himself. Maybe the telegram wasn't as bad as they had thought. After all, they could be jumping to conclusions. Maybe John was only wounded or something. Somehow he just didn't believe that.

The car suddenly jolted and bounced upward and back, to the sound of breaking glass. Herman swore. He took the car out of gear and got out, walking to the rear to investigate the problem. He had backed into a fire hydrant and smashed out his tail light. The hydrant was undamaged. Friday the Thirteenth's events had come a day late, he decided. Sullenly climbing back into his car, he drove the short distance back to the house and getting out, slammed the car door with extra vigor. The hell with it, he fumed. The hell with it all.

Back inside, he found Joe Miller with Jinny and Eff. He shook hands with Joe, each trying to force some semblance of a smile and good cheer. It wasn't easy. Nat Winokur arrived next, looking somewhat haggard. He knew this family and couldn't avoid sharing their anguish. He handed the sealed telegram to Jinny apprehensively. Trembling, she struggled to open it. It consisted of strips of tape pasted on a yellow sheet. The words all seemed to run together:

WESTERN UNION
W. P. Marshall, President

1951 APR 14

PA545
FQAO46 LOHG RX GOVT PD =
WUX WASHINGTON DC 14 1200P

MRS VIRGINIA ROBERTA THORNTON =
1026 VAN KIRK ST PHILA

=IT IS WITH DEEP REGRET THAT I OFFICIALLY INFORM YOU THAN YOUR HUSBAND LIEUTENANT /JG/ JOHN WILLIAM THORNTON UNITED STATES NAVAL RESERVE HAS BEEN REPORTED MISSING FOLLOWING ACTION IN THE KOREAN AREA. ON 31 MARCH WHILE PILOTING A HELICOPTER ON A RESCUE MISSION HE CRASHED IN NORTH KOREAN TERRITORY. HE WAS NOT OFFICIALLY REPORTED MISSING UNTIL THIS TIME AS IT IS BELIEVED HE WAS UNINJURED AND HAD JOINED A FRIENDLY PARTY. HOWEVER SINCE HE HAS NOT REPORTED

BACK TO HIS COMMAND TO DATE OFFI-
CIALLY HE IS TO BE CARRIED IN THE
STATUS OF MISSING. I AM MINDFUL OF
YOUR DEEP ANXIETY AND AS QUICKLY AS
ADDITIONAL REPORTS ARE RECEIVED
YOU WILL BE INFORMED
= VICE ADMIRAL L T DUBOSE
CHIEF OF NAVAL PERSONNEL

"Missing. They've got him as missing," Jinny
informed the others gloomily. A ray of hope
illuminated them.

"Then he's not dead. Well that's a hell of a lot better
than I expected. Thank God," breathed Winokur.

"God, what if he gets captured," Jinny said anxiously. "He won't cooperate with them. He told me
he'd sooner drop dead than do that." She thought a
moment more, her mood darkening again. "What's
to say he didn't get killed somewhere? May he won't
even *get* captured," she said pessimistically. She felt
very cold, and shivered. She was getting nauseous
again. Joe patted her on the arm.

"Want a cigarette to calm your nerves," he asked,
half joking. Jinny didn't smoke.

"Yes," she answered quietly.

Sunday morning Jinny awoke feeling exhausted.
The bad dream of yesterday's events was depress-
ingly still there. The reality of it could not be
escaped. A sense of hopeless finality gripped her as
she lay there in bed staring at the ceiling. A vision of
the rugged terrain of Korea formed in her mind. She
had seen it on the television newsreels and in the
papers and magazines. She pictured me in those
mountains, alone and forsaken in a brutal
wilderness. She saw a lifeless form lying on a hillside,
forgotten and unburied. She imagined the callous
winds of the highlands blowing across a still body as

the war and the world moved on. In her vision, I was dead—gunned down and shot to death in a cold and hostile land far from home. Far from her. She was overwhelmed again and cried bitterly, alone in her room. What would she do? How would she tell Jay? *What* would she tell him? How would he take it? He was so little to have to bear this sorrow. She got control of herself and once again imposed calm on her battered spirits. She would have to be calm for Jay's sake. He was such a little boy. Not even three. She would have to collect herself first before she could try to break the news to him. That would take her a little while.

A day or so later, she decided it was time he should know the whole story. Their abrupt departure from Avalon, the hasty drive home and an unexpected visit with his grandparents created an uneasy atmosphere that had not gone unnoticed. He seemed quite aware that something had gone wrong somewhere.

As his mother gave him the news, he quietly accepted her assessment of a future more uncertain than he had heard before. Daddy was lost in Korea but nobody really knew where. They hoped he would come back but couldn't be sure. He might be sick or hurt real bad. The Communists were fighting us in the war and they might keep him a long time if they wanted to. The child listened but somehow didn't believe his father would never return. He was sure he'd be back soon. His mother's distress was more disturbing to him than the news she bore which he didn't believe anyway. But Mommy was sad, real sad. He could see that, and it was this that frightened him more than anything. His father had told him to help her until he returned. This he would do. He would watch and take care of her. He would be all right as long as she was. Daddy will be back. He just has to fight those people, that's all. He wondered where Korea was anyway. It must be a very bad place.

Neither Jinny's vision or Jay's conclusion were far from wrong that day, as it turned out. I was in fact thinking of them both, lying on a hillside—not dead but feeling close to it. I was in the company of thirty-five captured ROK's who, for the moment, were of greater interest to our captors than I. They were being intensely harangued and questioned, and mercilessly beaten. One of them had befriended me. His were the first acts of compassion I experienced in captivity. He stole small fragments of meat and gave them to me. He had a little brass spoon and gave me that as well. He spotted my first few body lice and cleansed me. Yet sadly, his many humane actions toward me were noticed by the North Koreans. He spoke little English, but left me with one succinct phrase: "Communists no fucking good." He was right. For his treasonous acts in favor of an imperialist, he was condemned, beaten and finally—he was shot.

6

When sorrows come, they come not single spies,
But in battalions!

—Shakespeare
Hamlet

I was getting bored with the tedium of the local commissar's harangue to yet another town's populace and my legs were beginning to tremble from standing in one spot for so long. This was about the third village I had been to in the past couple of days. A busy itinerary of public appearances had been arranged for me by my captors. The routine was always the same, and frightfully disconcerting. I couldn't understand much of the speech but I assumed that the commentary paralleled the content of my incessant interrogations. I was a butcher, capitalist running dog, imperialist war monger, killer of women and children. After the street harrangue, I would normally be tried by a "Peoples' Court," pronounced guilty and hustled away under a hail of spit, garbage and fists. I had been lucky. Other prisoners had been summarily shot at the conclusion of the festivities.

Today's group of citizens was advised of my high crimes against the peace-loving peoples. The tone of the commissar rose gradually to a frenzied pitch and he was artfully carrying the crowd along with him. It was a tired routine to me but this time things seemed to be getting a little out of hand. There was a more vicious and restless shifting in the crowd, louder, angrier shouts and shaking fists. The commissar bellowed, pointing at me accusingly. It was this American butcher who had murdered their sons, destroyed their towns and made war on them. Justice demanded vengeance. The warmonger must pay for his crimes. The face of the crowd turned black and venomous. They were pressing forward, shouting. The commissar grabbed me and jerked me about. The mob's frenzy was reaching the breaking point. The crowd closed in and I began to feel weak. My heart was pounding and my breath got short as I awaited my own lynching. They were ready for the kill.

Without warning, a Korean suddenly jumped to the fore, screaming, and I ducked, expecting to get smashed in the face. But as I cringed, waiting for him to strike, no pain came. He wasn't screaming at me but at the crowd. What the hell was going on? He appealed to them for order and calmed them down. He turned to me and in a fatherly tone, informed me in English that the mob wanted to kill me. Not much news in that, I thought.

"You American," he said didactically, "you have brought harm to these people and their anger is justified. But I have spoken to them and know that they are willing to be lenient. These people here," he said, motioning to the sullen crowd, "they believe you are in this war against your will and that you are a peace lover in your heart. These workers you see believe that you do not wish to kill peace-loving peoples and fight only because the warmongers force you to. These peoples wish to give you the opportunity to learn the truth and abandon your aggressive ways. I have appealed for your life under the Lenient Policies of the Communist peoples of the world." I was grateful, but was led away from the smoldering crowd only to be tried once more, condemned, interrogated and taught again about my incorrect thinking. It was an endless cycle that wore my spirits thinner by the day.

As my reactionary attitude remained unchanged, the violent-crowd routine was rolled out time and again from village to village on the assumption that, sooner or later, I would sell out and beg for mercy under the push-pull emotional stress of repeatedly facing and then being "saved" from imminent death. The pressure was even kept up at night after such appearances, when the village elders and kangaroo-court officials would mosey out to where I was held. I was always an intriguing war trophy. They examined me like an animal and I felt degraded and ashamed as I sat there half naked, filthy and helpless. They goaded, kicked and punched me, having a jolly time of it. On one occasion, there was an outburst of laughter as one grabbed my ear and twisted it. I fended him off weakly.

"Thorn-ton," said another English-speaking Korean as he giggled. "This man wants to know if you capitalists have money in your ears. I told him to look for himself!" He laughed heartily and advised the ear-pincher that his joke had been relayed. They chortled, and after a few closing shots, departed full of joviality.

I was near the end of my rope. What the kangaroo courts and mobs had failed to do, this close-range taunting and jeering was achieving. My pride had been shattered and I was being reduced to little more than a starving, cringing cur. I had been stripped of my clothing and now my dignity. I was desperately lonely, not having seen another American since leaving Watson. I was on the brink of despair. Their control over my life was complete. My well-being was totally in their hands and they were allowing me to die slowly.

I hated them. I wanted to fight back but in my

anguish I couldn't imagine how. What weapons did I have, I asked myself, trying to take stock of an overwhelming situation. Slowly, like answered prayer, a few ideas seeped into my groggy brain. I decided I had at least four things going for me. First, God had remembered me before and surely he would do so now. Others had not survived captivity as long as I had and, brief as it was, that seemed a miracle in itself. In these troubled times, I decided that my fate would, indeed must, rest in God's hands. Where it would all end, I had no idea. Perhaps it would be in a shallow grave in the Korean hills, but regardless, I chose to believe that the decision would be God's to make, not mine and definitely not the Communists'. They would neither captain my ship nor master my soul. God alone would and to that I was resolved. Second, I had Jinny and a whole family at home who would surely know by now that I was in trouble. Spiritually, they would be pulling for me. Third, I had my will. Although it was close to breaking, it hadn't happened yet and that was cause for hope. Finally, I had my body. It was decrepit, but functioning, at least. I wasn't dead yet. So I figured I still had some weapons, some of them pretty powerful at that. I pledged to apply them all as best my scrambled wits would allow me.

Early one morning, I was jerked roughly to my feet and shoved ahead toward a small building where I had previously received interminable interrogations and indoctrination sessions. I had noticed that my intestines were beginning to act up strangely, gurgling and writhing inside my abdomen. By and large, I hadn't had any real food to speak of during the past two weeks. What little garbage the Koreans had offered sustained me, I supposed, just above the level of total starvation. As I staggered toward the building, I also recalled that I hadn't had a bowel movement during this entire period, either. No wonder my insides were in rebellion, I thought, but there was simply nothing solid in there. However, there was gas. Lots of it.

I was unceremoniously led into the interrogator's presence. The small six-by-eight-foot room was pleasantly warm, heated by flues running under the floor which transported air circulating through a firebox outside the building. The interrogator was seated behind a small table. He looked professorial, wearing horn-rimmed glasses and a neat, clean uniform. His English was fluent and he was obviously well educated. He glared at me hatefully.

"Thorn-ton, American dog, sit on the floor like one!" he ordered. I complied sluggishly but not to suit. "Too close, dog! Back there where I can see you!" barked the Korean. I slid backward. My stomach was gurgling ominously.

Satisfied that he could watch me comfortably without having to crane his neck, the interrogator commenced the session. The usual questions ensued. Who was with you in the hills, how many, what was your mission, where were you going when we captured you and so on. My answers were obtuse and unacceptable. The interrogator's patience was wearing thin. The room was getting stuffy and hot. I felt crampy and painful inside.

My intestines groaned and then silently convulsed. Slowly I was engulfed in a choking cloud of noxious flatus. As it began drifting throughout the small room, I looked at the interrogator and detected a slight frown. Flicking his nose, he pressed on, undaunted. My bowels were generating into the proverbial uproar. Another heinous quantity of intestinal gas groped its way toward daylight and quietly escaped into the atmosphere. It was worse than the first and I even offended myself. The

Korean coughed, interrupting his discourse as I sat innocently on the floor. Then, with machine-like efficiency, my lower tract began to manufacture outrageously acrid quantities of gas at rhythmic twenty-second intervals. Why fight it, I asked myself. Annoying the interrogator was an inviting prospect, aside from the fact that a good deal of physical discomfort was being relieved. I decided to assist myself more aggressively and began flexing my abdominal muscles. Silence no longer considered golden, I resonantly cut the cheese in the key of E-flatus.

The Korean snorted and seemed to want to gag. I couldn't blame him. He reached for his handkerchief, wiped his brow and droned on. The tiny room was getting hotter by the minute. I continued to respond to his questions stupidly, punctuating my remarks with raucous emission. A hideous pungency was stifling our quarters. The interrogator sneezed convulsively, then coughed again. I was roaring inside with laughter as he put the handkerchief over his nose and tried talking through it. I rejoiced in the discovery of a weapon whose effectiveness could not be denied. Another question from the Korean evoked another evil round which burbled down the pipes and issued forth with a sickly rattle.

The interrogation was in a shambles. The Korean's pace and train of thought had been completely thrown off balance. He had lost control of the session. Worst of all, he knew that I knew he had lost control. He peered at me over the handkerchief with cold eyes that were unquestionably tearing in the acrid air. Then, removing his glasses, he laid them carefully before him on the table. After wiping his eyes, he raised an accusing finger at me and said solemnly, "Thorn-ton, you are a gas-maker." Nodding in agreement, I fired a parting shot. The interrogator could bear no more. He summoned the guards and ordered my immediate removal.

I was elated at having farted my way out of a quiz session. I resolved to try it again at the earliest opportunity. It wasn't long after that the opportunity presented itself. As another interrogation got underway, I readied myself. The distress in my intestines had continued unabated but was getting more painful. I felt a familiar surge and flexed. Sadly, I hadn't recognized the early signs of dysentery and as the seat of my pants dampened, I realized that I had just crapped in my drawers. No matter. I was escorted out of the room.

Having little else to occupy my time, my perverse mind began inventorying other physical means of retaliation. I was committed to using my body-weapon to the hilt. But the gas option had become too self-destructive and was, therefore, no longer operative. As I mused over the important question of how else to strike back, I hacked up phlegm that was accumulating in my throat as the result of a cold I had contracted in my weakened condition. I snorted more in through my nose and spat it out on the ground. A light went on in my head. That was it!

I didn't want to insult my captors brazenly for fear of provoking a ferocious beating, so I promised myself not to spit at them. I would be more oblique. I recalled in my childhood joking with Italian boys about their "dago handkerchiefs." It consisted only of the thumb placed against one nostril, a sharp snort of air through the open one and then squeezing the two together for the final wipe-off. The wipe-off was vital in the unfortunate event that the mucus was not fully extracted during the blowing operation.

The guard came by and ordered me up. Quiz time again. The prim and proper interrogator stood me before him at his table and initiated the session. He had a little stack of paper before him that I was to use in writing my life history. We'd been through this before and I was immediately bored. I had no intention of giving him something I knew he would later use against me or my family at home through American Communists. The situation was irritating me. Standing up was irritating me. The neat little pile of paper was irritating me. So was the row of pencils tidily lined up side by side. Time for the dago handkerchief, I thought.

Leaning slightly forward, I raised my thumb to my nose and snorted out a horrible string of viscous phlegm that dripped onto the stack of papers. I excused myself politely as if not noticing the damage I had done and repeated the process with the other nostril. Looking down, I feigned shock at seeing the mess I had made. Apologetically, I stepped away from the table and cleared my nose again, this time on the floor. The interrogator was incensed by my vulgarity. As he leaped to his feet calling for the guards, I hacked obscenely and spat a massive lunger at the wall. It struck with force and hung there insolently.

His distaste was heightened as my physical condition deteriorated and my dysentery intensified. I became known as the dirty little old man of the camp. It was no laughing matter to me, though, as I had lost untold pounds of weight and could now readily span my thighs with my hands. I had also accumulated a vast population of body lice. I occupied my time by counting those I successfully picked off and killed. My best daily record was two hundred. None of this went unnoticed by my captors. Unsavory though I was, my condition presented them with another creative way to subvert my will to resist. On what was to be my last day at this camp, they offered me a proposal.

"Thorn-ton," said one of two English-speaking Koreans sitting before me, "we make you a deal. You are sick, dirty old man. You must be very unhappy. We wish for you to be happy. How you like to stay alive, have food, clothes, medicine? We give you even cigarettes and G.I. coffee. You want these things?" Something stunk besides me. They were setting me up, I knew.

"What do I have to do for all these wonderful things?" I asked, knowing that the price would be too high before he even answered.

"Very simple, Thorn-ton. We ask very little of you but we will reward you greatly. You will go to our capital, Pyongyang. You will be allowed to talk over the radio and let your family know you are alive and in good health." He's kidding me, I thought. "We will permit you to make recordings to tell the world that you are living happily with the peace-loving peoples and that you are being well treated."

I was a starving wretch, filthy, sick and covered with lice. Well treated? Perhaps they misread me, thinking that after being miserable for so long, I might be ready to give up and lunge at the opportunity to rebuild my broken-down body. But they had to know better. I had turned down similar offers before. Were they desperate? The North Koreans' reputation for prisoner treatment was an international scandal and perhaps they wanted to salvage what they could of it as quickly as possible. That had to be their motive and with my intelligence value to them growing increasingly stale, propaganda value was all I had going for me. But if I refused, I would be unneeded, useless and therefore probably dead.

"What else?" I asked, still assessing their motives and my options.

"We need leaflets written. Leaflets that urge your soldiers to rise up against their capitalist masters and join our cause. You can write these for us at the Peace Fighters' Camp. This camp has many good things for you, Thorn-ton.''

"You know I can't do that. You know it.''

"Why you can't do that, Thorn-ton?'' he asked patiently, his Asian eyes examining me intently.

"It's a betrayal. It'd be like shooting my family and friends in the back. You understand that.''

The Koreans didn't seem surprised or even upset. In fact, I thought they almost looked at me with an expression of respect. They hadn't misread me at all. They were just taking a long shot. The Korean sighed and shook his head mournfully.

"Thorn-ton, you are a fool. You will die here some-day.'' Rising, he moved toward me and with an ominous tone in his voice, announced his plans for my future. "Since you do not wish to go to the Peace Fighters' Camp, we see that you must have more indoctrination. You must be humble, search your conscience and learn correct thinking. When you have done this, you can go to the Peace Fighters' Camp. But since you refuse now to cooperate, you must be punished. We will cut your food in half. We offered you everything. Now you take nothing. Today instead of the Peace Fighters' Camp, we will send you to another place. You will learn your lessons there and have time to reconsider your ways.''

He called the guards and I was shuffled off toward my new home.

7

By the rude bridge that arched the flood,
Their flag to April's breeze unfurled,
Here once the embattled farmers stood,
And fired the shot heard round the world.

—Ralph Waldo Emerson
Concord Hymn

It was Patriot's Day, April 19, 1951. Forgotten in modern times by most Americans, it had been observed years back in remembrance of the Battles of Lexington and Concord and Paul Revere's midnight ride. Today, 176 years later, it found me limping on bloody, bare feet with frostbitten toes through more towns and hostile crowds on my way to an uncertain fate. I celebrated this day picking at my meager ration—a rice ball. It was also my twenty-ninth birthday.

As the day was drawing to a close, I was ten miles out of the last town, with three guards marching me down a country road. They were looking for a safe house to hold me for the night but it appeared they were disoriented and lost. They acted as if they were out of their known environment and were getting very jumpy. I could sense the tension and feel their increased desire to shed their responsibility—me. If I escaped, their lives would not be worth a plugged nickel. On the other hand, if I were shot while trying to escape they would be applauded for their alertness to duty. I would not be the first prisoner to be bumped off this way. Others had met their Maker in just such a manner.

It was shortly after sunset when the leader of the

trio called a halt and ordered me to lie down. We had stopped about two hundred yards from a farm house. Exhausted, I flopped down on the ground and sprawled out on my back just looking up at the beautiful April sky at dusk. As the words of a favorite poem, "High Flight," phrase it I "slipped the surly bonds of earth and danced the skies . . . sunward I climbed . . . high in the sunlit silence . . . hovering there . . . put out my hand and touched the face of God . . ."

My skyward hover was broken by a guard's boot, kicking me back down to the facts of life. I came out of my dream looking up into the faces of two North Korean officers. They were clean and dapper in their crisp uniforms. Their greatcoats draped over their shoulders, they wore Sam Browne belts with holstered Chinese machine pistols strapped over olive drab jackets. Dark blue riding breeches were tucked neatly into their highly polished boots. One officer reminded me of a 1930 movie matinee idol named Ricardo Cortez. What a contrast they were to grimy-looking me. Seeping through this clean and disciplined veneer, however, was the sadistic aura of two cats about to pounce on a mouse. I felt uneasy as they looked me over.

Suddenly, they jerked me to my feet to get a better look at their prey. My guards were not about to intervene on my behalf and silently stood aside. As the two officers surveyed me, they spotted my gold wedding band. Apprehension gripped me. While the ring had survived numerous shakedowns before, something kept telling me to start hiding it. But that seemed improper, even downright self-destructive. My wife, my marriage, were my strength, one of my weapons. The ring was a visible manifestation of that strength and my last tangible connection to it. To remove it, to hide it would somehow break the tie.

Besides, they had taken everything else I had. Surely they would allow me one small possession.

One of the officers spoke so-so English and informed me that he wanted to see the ring. "Mo-la" (no), I answered in Korean.

"You give the ring," he insisted.

"Mo-la, mo-la. Finger is puffed. Too big. I am a sick man. This ring will not come off," I lied.

"I will only look. This is beautiful ring. I wish only to admire this for you," he said trying to sound reassuring. "I give this back to you. Let me wear it for one minute."

"You look at it here on my finger. I will let you see. Look here," I said, extending my arm.

Without warning, he grabbed my hand and, nearly wrenching my arm from its socket, threw me to the ground. His fellow officer pulled out a knife. With the one firmly gripping my outstretched arm, the other prepared to amputate my finger. I tried to struggle but my emaciated frame was incapable of a meaningful response.

My mind raced. I was married. I was betrothed at the altar of God. I would remain so with this woman whose love for me transcended the miles. It transcended these swine who sought to desecrate the sanctity of our union. I struggled again, swore and called them pigs. The knife-wielder hoisted my head back by the hair to give me a clearer look, one last reminder of the blade and his intention. Scum. Stinking Communist scum. My spirit was seething in contempt and fury. I was breathless as much from rage as from the threat I faced. Take the goddamn ring, pig. Take it and *choke* on it.

"Wait a minute," I croaked. As they released their hold on me, I removed the ring and handed it over. Gloating, they passed it back and forth, examining it, trying it on and inspecting the engraved

initials 'VRT to JWT 9-16-44' inside the band. I
couldn't bear to watch. The ring was *mine*. It was *my
ring* and I wanted it back. Sensing this, the officer
extended the band to me. I reached for it greedily.
With a smirk, he pulled the ring away and returned
it to his own finger. They were enjoying their cat
and mouse game.

I demanded the ring. Nope. I swallowed my pride
and begged miserably. No dice. I was smoldering
again. I had no strength but that fact slipped
my mind. I summoned up all the power I had and
cursing, threw myself at them. The dirty little old
man moved in slow motion. Roaring in laughter,
they easily stepped aside and drew their weapons.
The one with my ring cocked the hammer on his
pistol and raised it toward me. He fired. I jumped
spasmodically as the gun's violent explosion stopped
me in my tracks, the bullet zipping past my side.
"Halt!" he commanded. I obeyed. Brazenly, he
swaggered over to me. Glaring at me viciously, he
spoke.
"You do not need this ring, dog. You are our
prisoner. America is far away. Besides," he said
with a sneer, "your wife is being unfaithful to you
now." Nodding toward the guards to take charge, he
and his friend turned to leave. The guards shoved
me to the ground as the laughter of the departing
officers seared my soul.

Grovelling in the dusty road, I broke down, my
spirits trampled. Cursing them, I prayed for the
wrath of the Almighty God to fall upon them and
their families. With seething vehemence, I spat out
every foul and poisonous oath I could dredge out of
my embittered mind. They had robbed me of the last
link to my home and my love. They had plunged me
into the the most profound depths of frightful
despair. I bellowed until I was hoarse. I sobbed and

cursed until I was exhausted and wept uncontrollably. Years later I would wish that a passage of the Fortieth Psalm had been etched in my mind just for that moment:

> *Let them be ashamed and confounded together;*
> *Let them be driven backward, and put to*
> *shame that wish me evil.*
> *Let them be desolate . . .*

The intensity of my sorrow was matched only by my hatred for them. I despised them with every fibre of my wretched body. My ring was gone.

In time, the wound of that day, like so many others, would heal over with a tough scar tissue of hateful determination. No, they would not prevail. They would destroy nothing in me, be it faith, love or my will to survive. My wife and I were bound by something more vital and enduring than the wedding band. Intangible, our love traversed time and distance. Echoing off the sun and moon, it reached me in my misery. I would live and I would love again. I would buy another ring. I would even keep my finger. I hadn't lost anything, I decided. By living to fight my enemy another day, I had won this round. I resolved to win the rest, God willing.

8

For God has marked each sorrowing day
And numbered every secret tear,
And heaven's long age of bliss shall pay
For all his children suffer here.

—William Cullen Bryant

I scooped up my broken body and spirits as the trek to my new interrogation center continued. It was now dark. As we walked along, a line of North Korean soldiers approached us moving in the opposite direction. They were carrying litters with moaning men in them. An even greater number of walking wounded limped along beside them. They were badly mauled troops and I revelled in their misery. Consumed as they were in their agony, they failed to observe my presence until my three faithful guards began bragging about their prize. Advertising the fact that I was an American pilot, they goaded the healthier troops to make amends in behalf of their mangled comrades. Fortuitously, they hardly had an opportunity to vent their rage as a captured American jeep rolled into the collecting crowd.

A North Korean colonel and a man in civilian clothes jumped out. They ordered the troops back and were quickly obeyed without dispute. The civilian was villainous in appearance. Somewhat crippled, he had a severe limp and looked like a gnome. He reminded me of Doctor Frankenstein's inept, brain-switching, hunchback assistant. Around the appearance of this bizzare-looking man, a night just as ominous and eerie was building.

The six of us climbed into the jeep and sped away. We drove a mile and upon reaching a roadblock, dismounted. The colonel and two guards departed, leaving the Gnome and the last guard in charge of me. Suddenly, as if on someone's cue, the nearby hills were brilliantly illuminated by flares dropped from U.N. night bombers. Their flickering glow cast spooky shadows and dancing forms across the rugged terrain. Then, like mythical griffins, night fighters swooped in from the gloom. Flying above the flares, they shattered distant, hidden men in firestorms of machine gun fire and rockets. Tumbling napalm cannisters fell from the planes like loose parts. Splattering across the ground in searing flame, they lit up the hills with an even greater intensity. The attacking fighters were met by red tracer rounds arcing skyward from anti-aircraft emplacements that groped for a target in the night. As the dying flares descended on their miniature parachutes and flickered out, they allowed the beleaguered mountains to retreat momentarily into the safety of darkness, their existence revealed only by the open wounds burning on their slopes. The process was then repeated—again and again. As we walked and watched, the guard became increasingly antagonized by the distant carnage, and every passing aircraft inspired him to punch me in the head and threaten me with his burp gun. The Gnome intervened to keep us apart and did so with enough success probably to spare me from being shot.

We continued to march for what seemed an eternity. Arriving at a small group of buildings, we took a path toward one of them. Suddenly, out of the blackness came the droning sound of a B-26 night bomber headed our way. We were about to be strafed. As we hustled off the path for cover I knew this would be a night to remember, if I survived it. The monotone of the B-26's engines rose in a harrowing crescendo as the plane dropped into its dive. Cringing in fearful expectation, we waited an eternity for the bomber to commence its attack. And then she opened up. Instantly, the buildings ahead of us seemed to erupt as they were engulfed by murderous fire. Chunks of the structures seemed to fly off as the bomber struck with armor-piercing rounds that penetrated walls and roofs. The terrifying sound of shattering glass and ricocheting bullets was compounded by the shouts of men caught in the hail of bullets. The plane shrieked deafeningly as it shot by overhead. Then, as quickly as it appeared, it vanished into the night, on its way to complete other tasks.

As the dust settled, the gooks tried to sort themselves out. A Korean in one building had been killed. Ten others crawled out unscathed but badly unnerved. My guard was trembling in total fright. While the attack itself had not physically affected me, its aftermath buoyed up my spirits tremendously. It was immensely gratifying to see my bullying captors reduced to the level of cringing, terror-stricken children. As time went on and other air strikes occurred, I marvelled happily at how even the very sound of an approaching plane would push them to the edge of panic.

By the time things settled down again, it was extremely late. Exhausted, I was ready to drop, but the Gnome had a better idea—more interrogation. At about the same time, a haggard looking ROK was brought into the building where I was held. It would be a two ring circus for the Gnome and a difficult time for the ROK and me.

Throughout that entire sleepless night, we were interrogated and beaten in alternating cycles—first him, then me. The ROK caught the brunt of it. He spent his last night on earth in brutal agony, but they never broke him. Finally, as the hours of darkness drew to a close, he stood condemned before his tormentors as a spy and an enemy of the Korean people. Wearing a face now resembling spoiled, raw meat more than human flesh, he was dragged away. In the quiet hush that settles with the dew before first light, a single shot announced his passing in the Land of the Morning Calm.

At dawn, still alive but on the verge of total collapse, I was ordered to my feet and we were on the march again. After a few brief stops that were interspersed with more quizzes, we halted for a longer spell. I had had enough. I decided that at the next order to march, I would refuse. Sprawled out on the ground, I wondered what they would do to me for disobeying them but I didn't really care. I couldn't go on. It was at this point that I joined up with the first American I had seen since leaving Watson. He was a mess. He was wounded three times in the lower leg and the shrapnel was still in. These untreated wounds and the mass of bruises that covered him from repeated beatings were evidence that he had not been cooperating.

We talked and I learned that he was a soldier with the Seventh Division. He was only nineteen. The Chinese had picked him up and stripped him of his belongings in the usual fashion. They had allowed him to keep one item though—his Miraculous Medal. Their reason was not so much out of deference to his faith as it was to prove a political, ideological point.

"You are wounded, American," they had told him. "You need medical attention. If you join the people's fight and condemn your aggressive ways, you will be helped under the Lenient Policy. If you refuse, then pray to your image, your god. Pray for a miracle. If this god does not answer your prayer and help you, then you will know he is a false god. Then you will see the real truth. If not, you will die.''

Despite the taunts, jeers, neglect and punishment, this young soldier had clung to his faith. But his body was going on him fast.

''Up! Up! We go to Pyongyang!'' shouted an officer at us.

''How far to Pyongyang?'' I asked, knowing it would be the same answer I had gotten for the past two days—only four kilometers.

''Only four kilometers,'' came the expected response.

''We can't make it. I've walked a hundred kilometers already going to Pyongyang. No more. I can't go,'' I said, still lying on the ground. I looked toward my young soldier friend and then back at the officer. ''He can't go either. Too sick. You must help him,'' I asserted.

''We help you both in Pyongyang. Up! Up!'' replied the officer impatiently.

''Blow it out your ass. We stay here,'' I said insolently. The officer unshouldered his burp gun and with an ominous snap, chambered a round. He aimed my way.

''Get up and march,'' he ordered. I shook my head negatively. He became furious and put the muzzle to my head.

''Get up quickly or I kill you now,'' he said in a low, earnest tone.

Bravado was the last thing in my mind. I was just fed up with it all. I didn't want to die, but I'd be damned if I was going to take another step. Pyongyang was no four kilometers away and there was no food, no medicine, nothing good waiting there for prisoners like me and my black-and-blue friend. Death seemed upon me whether I moved or sat, so I guessed it didn't really make any difference. Besides, I thought, the officer might be bluffing.

"Go ahead and shoot," I said glaring up at him. My response seemed to catch him off-guard or by surprise. A look of incredulous shock swept across his face and he almost seemed to stagger backward. His jaw dropped open and his hat even went cockeyed on his head. I reached my hand out toward his weapon. "Give me that. I'll shoot myself," I said, staring at him.

The officer was aghast. he lost his composure and didn't seem to know what to do. I assumed he thought he was dealing with a madman. Moments passed. Again we were promised a four-kilometer march—no more—and meat when we arrived. Even a truck was offered to carry us to a hospital for treatment. My friend and I were unmoved.

"No. We stay here. You bring the truck, *then* we go," came our response. More threats, then more promises ensued. Then came a closing statement.

"Four more kilometers and we will take better care of you." With that, they turned and left us both sitting in the middle of the road alone.

"They left us! The simple bastards left us!" said the soldier in disbelief.

"They know we aren't going anywhere. I can't get a hundred yards without falling on my ass," I bitched.

"Maybe some friendly natives will find us and sneak us across the lines," I said, thinking wishfully.

"I haven't seen a friendly native since I came to this fuckin' place," the soldier snarled.

"My goddamn leg is killing me," he said, wincing as he shifted it.

A deliciously peaceful interlude passed while we

rested and pondered our situation. Reluctantly, we acknowledged we were trapped in an inescapable prison formed by our own physical malaise.

"Right now I need something for this leg. I think I'm getting gangrene. Sonofabitch is turning blue," said the soldier, looking balefully at his festering limb. "Maybe they *will* do something. Maybe they'll feed us. Do you think they'll feed us?" I was bitter and angry.

"Carrot on a stick. That's just what it is, a goddamn carrot on a stick. The bastards egg you on that way," I fumed. We sat there silent for a time. "Shit," I said. "You want to try for the carrot?" The soldier paused for a moment, thinking it over. There were no alternatives.

"Yeah," he replied.

After painfully rising to our feet, we hobbled along the road and finally came to a check point where our guards smuggly waited for us. There was no food and no medicine, but they did produce a truck. We were advised that under the Lenient Policy, we would be driven to a hospital, given a bath, clean clothes, bed, and medicine, and nursed back to health. We were tossed into the back of the truck and rumbled through Pyongyang to the hospital, five miles to the northeast. It was night when we arrived. Getting out, I rubbernecked, looking all around for the bathhouse they said was here, where we would first get deloused and clean again.

"Where is it? Where's the bathhouse?" I asked again and again.

"This way. You follow," came the answer, and we were led down a winding path. I crawled and stumbled along on my ravaged feet, the soldier dragging along behind. We were too weak to help each other. Our journey finally stopped outside a small hut with a doorway leading into a little room.

"This is the bathhouse," they said, pushing us both in. It was pitch black inside.

"Well where the hell is the *bath*?!" I demanded. They slammed the door shut. Two voices emerged from the dark.

"There's no bath in here, buddy. Just lice, shit and us."

Two more Americans and a ROK were inside. One, an Army private, had a bullet wound in his ankle. The other American, a captain, had been shot in the knee. The ROK was also wounded and in bad shape. They had been captured a month before me and come daylight I would see that they looked twice as bad as I did. They were covered with lice and seeping, infected wounds, riddled with dysentery and starving to death. There had been no medical treatment for them at this "hospital."

On the 7th of May, sitting alone in a corner of this blacked-out room, I found my thoughts going stateside and back home. It was my son's 3rd birthday. Suddenly I heard the sound of anti-aircraft fire amid the drone of heavy bomber engines. Our guards ordered us outside to watch. It was a B-29 Superfortress raid striking North Korea's capitol city, Pyongyang, just to the south of us. It gave us a little sense of pride, a feeling that someone was hitting back at our torturers. Unexpectedly, one B-29 seemed to stop momentarily in the sky, next to a black puff of ack-ack. It was hit, damn it! It began to gyrate and fall. "Get it up, get it straight and level!" I wanted to yell out! This enormous plane was now in a flat spin, then the right wing sheared off. *"Get out, bail out!"* I shouted within myself. Having crashed fighters and helicopters myself, I knew too well the centrifugal forces at work. With their altitude decaying fast, I felt the impending doom in store for those air crewmen. Abruptly, this whirling mass spewed forth four dots from its side. Then I saw one, two, three and the fourth dot blossom only seconds before their mother ship disintegrated. The four U.S. Air Force crewmen had barely escaped with their lives, but I wondered, will they live? Their welcome aboard in this savage land will not be heartwarming.

Our guards were bragging ecstatically about two bombers being shot down. I yelled, "Bullshit! You couldn't hit a bull in the ass with a bass fiddle!" This half-understood statement coupled with a few of my choice Korean cusswords got us all thrown back viciously into the dark room. Back in my corner, thinking homeward once again, I knew son Jay had a Happy Birthday, 'cause I knew his mother would make it so.

We spent the next few days delousing each other, picking the lice off one by one and mashing them between our thumbnails. They were rampaging in our hair, beards and under our clothes. We'd kill two to three hundred a day. Failing to do this would have been to allow one more slow, piecemeal loss of blood to sap further what little strength remained in us. I would later see sick men who hadn't the strength to delouse at all and after three to four days, their chests would be as white as the driven snow—covered with lice. Our dysentery was fierce and uncontrollable. We had somehow learned to eat and keep down garbage found on the roadside, even maggot-infested garbage. We could, in a small way, deal with starvation, but the dysentery was beyond us. It enervated and dehydrated us as we sat there in our own excrement and slowly withered away.

After a few days of this, my friend's leg was eaten up with gangrene, as he had feared it would. It was blue and puffed, and stank. The infection was massive and as it began to rage through his fevered body, he began to deteriorate rapidly. He was wracked with periodic seizures and would writhe on the ground in spasmodic fits. His pain was intense and inescapable. Gradually, he began to slip from occasional incoherence into almost complete delirium. We appealed to our captors repeatedly for medication, attention or something we could administer ourselves. We begged for anything we might use to extract the shrapnel from his wounds. Our pleas were rebuffed with sadistic smiles that always said no.

My friend was dying and yet in his growing insanity he seemed to find a refuge from the ugliness of his plight. And strangely, despite his loss of contact with this world, his contact with the next seemed to increase. He clung to his Miraculous Medal and his faith. Physically and mentally, he was being torn loose from his earthly moorings. And yet spiritually, his faith—such a powerful, unswerving faith—became ever more solid and unshakable.

Then came another day, we were allowed outside our cubicle to blink at the sun for a few precious moments. It was May and a beautiful spring. The birds were singing and flying above us free. You could almost—almost—lift yourself out of the pigpen you lived in. Without warning, my friend convulsed grotesquely and collapsed to the ground. He was having another seizure and writhed in agony. The two other ailing G.I.'s and I stumbled toward him to try to move him back to the cubicle, but our efforts were futile. He weighed only a hundred pounds by now but we were too weak to budge him. We asked the guards to help. They looked at us with sinister expressions and then shoved us away. What then occurred was the single greatest horror of my life.

One guard had a captured American M-1 rifle, a long weapon with a heavy wooden stock. It made an excellent club and was employed accordingly. He smashed it brutally into the soldier. Gleefully, the other guards joined in, kicking his shattered body across the ground like a rag doll. Again and again, they pounded him, kicked him, punched him and spat on him, using him for a soccer ball and laughing as if it were just a game to pass the time. The sound of boots crunching and thumping into him sent a tidal wave of rage and nausea surging through me. The look of it was ungodly. The violent emotions I had felt at the theft of my wedding ring were compounded a thousand times as I was swept back and forth from fury to horrified grief and back again. I cursed, wept, begged and threatened as I tried desperately to move to his aid. I could barely stand, let alone fight them off, and the other two G.I.'s knew it as I began moving toward the cackling guards. Two weak and wiser men restrained a third less wise one and together we watched in helpless anguish as a dying youth was demoniacally brutalized.

Finally, the game was concluded. Their fun over with, the guards gathered up the unconscious human wreckage that was once a whole man and dumped him in our cubicle as if he were rubbish. He never came out of it. Two days later, clutching his Miraculous Medal and clinging to his faith, he mercifully died.

A few days after that, the private and the ROK followed him.

9

*I waited patiently for the Lord; and
He inclined unto me, and heard my cry.
He brought me up also out of an horrible
pit, out of the miry clay and set my feet
upon a rock, and established my goings.*

—Psalm 40

"Han! Hey, Han!" I shouted weakly to summon the Honsho in charge. The effort nearly exhausted me. Han, a North Korean major, was informed of my call and finally appeared. We had been pestering him for days to get us out of the Hospital, complaining of the filthy conditions, lack of care and most of all the callous neglect and brutality that had killed three of our fellow inmates. Our appeals were dismissed on the grounds that we were "not well," that further "rehabilitation" was necessary and that our recovery would be reflected in more positive attitudes toward the peace-loving peoples. We got the message. We were not cooperating and did not have the correct cognition. The lesson would have to be drilled into our minds. In order to get out of here we would have to demonstrate the proper thinking. The two of us decided to feed them a little rope if it would get us out of the Hospital and perhaps into less miserable surroundings—someplace where we might have slightly better odds at surviving.

"I understand you wish to leave the Hospital," said Han in perfect English. His manner seemed to suggest that the subject had never been discussed before. We nodded affirmatively. "Have you been well treated physically and mentally under the Lenient

Policy?'' he asked with a straight face. We were dying of malnutrition and dysentery and covered with festering wounds. Mine were from the unremoved shrapnel left over from the crash, and my friend's from his shot-up knee. Like that of the first man to die in our midst, his leg was beginning to turn ominously blue.

"Yeah, we're in great shape, Han. Healthy and hearty," replied the captain.

"And you, Thorn-ton. Have you also recovered?" asked Han.

"I'm great, just great. Weight's down, bowels are moving well and I can even support a good-sized population of lice. You should show this place off to the Red Cross, Han," I answered hoping he didn't understand sarcasm.

"Get us outa here, Han," demanded the captain almost threateningly. Han nodded with approval, probably on the assumption that we had been adequately softened up for bigger and better things.

"O.K.," he said, "You have had good treatment." He turned and left.

A short time later, we found ourselves hobbling down a road away from the Hospital. My crippled-up friend was using a makeshift crutch that was cutting him a third armpit. We walked east for a painful five miles and arrived at another interrogation center near Pyongyang. The place had at one time been a brickyard surrounded by small Korean houses. The brickyard and its related structures served well as a P.O.W. compound and the houses were pressed into various auxiliary services including housing for our captors, administrative areas and other facilities related to interrogations and indoctrination.

While the chief administrator of this North Korean compound was a Colonel Lee, the dominant figure was the chief interrogator, Major Pak. Pak was an expert in his field. He was also a sadistic animal who should have been in a cage. It was his unique style of perverse brutality that compelled those of us under his heel to dub the camp Pak's Palace.

The captain and I were placed in a cubicle measuring about six feet by eight feet. Inside, four other prisoners already languished, stuffed in like sardines. A light bulb dangled from the ceiling and burned continuously day and night. To even touch it, let alone turn it off, was forbidden, a capital offense punishable by beating, solitary confinement or banishment to the Holes. Most of the Holes were former outhouse pits that were now reserved for the confinement of uncooperative prisoners. During the night, to add to our misery, the guards would enter our cubicle, wake us, take roll call and then leave. Thirty minutes later they would be back again with the same routine. It was measured, methodical harrassment, courtesy of Major Pak. Permission had to be obtained to use the one and only latrine available to the thirty-six men riddled with dysentery that stayed in our area. Frequently, humble requests to make a trip were haughtily refused by smiling guards who would deny all defacating and urinating rights. Our bowels being completely out of control led to the obvious result—we sat and slept in our own disease-ridden filth. We were six men in a six-by-eight cubicle in the warmth of spring with flies and lice for company.

My four new cellmates turned out to be B-29 flyers. They were, in fact, the four dots that blossomed into parachutes on that fateful day of Jay's third birthday. I told them it was nice of them because it got us out of the dark room and into the fresh air and sunshine. Sadly, one of them was never to leave this place alive. But the others and I were to be together for more than two more years. Having ascertained me to be a helicopter pilot, one of them, Captain McTaggart, decided that I be dubbed "Rotorhead" since I was always in a rotating configuration while spinning off to the crap hole.

Pak's insidious scheme was as logical as it was brutal. By carefully blending beatings, torture, starvation, disease and total degradation, he expected our mental faculties and in turn our resistance to slowly to erode. To help blur our ability to distinguish friend from foe, right from wrong and shift our dependence from each other, our God and our principles to our captors, Pak employed other techniques. A friendly pat on the back from a guard, a surprise hard-boiled egg from an interrogator, a cigarette from another and the bad guys began looking like good guys. A bowl of rice without weevils, a piece of fish without maggots, turning out that damned light. They were given now and then to throw us off balance, at "no cost" with a promise that more would be forthcoming. We were told that little was asked of us to open the cornucopia, so very little. Existing in a haze of fevered disease, weakness and starvation, our ability to remember who did what to whom, which of last week's bastards were this week's deliverers became fuzzy. Helpless as babies, we began to exist on a level where values seemed to be irrelevant since they didn't fill bellies or heal wounds. To eat something decent, to have clean clothes, a good night of uninterrupted sleep or unlimited latrine privileges were such precious, yet distant treasures that they became obsessive, all-consuming and irresistible. We needed these so desperately. They were *available*. We could *have* them. We were reminded of this over and over again. All for you—if only you will cooperate. With the constant pressure and manipulation of need, task and reward, a Pavlovian environment was created that could quickly inundate and wash away an individual's sense of loyalty to anything but his own survival and those who could guarantee it. It was a carefully constructed and meticulously managed trap to which many fell victim. Others didn't. And others died. And as they died, the will of the survivors to continue to resist was chipped away just a little more—one life at a time.

Pak's best assistant interrogator was known to us as the Professor. The Professor would commence his session with mind-numbing, interminable political harangues. They would be followed by seemingly innocent requests to fill out questionnaires for the more insidious purpose of extracting shreds of personal information or insight on personality traits that might be of future manipulative value. Endless questions, both inane and of intelligence value were asked. The carrot-on-the-stick was there along with cajoling and appeals to reason. Failing here, a severe beating would ensue. For starters, a cigarette might be snuffed out on an arm or in an open wound. Fingernails were ripped out, faces smashed, teeth knocked loose and backs pounded with rifle butts. Limbs would be twisted, dislocated or even broken. A snotty-acting P.O.W. might be quickly put in his place with a savage kick in the genitals. Retching on the floor, he would be reminded of his need to show the proper respect and to have the correct thinking. Unconscious men would be dragged back to their cubicles, their faces bloody pulps, their eyes swollen shut. Then it would be your turn. Hell was not in the center of the earth. It was right here on the Korean peninsula at Pak's Palace where men were dying like flies.

I had been singled out by the Professor for special

treatment. I had not been cooperating and was getting a very ugly reputation in the camp. I was setting a bad example for the other prisoners and needed to confess to my past and present crimes. One particular interrogation didn't go well at all for the Professor. He was displeased with my refusal to answer his questions or criticize myself for my reactionary behavior. I was banished to the Black Room to contemplate the errors of my thinking.

The Black Room was a totally blacked out cubicle, devoid of light. I was shoved into a corner and left there. No water, no latrine, no food was made available. In some cases, this could go on for days. This time, for me, it was only several hours and was something short of a fully qualified stay in solitary confinement. After awhile, I received visitors with more questions. They were very unhappy with me. I was feeling especially balky and wouldn't produce acceptable replies. Scuffling and loud, angry Korean voices filled the darkness as I was pushed around and popped in the face, stomach and kidneys.

"Thorn-ton! You answer! Confess to your crimes, capitalist dog!" bellowed one.

"Do not turn your head! Put it back in the corner!" shouted another, hoisting me up and grinding my face into the wall. "We will *kill* you now," he hissed, trailing off with a stream of epithets. Half-dazed, I sagged into the corner as he drew his pistol and put it near my head. I couldn't tell if he was pointing at me or away from me. Click. Click. Click again. "Search your soul, war monger. Be humble. Learn the truth. Self-criticize and confess. Do these things and you will live. Resist and you will find a loaded gun at your head." The grievance committee released me and stormed out of the Black Room. As the door slammed shut, I was plunged back into the darkness and slumped down to the floor, exhausted.

Time passed. More visitors. More quizzes. In and out of the Black Room. No progress was being made at all on my case. Into the Black Room again. Standing in the corner, I heard the approach of another entourage. Yet another shouting match ensued and more beatings. Thrust into the corner once more, I heard a different voice come out of the gloom, one rather unfamiliar but I had heard it before, nonetheless.

"Thorn-ton. You are a liar. You refuse to cooperate. We have no use for prisoners who will not cooperate. You are a troublemaker . . ." A wave of anxiety swept over me as I remembered whose voice that was. It was Pak! Pak himself was giving me his personal attention. I knew I was in for it now. Pak had made me his own special case and by failing to break me, he and the Professor had lost face. They would have to make amends now. I heard the sound of a pistol being drawn and cocked. A tiny draft chilled my neck as he raised the gun to my head, just behind the ear. Pak was a known killer. I stiffened with apprehension. My heartbeat doubled. "I will shoot now," Pak announced indifferently. I closed my eyes.

He pulled the trigger and the whole universe seemed to explode around me. I convulsed involuntarily, my muscles flexing into cramping knots. There was a loud, roaring noise in my head. After the explosion passed, I realized I was still standing and slightly deaf in one ear. It stung from the powder burn. I was a little dazed and disoriented but I knew I had called his bluff. I knew I was still alive.

"Thorn-ton," said Pak with cruel sincerity, "since you are a reactionary and will not cooperate, you will suffer the consequences." Turning away, he left me in the Black Room, facing the corner to think. Sometime later, the Professor returned.

"Thorn-ton, you are not progressing and there is no joy in my heart. But tonight I will let you return to your comrades and stay with them in the compound. You must search your conscience this night. Tomorrow, after your thinking is correct, I will come for you, you will confess and become more cooperative." He added a closing good-night remark. "If you do not cooperate tomorrow, I cannot help you. Pak will surely kill you."

On that happy note, I was returned to the compound. There waiting to help me was Air Force Captain J. B. Smith. He, our cook, had saved a piece of dog for me. He had softened the meat—by chewing on it. He had tenderly tenderized it and thoughtfully saved it for when I would return. It was good. I was left unmolested throughout the night and most of the next day. Finally, the Professor came for me and took me to a building where the guards stayed which we called the Big House. I was ushered into a small room. The Professor immediately went berserk, launching into a flaming political tirade that is etched in my memory.

"The struggle of the North Korean people against U.S. aggression and for national salvation is now the focus of the people of the world! The determination of the Chinese people and the Korean people against the capitalist war mongers is unshakable. No matter what U.S. imperialism may do to expand its war adventure, the Chinese people will do everything in their power to support the Korean people until every single one of the U.S. aggressors is driven out of Korea!"

The Professor droned on with his harangue as he had so many times before. I felt exceptionally irritable and his ravings weren't sitting well today. I bit my tongue trying to maintain my silence and composure as he shifted gears into a lecture on Marxism-Leninism.

"All actions of Man are determined by the economic system. What we think, what we feel, what we believe, what or whom we worship is an expression of economic forces. Nothing more. Man is matter in motion, no more, no less. He is completely describable in terms of chemistry, physics and the Laws of Nature. He has no soul, no spirit, no individual value. Man is subject to modification and transformation by the established laws of animal husbandry."

The Professor's pitch was intensifying. I was growing increasingly inflamed by his shrieking, not to mention the garbage he was espousing. He ranted on, moving into a discourse on religion. He was touching a nerve and I began arguing with him. Angrily, we debated back and forth until finally the Professor made his determined summation.

"There *is* no God. There is no *moral* law. There *is* no absolute standard of truth. Communism is free to erect moral and ethical standards as the occasion demands! Thorn-ton, if your god is so great, so powerful and good, why does he permit you to live like this? Why don't you just pray to him and ask him to perform one of his great miracles I hear about? Why does he not save you from this life of a pig you are living?"

"My God does things for a reason," I replied. The Professor scoffed at this and snapped back.

"What is the reason your god has for you to be here?"

"So I can learn how to fight you sons-of-bitches better," I responded arrogantly. The Professor went wild. He leaped from his chair, spitting, fuming and screaming in a high pitch. He was in an unprecedented rage of frustration with me. Glaring at me, he shouted in my face furiously.

"Capitalist *dog!* You are hopeless! You will not be humble and learn the truth! You refuse to examine your conscience and confess so we must do *away* with you! We have given you many chances to self-criticize yourself but you will not do this. Because of this, we will make an example of you for the others. We will *shoot* you! Tomorrow at dawn you will be taken out in the rice paddy behind this house and be *shot* for your lack of cooperation and for your *insolence!* Tomorrow I promise you will die. You will also spend your last night in the Hole." He motioned for the guard to take me away.

I was led to the Hole, the one chosen for me being among those which had once served as a latrine pit. It was dreary out and raining. Before throwing me in, the Professor offered me one last thought.

"Thorn-ton. I *never* believed, I *do not* believe and I *will* not believe!" he hissed.

I was shoved into the Hole. It was so narrow that I could only slide down the slimy sides to squat in the muck. The stench was choking. It was impossible to stand except with my head bowed as a cover of wooden slats was pulled across the top and secured. The rain dripped through the cracks in the cover and ran down my neck. With the Professor's arrogant sign-off implanted in my mind, I pondered my fate. I knew of three men who had been in the Hole for twenty-six days. Two came out alive. A marathon in the Hole was not, of course, in the offing for me. Tomorrow, I would be shot. This time I didn't think they were bluffing. I believed them.

Night fell and I sat alone in the blackness of a latrine pit. The rain continued to drip on me and I was soaked. I stank hideously. As I sat in the human manure that was my only resting place, even my lice were disgusted. They began crawling up my body, away from the filth that lapped about my lower extremities. I had reached the nadir of my imprisonment, the greatest depths of my anguish. I was a miserable, broken-down wretch, covered in so much feculence that it was difficult to tell where it left off and the person began. The dampness made me shiver and the cold swill turned my feet into blocks of ice.

I prayed and asked God if this was the end of the line for me. I trusted that my fate lay in His hands, not the Communists', but still, I was spiritually shaken. I asked Him how I would get out of this one. Greater strength than my own had come to aid me in the past but even then, there always seemed to be some small degree of personal control or choice of action in each incident. But this situation left me completely helpless. How would I stop the bullets of a firing squad? There was no verbal response from the Almighty.

The Professor's words kept coming back to haunt me. 'I never believed, I do not believe, I will not believe.' Bastard. Sleezy, stinking bastard. I would not yield to the likes of him. There was a time for living and a time for dying. That was somewhere in the Bible. I wondered what time it was for me and guessed it might be the worse of the two. If I were to live then my future days of captivity would take care of themselves, I figured. But if death were my lot, I felt I had better prepare myself for it. I decided I would recite a prayer, the Twenty-third Psalm:

The Lord is my shepherd. I shall not want. He restoreth my . . . No that wasn't it. Yes it was. No. Well, just start over. *The Lord is my shepherd. I shall not want . . . My cup runneth over . . . Damn!* How the hell does it go?! Try another. Lord's Prayer this time. *Our Father who art in Heaven, hallowed be thy name. Thy kingdom come, thy will be done on Earth as it is in Heaven* . . . I lost my place, thought a minute and then continued. . . . *Surely goodness and mercy will* . . . No, no, *no!* That's from the other one. What the hell are the *words?!* Frantically, I searched the recesses of my memory for the right phrases, the proper sequence. I just couldn't remember. I was in dire need of these comforting words but was completely unable to recall them. Again and again I tried and failed miserably. My brains were scattered and scrambled. Remorsefully, I wondered if my captors had done such a good job on me that they had erased my religion. Or was I just such a poor Christian that I had never really known two of its most basic prayers from the Old and New Testaments? I rummaged through my mind desperately trying to dredge them up. It was no use. I couldn't think straight. I wept in despair and frustration. A fine example *you* are, I thought. You're in a shit hole, five feet underground and it may as well be your grave. You shot your mouth off in a fight over religion and you can't even say a simple damn prayer. You're going to be killed for it and you can't even remember. Some Christian. Some stupid ass.

The hours dragged as the night wore on. Between thinking about my wife, home, and family, and persistently but unsuccessfully trying to sort my prayers to God, I detached myself from my slimy surroundings. I thought of many things that night. I thought of America and its principles. I thought of communism and *its* principles, or lack thereof. There were many Americans here, I thought, and in battle all across Korea. They, for the most part, were willing to risk their lives because their country had asked them to. But did they really understand what they were defending? How deep was their grasp of their nation's moral and spiritual foundation, its heritage of personal freedoms? Once captured, it seemed that in too many men, their grasps were too weak, their understanding too shallow to withstand the ideological onslaught of their communist captors. Though citizens of a nation blessed with prosperity and liberty, Americans too often had no answers when confronted with the weaknesses of their capitalist system or the untended ills or shortcomings of their free society. Silent acknowledgement that some of the problems their captors pointed out did, in fact, exist was only another political source of dangerous confusion. One small, isolated truth would serve as the cornerstone for a larger structure of lies that would call everything into question. Some men might begin to wonder, in the absence of a rebuttal within their own knowledge, whether maybe they had been deceived all these years. Maybe the system *was* totally corrupt. Maybe they *had* been lied to. Maybe America's leaders were just so many crooked politicians and greedy businessmen that were squeezing taxes and profits out of American workers' sweat and gouging wealth out of the impoverished nations of the world. Maybe they *were* all a bunch of lousy, callous capitalists sitting at home sucking on their fat cigars and counting their money while their soldiers rotted and died in a forgotten hellhole. Maybe none of it *was* worth dying for. And it could easily follow that it wasn't worth suffering for either—not the way they dished it out here. Besides, who would know if they broke? And if it was known, who would give a damn? Who would remember? The winds of time would eventually blow away the memory of treason and sacrifice alike. So sign the confession. Tell them whatever they want to know or hear. Rat on another prisoner. And *live*.

But in the here-and-now, I couldn't reconcile myself to caving in. I remembered the ROK they had shot for being kind to me and the other they brutally murdered the morning after my birthday. Most of all I remembered the young soldier they had used as a soccer ball and horribly killed as well. All of them had died rather than yield. Still others lived and continued to fight back and pay the consequences. I could do no less.

I believed in my country, and as my brutal captivity progressed, I increasingly understood what America was fighting against, here in Korea. I knew why I was here. Accordingly, the thought of giving in was unconscionable. Believing our cause to be right, I figured that I would have to answer to God if I broke faith with it. But even short of that, to yield in exchange for my life was no kind of an acceptable alternative to me. For the rest of my days, the same face would be staring back at me in the mirror each morning as I shaved. To give in to swine whose ideologies I abhorred, whose execution of those ideologies was barbaric and who had starved, beaten and neglected the sick and dying, was repugnant. I could never do it and if I did I could never live with myself. I treasured life but living with a conscience I knew would be rabid with the guilt of betrayal was not living at all. If dying was the only other alternative, I was reconciled to it. I had lived almost thirty years and had drunk deeply the joys and sorrows of this world. I had loved and been loved. I had known freedom and now captivity. I had hated and been hated. I had killed and would now myself be killed. Perhaps a balance had been struck, the circle closed. Alone in the Hole, enveloped by the darkness of a rainy night, I came to peace with myself. I was ready.

* * *

Halfway around the world, Jinny stood on the front steps of our row house in Philadelphia talking to her neighbor, Peg Miller. It was a pleasant, warm spring day in early June. She had received no new word on my status or whereabouts since the telegram. I was just M.I.A.—missing in action.

A delivery truck pulled around the corner onto Van Kirk Street. A strange feeling came over Jinny as she watched the truck's approach. It stopped at the curb in front of the house. The driver emerged and climbed the steps toward her.

"Mrs. Thornton?" he inquired, looking back and forth from Peg to Jinny.

"I'm Mrs. Thornton," my wife replied.

"I have a delivery here for you, Mrs. Thornton. We'll bring it in for you if you'll sign the receipt here," the driver said holding out a pen and pad.

"What is it?" she asked reaching to take the pad. The driver retracted it to remind himself.

"It's a big wooden box," he said as he searched over the message on the receipt. "It's, ah . . ." He paused for a moment, then frowning said, "It's your husband's . . . um . . . personal effects." He handed the receipt back glumly, his eyes avoiding hers. "Would you like us to bring it in now?" he asked, wanting very much to conclude this sad transaction.

The men delivered my cruise box to the living-room and left. Alone with our son, Jinny opened it and began removing its contents. She found my hairbrush, laden with hair from too much use and too little cleaning. Tears began to well up in her eyes as she combed out the hair and placed it in an envelope to save and touch. She found my slippers, which inside still bore the impressions of my feet. Her sorrow deepened. She found my dress hat. Neatly folded inside it was a silk reproduction of a wallet photo of her and Jay that I had made for me in Japan in better days. The final blow came with a set of pajamas, the last I had worn. They hadn't been laundered and still carried my scent.

Quietly weeping, she carefully folded the pajamas, carried them upstairs to the bedroom and put them beneath her pillow. That night, she grieved more profoundly than she had since first receiving the bad news. A sense of death was strangling her.

* * *

The long night passed and dawn gave light to my Hole. Morning went by and then the afternoon. There was no Professor. No firing squad. The daylight was waning when a slat above my head was moved back. Silently, the arm of a guard was thrust in toward me. He held out a handful of something. I took it. It was my dinner—seaweed. The slat was shoved back into place. The sun set and once again, darkness descended. I had lived another day.

The second night passed much like the first. More searching for the right words of prayer, thinking of home, hoping I would live through tomorrow. The second day came. And it too passed.

On the morning of the third day, the Professor appeared. I was pulled roughly out of the Hole and marched to the rice paddy. Confronted by my captors, I knew the moment of truth had arrived. We stood there for a time in strange silence. I supposed they were waiting for me to grovel and plead for my life. I would deny them that satisfaction. Then suddenly the Professor spoke up in a loud and angry voice.

"Send him back to the compound! Under the peoples' Lenient Policy we do not harm prisoners. He will be allowed to live."

I couldn't believe it! As the realization of my

deliverance sank in, my heart began to soar. I almost exploded in joy. It was like celebrating my own personal Easter. On the third day, God had raised me from the dead and brought me out of my stinking sepulcher. These bastards hadn't allowed me to live. *God* had! And he didn't even fault me for not knowing my prayers. Once more I had survived by His intervention.

* * *

Twelve thousand miles away, Jinny began to sleep a little better as time went by, for some reason she didn't understand. The cruise box had really gotten to her but now it was behind her. She guessed it was just one more cycle of her ups and downs. The blues had passed again for awhile.

10

To die—to sleep—
No more; and by a sleep to say we end
The heartache, and the thousand natural shocks
That flesh is heir to.

—Shakespeare
Hamlet

I was herded back to the compound just in time for the morning feed. Except for the seaweed, I hadn't eaten in three days. My ration of millet and more seaweed was handed to me and I eyed it as if it were steak and caviar. I was preparing to gobble it down when the Professor rushed over to me.

"Thorn-ton! Come!" he shouted.

"I'm not going anywhere!" I snapped back. The Professor was angry.

"You cannot eat! Eating is not for your kind!" he said, lashing out at me. He knocked the food out of my hands to the ground and then stomped it into the dirt with his boot.

I was dragged back to the Big House for more interrogation and God knew what else.

"Thorn-ton. You are a great trouble to us. You are a liar. You are insincere. You must be punished until your thinking is correct," said the Professor for the umpteenth time.

"I don't care. I want food. Give me something to eat before I starve to death," I replied sullenly.

"You will get no food, liar! As long as you lie and refuse to cooperate you will have no food!" The Professor motioned to the guards. It was back to the Black Room again. "You will stand in the corner, Thorn-ton, and search your conscience again. You will self-criticize and mend your ways." He left me, and again I was alone in the dark.

To my surprise, after standing in the same spot for only three hours, I was visited again by the Professor. He told the guard to take me back to the compound. I shouted to him before he was out of range.

"I want some *food!* Gimme something to eat!" Looking back over his shoulder, the Professor replied to me.

"Be patient," he said. "In an hour or so you will be given a lot of fish from the people's food. You will have a feast."

What was this? Another trick? I was astounded. Fish! If it was true, this was wonderful. I got back to the compound and waited expectantly with the other P.O.W.'s for an hour—then two. The fish finally arrived. It was fish all right, but it was anybody's guess how long it had been on dry land. Beggars can't be choosers so we accepted this pungent offering. It was covered with mold and maggots. To pick it all off would have left only bones. So we ate a three-course meal—rotten fish, mold and maggots. It was disgusting and many P.O.W.'s couldn't contend with smelling it, let alone eating it. But garbage like this was standard fare at Pak's Palace. It fit in perfectly with the general conditions of our captivity here which were at once merciless and lethal.

There were those who couldn't or wouldn't adapt to the despicable environment that characterized prisoner life in the harsh, early years of the war particularly at the Palace. We came to name this refusal or inability to cope Give-up-itis. Springing from the constant harassment, beatings, disease and lack of food, men who felt they had no other reason to go on simply gave up—and died.

The first case I saw of it, long before we ever

named the malady, involved a G.I. who had been in fairly good condition when I rolled into Pak's Palace. As time went on, however, he began to retreat into a kind of dreary despondency, willing to do less and less for himself, including eating. I appealed to him to come out of it.

"Aren't you gonna eat? You gotta eat when you get it. You don't know when it'll come around again." The G.I. didn't seem to be listening. "Did you hear me? Just gulp it down."

"I can't eat that shit. Pigs wouldn't eat that garbage. You take it," he replied, turning away into the corner where he slumped.

"C'mon, get outa that corner. *Pak* puts you in a corner. Don't do it to yourself. Please, will ya? *Eat* this. I know it's lousy but it's all we got." He ignored me. "You'll *starve* if you don't." Silence. "It'll keep you alive! You want to live don't you?" Again I got no answer. "You want to die?" More silence. And then,

"I just don't give a fuck. We're all gonna die here sooner or later. Maybe I'd rather go sooner, that's all."

"You don't *have* to die! You don't have to do shit except fight these bastards and *eat!* Don't you want to get the hell outa this place? What . . . what if they spring us outa here next week or something and you're dead? I get out and the pigs are munching on your dead ass? What then? What about that, huh? Answer me!"

"You're full of shit and you know it," he said disconsolately. "Nobody's coming after us and this war is nowhere near over. We're dead meat, all of us. And I want out. So just fuck off, will ya? Go eat your goddamn garbage and mine with it. Just leave me alone."

"You've got a wife and kids. You don't give a shit

about them? What the hell happens to them?'' The
G.I. laughed weakly and glanced back at me.
''My old lady was running around long before I
came here. She didn't give a damn about me then
and she sure as hell doesn't now. The kids'll get the
insurance when I'm gone. They'll do all right. So
fuck it. And fuck you. Get lost.''

I left him with the rancid food in the hope he
would change his mind. I and others continued to
plead with him over the next ten days, but to no
avail. He withdrew himself and broke contact with
the outside world, a world that he had grown to hate
and fear so hopelessly. He steadfastly refused to eat,
rejecting even our efforts to spoon-feed him. In time
he became completely incapacitated. As he weakened and sickened, we began caring for him like a
baby. He couldn't move to go to the latrine and lay
in his own filth curled up like a fetus in his corner.
We changed his clothes for him as he defacated and
urinated in them uncontrollably. Finally, he went
over the edge. Beyond the reach of friend and foe
alike, the spark of life went out in this piteous,
broken man.

My stay at Pak's Palace spanned less than a
month. I had been greeted by this man on my arrival
May 27th. It was now almost the end of June and he
had managed to destroy himself in something under
two weeks. He felt he had nothing to live for and died
because of it. I believed I had everything to live for
and so fought back and survived.

A few days later, we would move to another camp
and after that yet another. There would be more
barbarity, more starvation, more beatings and more
disease on the long road home. The G.I. could have
endured it if he had tried; if he'd had the will; if he'd
had the purpose. But he didn't. He never left the
Palace.

11

For many walk, of whom I have told you
often, and now tell you even weeping,
that they are the enemies of the cross
of Christ: whose end is destruction . . .
and whose glory is in their shame . . .

—Philippians 3: 18, 19

"Take all and come with!" order Major Pak at 2:00 a.m. on June 22nd. Sleepy-eyed prisoners stumbled about in the darkness trying to find their way around the compound to make a formation of sorts. Pak began calling names. There was to be a shift of bodies to other camps. The future in any case held little hope for improvement, but getting out and away from Pak would be well worth risking the unknown. I was willing to try anything compared to the Palace. My weight had fallen under ninety pounds, the lice and dysentery were continuing unabated and I had now contracted beri-beri which swelled my legs and genitals painfully.

Finally, my name was called, much to my relief. Some new prisoners were brought in and added to the travel group which numbered eighteen officers and five enlisted men. We "took all" which was nothing and "came with" our new officer-in-charge, Major Han, the one who had brought us to Pak's. Han informed us of our destination.

"You Americans are most fortunate for you have been selected to attend a great school of communist learning. You will be traveling a great distance to Pyoktong University." Nice name, I thought. The initials were appropriate enough—P.U. Han continued. "You are no longer prisoners of war. You are now students and will learn the truth. You will be studying very hard and we will give you good food and living conditions. This school is very far away and to demonstrate our interest in your well-being, we will drive you there. First, you must load the truck with your provisions.''

Perhaps they were serious this time. We loaded four sacks of rice, three sacks of salted fish, a fifty-five gallon drum of gasoline and a spare tire. It took all eighteen of us to do this small amount of work, we were so emaciated. Once the loading was completed, Han and three guards climbed into the truck, hogging most of the space, with the rest of us jammed into what little room remained. Pyoktong was two hundred miles north on the Yalu River that divides Korea from Manchuria. Sick as we were, a forced march would have wiped out the entire student population, so the truck was a welcome break to us. Even so, three students died.

We traveled until dawn, stopping at a town called Kuna-ri. It was mobbed with enemy troops and materiel. We were herded into a small hut next to a railroad track, wondering all the while how Kuna-ri had escaped attack. It was a prime target. No sooner had we settled in when our question was answered. A flight of F-80's appeared and immediately began working the place over.

Our hut's roof had been knocked through, apparently in a previous attack, and we were thus able to observe the full onslaught. The F-80's blue noses were pointed our way and as their fifty-calibre machine guns opened up, we figured we'd be killed with the gooks. Since the Communists dispensed with the formality of prominently showing ''P.O.W.'' on trucks and buildings holding prisoners, we, the hut and our truck were just that many more targets in the thick of it.

Kuna-ri was mangled before our eyes. Rockets

whooshed over our building, slamming into the
tracks and rolling stock. We watched the destruction
with a mixture of pleasure and anxiety. All that
would be needed to wipe us out was one pilot
skidding off his flight path. His stray rocket would
miss the railroad and explode in our hut. Han must
have read our minds for as the destruction closed in
on us, he advised that our friends were trying to kill
us to prevent us from learning the truth at P.U. But
to our amazement, the F-80's never touched us.

By the time it was all over, the Koreans were
emotional wrecks, just as I had observed in earlier
raids. One of our rottenest guards, known as Dinny-
Dimwit, was quivering all over. He couldn't keep his
teeth from chattering, so intense was his fright. The
whole show did wonders for our morale though,
especially since we emerged unscathed. Luckily, our
truck also survived undamaged along with its cargo.
But before we departed, Major Han had some
business to tend to. The raid had not affected his
sense of commercial enterprise and apparently his
customer base was still intact. He had us unload one
sack of rice and quietly completed a transaction off to
the side.
"You don't think the Major would be into the black
market, do you?" asked one P.O.W.

Of course not. By the time we reached Pyoktong,
he had sold off every last bit of our provisions—
unopened—splitting the proceeds with the guards.

Three days later we were still on the road. Han
gave us a rare rest stop off the truck and I decided
to take advantage of the opportunity to respond to
my dysentery. But just as I was settling in, he
ordered us back inside. I couldn't turn myself off
that easily and so stayed put. Han was nonplussed.
He was a huge, six foot tall Korean and walked over,
demanding my immediate return to the vehicle.

"Get up and *move*," he growled at me. I was in no mood to cooperate. I'd be damned if I was going to dump in my drawers if I didn't have to.

"I'm not *ready* to move and I *won't* move until I *am* ready!" I shot back brazenly. Han, much like Pak, was not to be toyed with. He had killed prisoners before with little provocation. He drew his pistol out and ordered me again. Surprisingly, he attempted to reason with me a little.

"You don't want us to leave you behind do you? Your American planes will shoot you here on the road." There wasn't a plane in sight. Unwisely, I lost my temper.

"I don't give a goddamn if you *do* leave me here, Han! I hope the hell you do! I hope the planes *do* come back and blow your fuckin' *ass* off!"

Han was incensed at my blatant insubordination. He hauled off with his pistol and smashed me in the back of the head, knocking me flat. Dazed but still conscious, I lay there like a paralytic. The other P.O.W.'s waited tensely for the gunshot they knew was coming. But then Han stopped in his tracks and to the immense shock of everyone, relented. In a manner totally uncharacteristic of him, he allowed two other prisoners to come to my aid, lifting me up to finish my crap and then dragging me onto the truck.

By all rights and past behavior, Han should have shot me outright. He had done so to others, many times before, we knew. Three were already near death and a fourth was not desirable. He would have looked bad if all his students died on the way to school. But he was an impulsive killer with a short fuse. I never knew what actually turned him aside, but I credited God with bailing me out again.

About 3:00 a.m. the next morning we pulled into the town of Kang-ye, a big railroad center. Our group was divided and put into two old storehouse rooms. Large crocks, four feet high and two feet in diameter were already in the rooms so we had to squeeze in between them to sleep. As we were just settling in, all hell broke loose. It was another air raid.

We were locked in and couldn't get out, so win or lose, the storehouse was our bomb shelter. As the explosions intensified, it soon became apparent that many buildings were being squarely hit and set ablaze. We could see the flickering flames through the cracks in the door planks. The raid lasted about thirty minutes and when it was over, there was a great commotion outside. Our door was being hurriedly unlocked. It was Han and the guards and they were extremely agitated. Shoving and pushing, they hustled us out of the storehouse in a rush. Once outside, we quickly understood why. The local citizens had learned that American prisoners were in town and after the shellacking they had just taken, they were organizing a lynch mob to seek their revenge. We were the goats.

We didn't need much encouragement from Han as we saw the screaming crowd bearing down on us, backlighted by the inferno that had once been their town. Kang-ye was totally engulfed in flame. Entire blocks of buildings were ablaze and railroad yards, warehouses, locomotives and railcars were burning out of control. Ammunition dumps were being torched off sky high. The night glowed red.

Han's concern for us was surprising, if something less than heartwarming, as he piled us into the truck. We roared out of town, one step ahead of the approaching mob.

All through the next day as we traveled on, there seemed to be growing confusion as to where we were to be taken. Han said he had been informed that

Pyoktong might be out and that a debate was underway as to whether we would go there, to another camp to the northeast or—worst of all—across the Yalu River into China. The prospect of being taken into China was a horror. There we would be totally out of U.N. reach and, we feared, lost to the world forever.

The debate failed to be settled enroute, so we were held up in another railroad center while the gooks sorted out the situation. The town was Mampo-gin, lying along the banks of the Yalu in President Truman's "sanctuary area." Off-limits to interdiction and air strikes, the sanctuary was used by the Communists to the hilt. As we rode into town, we could see war supplies piled high everywhere across the river, surrounded by anti-aircraft positions manned by Chinese and uniformed Russian military. It was a frustrating and pitiful sight. All of what we could see had helped bring each of us to our present misery and was doing the same or worse to other American and U.N. troops. Even more depressing to us was the realization that if the U.N. allies were unwilling to broaden the war here and fight for their own protection, they'd never risk doing it to save our skins. Crossing the Yalu into China would be the kiss of death. We'd never get out. Our anxiety mounted as we waited.

We were off-loaded from the truck and confined in a school yard on the south side of Mampo-gin. Idly, we milled about, awaiting further news on our destination and ultimate fate.

A hundred yards beyond the school yard's fence was a small, white, stuccoed building. It had once been a tiny Christian church with only one room. Our captors proudly proclaimed and explained that the teachers and missionaries of this capitalist outpost of exploitation had been liquidated or imprisoned by the peoples' liberation forces. We were assured that the struggle for liberation would never cease until the myth of God had vanished from the minds of men. Unfortunately, by taking advantage of an apparent oversight, God had not cooperated in this endeavor. He hadn't quite vanished from the little ransacked church.

True, the bell tower had been stripped of its bell and cross and the church's interior gutted. But there was something obvious about the back of the church, which faced onto the school yard where we stood. Inside that wall was where the altar must once have stood, with a large cross mounted above it. The cross had apparently been deeply imbedded in the wall, for when the church was desecrated and the cross ripped down, it tore out the stucco surrounding it all the way through, like a cooky cutter. The cross had left a hole in its exact shape penetrating the full depth of the wall to the outside. A perfect image of it remained. Despite their efforts, the Sign of God was clearly visible. In trying to destroy the cross, they had only made matters worse. No one could have seen it inside the building. A lock and key would have denied it to every eye. But now the cross's ghostly image, there in the broken-out plaster, stood out for all to see from far away—people like us, people like the natives, people unlike the Communists, for they didn't seem to notice. But *we* did and were once more inspired by the tenacious presence of a God who would not be vanquished.

And it was here in a school yard, in the shadow of the Church of Mampo-gin that we learned a little more about faith, and about our future. We were ordered, not north to certain oblivion in China, but west—to Pyoktong.

The Communists bragged that there was no God. We knew better. We'd just been to Sunday school.

12

Therefore, be prepared to fight if you
desire to gain the victory . . . If you
will not suffer, you refuse to be crowned.
If you desire to be crowned, fight manfully,
and endure patiently.

—Thomas à Kempis
The Imitation of Christ

On June 27th, after nearly three months of captivity, I, and the other surviving members of our party, finally arrived at a genuine P.O.W. camp, Pyoktong ''University.'' The student body numbered about 3400.

The summer monsoon arrived in June along with us. By July, high humidity, cloudy and rainy weather dominated the area. Intermittent and recurrent thunderstorms flooded streams, rice fields and highways, hindering road traffic and transport. The rain most characteristic of the area, called the Plum Rain, was a light one of low intensity but great persistence. The name was derived from the rains' annual arrival coinciding with the maturing of the plum fruit—a fruit which prisoners never got to eat.

Pyoktong was a small town located on a southern inlet of the Yalu River. It was a self-sufficient entity based on an agricultural economy. Sitting at the edge of a clear blue reservoir, the town lay nestled among the wooded hills that surrounded it. The brownish-yellow slopes wore a mantle of shrubs and broad-leafed trees at the lowest levels, then rose into towering three-thousand-foot peaks covered with tall pines, spruce and at the highest elevations, aspen and birch. The houses ran along one side of a rocky spur that jutted out into the reservoir. They were of crude construction using local materials such as stone, rough-hewn wooden beams, mud plaster and rice-straw thatch. Some homes, such as those occupied by the more affluent Honshos, had slate in place of straw for roofing materials, or even tile. Perhaps the most ironic feature in this communist society was the homes' private courtyards surrounded by protective fences of either earth or stone. Sometimes there would be only a lone gate, standing ten feet in height and width, with no connecting fences. But the message of "private—keep out" was clear enough, the invisible property line being carefully respected by all. It was a picturesque little village when seen from afar but the mountains that enclosed it formed insurmountable prison walls for weak and dying prisoners yearning to be free.

Our prisoner housing for the most part consisted of the typical Korean dwelling. They had been abandoned long years before our arrival, though, and were in extremely poor states of repair. As a result, many prisoners in the winter preceding my capture had frozen to death when temperatures fell as low as forty below zero.

The building which was designated as the camp hospital was in the same disrepair. Cold air entered between warped and separated wall planks, resulting in a virulent situation. Prisoners who went in rarely came out. The hospital was for all purposes a death house.

Pyoktong University was a high-powered interrogation center, and an exclusive one at that—P.U. was reserved strictly for non-Korean captives. It was an all-business college. The faculty quickly informed us that they *meant* business and would *give* the business to anybody that didn't learn their lessons properly. The welcoming remarks we received made it all very clear. A high-ranking interrogator addressed us.

"Cooperate," he said solemnly. "Become good students. Get the proper cognition. Learn the truth. Do these things and you will be sent home at an early date." He paused to let these positive thoughts sink in. Then he became more menacing. "If you keep your reactionary ways, if you do not cooperate, we will dig a deep hole. We will bury you in that hole and cover you with much dirt so you will not stink up the countryside as you rot."

They meant what they said and kept their promises. Before P.U. would close its doors at war's end, more than two thousand men would die here and be buried nearby. Every day during late spring and early summer, ten to fifteen men died, men whose last strength had been used fighting for life during the terrible winter of 1950-51 when there had been neither accommodation, food nor clothing for such temperatures. The North Koreans and Chinese had refused to permit the International Red Cross to come in with any form of comfort or aid for the prisoners.

Worse, those under interrogation who did not answer satisfactorily, or others who resisted or shot their mouths off against the indoctrination efforts, suffered a variety of punishments tailored to take advantage of seasonal climatic conditions. In summer, the Sweat Box was employed for lagging students to consider their errors. These were little hutches in which a man could neither sit nor draw up his legs. Come winter, slow learners were offered the solitude of the same facility which the weather had now transformed into the Ice Box. Here they could reconsider their shortcomings in the agony of sub-arctic cold. Sometimes the wretched offender didn't reconsider in time and was removed to the hill to join a growing mound of unburied corpses. The frozen ground was hard as rock and permitted only shallow graves at best, covered with a thin layer of dirt and stones. With the arrival of spring's thaw and later the Plum Rain, these graves washed out, belching up their corpses and leaving them exposed above ground. The nightmare was compounded as Korean pigs and dogs were set loose upon them to feed. Our captors sadistically informed us that this was all we were good for—pig slop. Even our dead were not allowed to rest in peace.

As bad as it had been during my first three months of captivity, the full extent and enormity of the communist carnage was still largely unknown to me. At Pyoktong, the shared experiences of thousands of U.N. troops served to enlighten us quickly as to the methodical butchery that had bloodied the North Korean countryside since the war's beginning.

I learned of one march in which seven hundred men had set out from the front to camps in the rear. Eighty-one were shot in the back of the head in the first ten miles of a two-hundred-mile march. At its conclusion, one hundred and forty-one were still alive.

A British P.O.W. related another story that spoke of both savagery and selflessness. The incident took place in "the Caves" at Kang-dong. The Caves were abandoned coal mines in this North Korean mining town, pressed into service as prisoner quarters. Hundreds of U.N. prisoners were crowded into these leaky, damp holes underground.

Two main prisoner columns had been led north from the Imjin River in the summer of 1951, and straggling behind were the shot-up remnants of "A" Company, Gloucestershire Regiment. The last surviving platoon commander of "A" Company, suffering from a leg wound and head injury, shepherded his men along, caring as best he could for other more seriously wounded men. By the time they had reached the Caves, his condition and that of his men had deteriorated badly. They had received no medical attention enroute and many still wore the same dressings, now filthy and ragged, first placed on their wounds by Gloucestershire medics prior to capture.

The officer and a sergeant of their machine-gun platoon were placed with several others in a cave already crowded with South Koreans, themselves dying of disease and starvation. Except when two daily rations of boiled, cracked corn were passed through a small opening to their cave, these men sat in almost total darkness. A subterranean stream ran through the cave, adding to their anguish and discomfort. It soon became difficult to distinguish the dead from the dying.

One day a North Korean colonel visited, offering a proposition. "We realize that your conditions here are uncomfortable. We sympathize. I myself am powerless to help you unless you are prepared to help us. If you will join the peace movement to fight American aggression in Korea, we can take you to a proper camp. There you will have better rations and improved accommodations, and your wounds will be cared for by a surgeon."

All refused this offer, individually. The platoon commander pondered the prospects overnight, and in view of the continued, rapid loss of life, arrived at a decision. Next morning he drew the sergeant to one side. "I've thought it over," he said. "I've decided that you must go over to their 'Peace Fighters' Camp.' You and the rest might survive there. Just do as little as you can and don't ever forget that you are British soldiers."

"And what about you, sir?" asked the sergeant. "Won't you be coming as well?"

"No. No, I'm afraid not. I'm an officer and we—all of us—will be judged by what I do. Or don't do."

"Sir, you'll die here! We can't abandon you; the men won't have it! You *must* come along with the rest," the sergeant pleaded. The officer shook his head sadly.

"No, it's different for me. The men are in your charge now, sergeant. I order you and them to go. I'll say behind. I must."

The North Korean colonel returned to make his pitch again and was informed of the decision. The men were removed from the cave with a number of Americans. He spoke to the officer. "Englishman," he said, "You should be with your men at the Peace Fighters' Camp."

"I'm not going. I'm a British officer responsible for my actions in behalf of Great Britain. I will do nothing that could be used to dishonor me or my country." The North Korean was unimpressed by this, taking it as senseless bravado.

"I will let you think about this foolishness. Perhaps your thinking is not clear so I will not accept this as your final refusal. I will return later and we will discuss this again."

He returned four times with promises of medical treatment, a special diet of eggs, milk and meat, and better living conditions. Each time, he was rebuffed. The young officer, recently graduated from the Royal Military Academy at Sandhurst saw himself for what he was—an officer representing the Commonwealth in enemy country. He was given a choice: life, and agreement to reject, if only outwardly, the principles which had brought him to Korea; or steadfast adherence to those principles, and death. Bravely and loyally, like the gallant British officer he was, this young subaltern chose to die rather than be tainted as a collaborator.

And so it was. He died in the Caves—along with nearly three hundred others.

Fighting against our oppressors took place at all levels, from that of the individual where it was absolutely essential—and sometimes fatal—to the group level, where the possibility of mass reprisals and killings was always a risk. Yet the risk was taken because the alternative of yielding to total subjugation was as repugnant as outright collaboration. One particular group which resisted to the very brink was comprised of Turkish prisoners. More than three hundred were captured in the war, most of them wounded. To be picked up otherwise, to the Turkish way of reasoning, could be tantamount to disgrace. Many of these men were in Pyoktong in 1951.

Intense pressure was being placed on the Turks for the value of their propaganda as oppressed minorities in the event they gave in. The guards were constantly on their backs, increasing their workloads, shorting their rations and giving them only pork, on those rare occasions when meat was on the menu, in violation of the Turks' Moslem religious prohibitions. Particularly petty and irritating were the harrassing headcounts made every hour of every night.

Hamid Yuksel, holding the rank of Yuzbashim (Commander of One Hundred), was an instinctive leader of tenacious courage. To the man, he and his troops harbored a profound hatred for their atheist, communist captors. This was the unavoidable result of their strong Moslem faith combined with the close proximity of their homeland to the Soviet Union. Accordingly, they were unruly and rebellious prisoners who would ignore or disobey even the more reasonable requests of the camp cadre. Their behavior was far more than mere spitefulness, however. They were engaged in a war of their own and their goal was simple. If they were to be in captivity, it would be on *their* terms to the fullest extent possible. Armed with a sense of mutual commitment, fearlessness, and a spiritual faith that was unexcelled, they launched their first offensive under the able leadership of Yuzbashim Yuksel. Their first target would be the hated headcount program.

The Turks were housed in a long, rectangular building with only one door, located at one end. All windows were covered with blackout boarding and, there being no interior lighting, the inside was pitch black. While the absence of doors and windows made it easier for the guards to maintain security, it created some disadvantages in the execution of their nightly headcounts. Armed only with a pistol and a flashlight, it was like going into a blind alley. The inspection was handled by a single guard who entered the building through its only door and walked down a central aisle. Twenty-five Turks lay on each side. Upon reaching the end of the aisle, the headcounter would turn and walk back toward the door.

The word was passed among the Turks that the headcount would be terminated. The order and manner of executing this operation originated with Yuksel and was eagerly obeyed. One moonless night, the headcount guard opened the door to the Turk building. Cautiously he walked through and into the black interior. Slowly moving down the central aisle, he flashed his light along the sleeping forms that lay along one side. He didn't hear the door quietly swing shut behind him. Completing the first half of his walk and reaching the end of the aisle, he turned. Silently, the Turks nearby rose up, grabbing his pistol first and then his flashlight. It was quickly extinguished and the room was plunged into total darkness. The Turks then proceeded to administer a savage beating on the guard, passing him down the aisle so that each could enjoy his own long-awaited satisfaction. Fifty Turks punched, kicked and pummeled the guard down the entire length of the building. Yuksel had ordered that the guard not be killed, and he wasn't—barely. He was thrown bodily out the front door in a crumpled, bloody heap.

Whistles and bugles immediately started blowing and in the wink of an eye, the entire guard contingent was on alert. Machine guns and even mortars were hastily set up and trained on every P.O.W. building. All prisoners were ordered outside in their respective formations, surrounded by the heavily armed guards whose weapons were cocked and ready for firing. It would have said little for the Lenient Policy, not to mention the treatment afforded minority captives, if no Turks returned home from the camps. A mass execution was therefore not a good or even probable alternative. The ringleaders would have to be identified. Once this had been done, it appeared certain that the Turks would have some of their numbers shot for instigating a high crime against one of the Peace Loving Peoples.

The camp commandant, in a loud and angry voice, ordered the troublemakers to step forward, confess and save everyone from severe punishment. There was no movement within the Turkish ranks. An hour passed and then two. The entire P.O.W. population was held at attention, but nobody minded too terribly. There was silent admiration for the Turks. Three hours passed. Still no admissions of guilt.

Our captors were getting nowhere and were losing face badly. The tension was mounting. The cadres decided that if no one would admit to being a ringleader, then they would decide who it was. The commandant walked down the first Turkish rank. Pointing at three Turks, he ordered them to step forward. They did—and so did forty-seven other Turks in unison. The commandant then ordered three guards to pull the three Turks out of the ranks, physically. They did, and the entire Turkish formation moved with them. The air was electrified with tension so thick it could have been cut with a knife. The guards were getting jittery and were now aiming their weapons directly into the ranks—all ranks. The Turks were unyielding and the entire camp was backing them up. A riot was in the making. Suddenly, the camp commandant relented.

"We will not be duped into hurting these good people of Turkey. This is the result of a language barrier, which explains such misunderstanding. We wish only to be friends with the Turkish nationalities who have been deceived by the U.N. and forced into fighting the Peace Loving Peoples." The commandant paused and contemplated a peace offering. "Inspections of the Turkish company will stop. Further, in respect to the Moslem faith of these Turkish peoples, we will no longer give them pig to eat. From now on they will have chicken."

By blaming the problem on the language the commandant had resolved the crisis without undue loss of face. The formation was disbanded. But from this point on, having exercised their territorial imperative, the Turks staked out their claim. Here, and wherever they were held prisoner, would be sovereign ground, a bit of Turkey, theirs by right of conquest. Like the fenceless gates that guarded the privacy of the Korean houses, an invisible line had been drawn around the Turks, and was honored by all.

13

If we must die, O let us nobly die,
So that our precious blood may not be shed
In vain; then even the monsters we defy
Shall be constrained to honor us though dead!

—Claude McKay
If We Must Die

"Are your wounds feeling better now that they have been treated?" asked the friendly interrogator.

"A little," replied Captain Milford Stanley, warily. Stanley was taken prisoner in 1950 with multiple shrapnel splinters imbedded in his flesh. "There are others guys worse off. You helping them too?" he asked. The interrogator ducked the question.

"We feel a particular concern for you, Captain Stanley. You are special to us," came the oblique reply. "We are prepared to put many good things at your disposal. Good food, clothing, more medical attention. Would you like some hot tea?" Stanley had heard this tripe before. The interrogator continued. "Tell me, Stanley. Why do you fight this war?"

"You know why. Because I'm an Army officer. I'm an American," replied Stanley, suspicious of what was coming.

"This is not your war. You have no interest in this business. On the contrary, your true interests lie with us. We fight on behalf of oppressed peoples everywhere. You must join us, Captain Stanley," said the interrogator.

"Why are you so interested in what I do for you? Why me, I mean how come I'm so—special," asked Stanley. Today's session seemed to have a slightly different wrinkle to it.

"Because you, like other oppressed people, have been denied your freedom. Your rights have been trampled on and you have been exploited by the capitalist class. You know this to be so. Consider this and you will understand why you are important to us."

"I'm just one more American soldier. I'm no different from anybody," said Stanley, beginning to get the drift.

"No. You *are* different. Your color is not the same as the others. We know that you Negroes were slaves and that you are still slaves. You have no freedom. You are treated differently by the whites. Do they not have a name for your people? We know they call you 'nigger.' And do the whites not deny you the benefits which they enjoy themselves?" Stanley was stung by this. They were playing on his color, demeaning him in a way which incensed him. The interrogator entreated him further. "We will give you all that the whites have denied you. You are under the protection of the Peace Loving Peoples of the world. You have nothing to fear. The good life can be yours if you will help us strike back at the oppressors." Stanley wasn't taking the bait. "Food, Captain Stanley. Clean clothes. Medicine. It will all be yours if you will help. Everything you need is within your grasp. Think of the whites and what they have done to you and your people. Do you not yearn for revenge?"

Play their game or lose it all. It was the usual theme, this time with a racial twist tailored just for him. He was different and special all right, singled out for a cruel yet subtle approach that a lesser man would have fallen for. They were pandering to him condescendingly, using their oppressed-peoples-of-the-world line. And Stanley recognized it for just that—a line. It angered him that they would play on his color to lure him into collaboration. It was veiled racism and he rebelled against it with contempt and disgust. He answered the interrogator.

"Yes, I'm a Negro. It's true I'm a different color than the others. But I'm still an American and I'm no different a man than any of them. I don't need any special favors from you. You can treat me like the rest."

"Very well. It shall be as you wish," replied the interrogator. Tired now after trying this and other approaches on Stanley without fruitful results, he had him removed to be treated like the rest. Stanley's determined loyalty was rewarded with a savage beating. His wounds were never touched again, the steel splinters left where they lay, festering in his body.

Singled out repeatedly because he was black and because his captors thought they were toying with an unsophisticated mind, Stanley was forced to carry a uniquely insidious burden throughout his captivity. And sadly, his success in bearing it might have been a result of confronting similar challenges at other times in his life—at home. But he had chosen to cope with these evils with insight and understanding. He was one of those prisoners who knew that the unkind attitudes of some of his fellow citizens and the imperfections of his country were insufficient grounds for a wholesale indictment of America. That being so, it had produced a certain strength and immunity to withstand the psychological offensive thrown at him in his Korean enslavement. He was a graduate of a tough, down-to-earth school which had taught him that hard times and ugly slurs couldn't break a man if he didn't allow it. It made his resistance that much more admirable and heroic. He never allowed his captors to drive him to the point of breaking faith with his country or his fellow P.O.W.'s—most of whom were white.

He fought back in what might have seemed a solitary struggle. Yet Stanley knew he was not alone. He had the help of his God in whom he placed a great and intimate faith. Any time, day or night, Stanley would call on his God as the need arose. It was almost a casual relationship he had, for without the benefit of preacher or ritual, Bible or prayer book, he could reach out with a personal, man-to-Man faith that was an inspiration.

Milford Stanley never allowed himself to be ruled by cynicism, pessimism or self-pity at a time when he could have done so very easily, and as some P.O.W.'s of both races did. Likewise, he refused to be defeated, and never permitted himself to be the putty his oppressors thought they had in their hands. Stanley was a soldier. Most of all, he was an American.

14

For those who fight for it, life has a
special flavor the protected never know.

—Anonymous Marine
Khe Song, R.V.N. 1969

As the summer wore on at Pyoktong, our conditions, both physical and environmental, reached a low ebb. Medical treatment from our captors was non-existent and in its absence, our numbers steadily dwindled. Prisoners were permitted to die without any attempt by the Communists to give them relief.

The medical facilities, if they could be called such, were abysmal. One "hospital," for example, contained stalls in it like a stable with bare floor boards serving as the patients' resting place. The sick and dying were tossed into these stalls, often naked and coated with lice. One man visited two of his friends in the hospital. To his horror, he found them covered with maggots that crawled in and out of their noses, ears and eyes. Blowflies harrassed them, crawling about their mouths. Too weak to move or even roll over, these helpless men agonized, completely unable to cleanse themselves of their pestilence. They were the living dead.

To ask the communist doctor for help would accomplish little more than eliciting an unconcerned "Later," in response. In many cases, it was probably for the best. An Army sergeant by the name of Treffery had been suffering from frostbitten toes since shortly after capture when his boots were taken from him. In time his toes began to rot and he sought treatment from the communist doctors. What he got was a multiple amputation from a Chinese nurse using a pair of garden shears, all without benefit of anesthesia. Later, as other toes worsened and an increasing number of patients entered the hospital never to be seen again, Treffery decided to treat himself. He broke off the remaining toes with his fingernails.

One treatment frequently applied by the Chinese was credited to Soviet medical science and was hailed as a panacea for various wounds and ailments. In the tissue operation, as it was called, an incision would be made on the prisoner's side, maybe three ribs up. In the incision would be placed a chicken liver. The incision would then be sewn up. That was it. Before long, the chicken liver rotted, the wound festered, and the healing effect? Infection.

Fortunately a handful of American Army doctors were among our company. While they were given little if anything in the way of tools or medication, these doctors worked miracles. Two in particular in our compound were Majors C. L. Anderson (known as Doc Andy) and Sidney Esensten (known as Doctor Sidley). They set broken bones, pulled abcessed teeth and removed strange, tumorous growths. They performed one amputation and even an appendectomy.

The appendectomy was done for ailing Captain Paul Bromser whom the Docs, without benefit of anything except their own medical skills, had correctly diagnosed as suffering from acute appendicitis. The Chinese could not have cared less if Bromser died, and offered no help. Doc Andy and Doctor Sidley proceeded as best they could and operated with what they had. Their tools consisted of one blade of a broken scissors found on a road during a work detail; a knife made from the steel arch of an old G.I. boot honed down to razor sharpness; a needle hammered down with rocks from a piece of wire; and a shredded nylon shoelace for thread. There was no anesthesia. The operation was a success owing to Doc Andy's and Doctor Sidley's incredible expertise and knowledge, not to mention Bromser's ability to withstand the agony. He healed and lived to be a free and healthy man once more.

Our doctors could count on support from us in return for their life-saving efforts. Marine Major Gerry Fink fashioned a wooden leg for Lieutenant Colonel Tom Harrison whose leg had been torn off during a high-speed bail-out from his disabled jet. He walked around on it quite comfortably. Army Captain Ralph Nardella created a stethoscope from some stolen tubing and a resonant piece of wood. It worked and was put to good use by the doctors.

Without the heroic efforts of these two doctors and others like them, more men might have died. But there was little they could do as disease and malnutrition took their toll, especially in the aftermath of the brutal North Korean winters. By the time the summer of 1953 arrived those who survived were physical wrecks. Our hair was turning grey and falling out. Our bones became those of seventy-year-old men, snapping like dry twigs. I alone broke a finger, wrist and another rib. Our teeth were abcessing and falling out of our mouths. We were mere skeletons as our bodies consumed what was left of themselves. As our metabolisms collapsed, dysentery, beri-beri and a host of other diseases would pounce upon us again and again, taking advantage of our weakened conditions. Night blindness from vitamin deficiencies would set in followed by day blindness. Every year of this we endured probably cost us ten in longevity. And yet for it all, there was some humor to be found in the misadventures that our shabby conditions gave rise to. We had to laugh. If we didn't we'd have cried.

By September, 1951, my dysentery had reached the peak of its ferocity. I was forced to defecate as often as fifteen times a day, generally with little advance warning. The prisoner house I lived in was about two hundred yards from our assigned latrine. Midway through this distance, a low, broken-down foundation wall had to be negotiated to reach the crapper. I had little bowel control and had great difficulty in preventing a premature dump in my drawers. Accordingly, it was necessary to make my way gingerly to the crapper, squeezing the cheeks of my behind together to hold back the flood. This always worked well until I reached the little wall. As soon as one leg was lifted for the hop over, the job was finished on the spot, covering me and the wall with filth. Choosing to avoid soiling my clothing, I began making my run naked from the waist down. Yet the results were always the same at the wall. To make matters worse, I had to clean up the mess I had made to prevent the spread of disease.

Frustrated by my repeated misfires, I opted to break the camp rules and use a different latrine, in a nearby area. It was downhill, close to another prisoner house. There were no walls to obstruct my passage and the downhill walk enabled me to keep my rectum clamped shut. The main disadvantage was the need to be surreptitious. This particular crapper enjoyed considerable popularity as other rule-breaking mavericks had discovered its merits before I had, much to the dismay of the resident prisoners who had to clean it out. Heavier use demanded more frequent cleaning, a task which under the best circumstances was galling enough without having outsiders fill it up at an accelerated pace. Suspecting they were being had, the downhill prisoners let their anger be known. I was unimpressed and chose to make use of their latrine anyway. Not being a total fool, my discretion compelled me to limit my visits to the hours of darkness. Rumors began spreading of a nefarious "Night Shitter" who was gumming up the works down in the Lower Forty. Warnings were advertised that this person had literally better watch his ass. But, throwing caution to the winds, I ignored these seditious whisperings and continued. The downhill gang finally lost their patience. They posted a mid-watch on their crapper. Late one evening, they caught the Night Shitter in the act. It was all over for me. I not only was banished to my old latrine and the much hated wall, but worse, to *two* honey-bucket details instead of just one. I not only had to clean up my own latrine *and* the wall, but the downhill commode as well. Prison life was hell sometimes.

No one knew this better than Air Force First Lieutenant Waldron Berry. A graduate of West Point and a fighter pilot, Wally was a proud and meticulous man. Despite our filthy environment, he was always able to put forth a good appearance, as he painstakingly cleaned himself. He tried his best to maintain his physical condition as best he could, and, standing five feet, eight inches tall, with dark hair and a healthy complexion that seemed perpetually tanned, he looked remarkably well. Owing to his extremely good morale, Wally had big plans for the future. Confident that he and the rest of us would survive and go home, he looked forward to a renewal of his bachelor life and the droves of women that he *knew* would be begging for his company and recitals of his brave exploits during captivity.

Despite his good efforts, Wally, like the rest of us,

was unable to avoid contracting the Trots. One
evening, long after sundown, Wally approached me.
"Hey John."
"Yeah."
"Gotta shit again. Wanna go?"
"Sure," I said, getting up, tired. "I may as well do
some business too. It's now or later." We went
outside headed for the latrines.
"I'm sure glad we got those white latrine covers
now. The chinks got so sick of listening to the blind
guys complaining about not finding the holes in the
dark, they finally broke down and gave us the wood
and whitewash. You aren't night blind yet are you?"
I asked Wally.
"No. I can see pretty well, really. It hasn't happened
so far anyway. I can see good right now, can you?"
"Yeah," I replied as we neared the lean-to that
stood over the holes. The night was moonless and
black, but we could see the white covers lined up in a
neat row.
"Yeah, hell, John. I can see the covers great, no
problem. Guess I'll get down to the brass tacks," he
said striding over to his chosen hole.
   One of the many rules governing latrine usage was
that the white covers should always be put back in
place by the user at the conclusion of his business. As
Wally pressed on, it appeared to me that the particular cover he was headed for was not quite in line
with the others. Wally didn't seem concerned,
though, and was close enough to see, so I dismissed
it. But then he seemed to hover in mid-air, and then
abruptly disappeared. There was a splash and some
gurgling. A moment later, two hands appeared at
the edge of the uncovered hole and the meticulous
Wally began to emerge. Something resembling Al
Jolson's minstrel-man face rose up from the five-feet-
deep hole. He was covered in filth so acrid it brought

tears to my eyes. Laughing also brought tears to my eyes. Prisoner humor being what it is, I couldn't control my hysterics.

Cursing, Wally stormed off to try to restore his former state of cleanliness. He would not fully succeed in doing so for quite some time. In the absence of regular bathing, we all smelled rotten, but Wally's aroma was sadly compounded. He caused much consternation in the camp, particularly among those with whom he slept. He was generally encouraged not to pray for peace, at least for a time. An early repatriation would clearly dash his dreams of a vigorous bachelorhood back home.

Distasteful as it may seem, Wally's "fall from grace" became a fabled, humorous tale that gave everyone a huge laugh at a time when laughs and good humor were hard to come by. His sad story was told time and again around our meager stoves on cold winter nights and warmed us with the delight of slapstick comedy. Best of all, Wally was able to laugh himself, once he had cleaned up, of course, and never resented being the object of endless, off-color jokes and wisecracks. He and the rest of us began to recognize that humor, no matter what the source, was a key element in our struggle to survive. In time it would become a key weapon in our efforts to resist.

* * *

In October of 1951, we were moved from Pyoktong to Ping-chong-ni. Established that same month, the camp was reserved for all officer and warrant-officer P.O.W.'s not held back for further interrogation at P.U. A few Air Force noncommissioned officers were also brought in. It would be our home for the next two years until our repatriation in September, 1953.

Ping-chong-ni was a village some ten miles east of Pyoktong and four miles south of the Yalu River. The prisoner compound was in the main schoolhouse complex of the village. The schoolhouse, which lay in an east-west position, was a long building of timber and mud construction built during the days of the Japanese regime. It was in an area measuring about three hundred feet by two hundred feet, enclosed by barbed wire fencing, with sentries posted at intervals. The main entrance to the building was in its center where a wide passage ran back to a classroom corridor running the entire length of the building. At the rear, off this corridor, sliding doors opened to what had once been classrooms. These were our quarters. Nearly three hundred British, Turkish, American and other U.N. officers lived here. The classrooms were divided by wooden partitions into cells holding squads of thirty men.

Except for a narrow aisle down the center of each room, the floor boards were covered with rice-straw mats. There were no individual sleeping bunks until February, 1953. Mainly cosmetic, they served for the last six months to look good in the event of an international inspecting body visited pursuant to a negotiated truce. Prior to that, however, fifteen men slept along each wall on the straw mats, each covering himself with a thin quilt or blanket against the penetrating cold. In the sub-zero weather of winter, it was difficult to keep warm, and many weary hours were spent crouching around each squad room's tiny wood-burning stove. The small ration of wood provided to heat wash water for both bodies and clothes was almost always put to use for heating our quarters. The obvious result was some gamey body odors come spring.

At the western end of the building was a double classroom known as the Library, which contained all of twenty books and a few three-month-old copies of The *Shanghai News,* the New York and the London *Daily Worker* and the *San Francisco Peoples' World.* As the books were all either treatises on Marxism or translations of Russian novels, the Library had a definite political bias. Plastered around the walls were portraits of all the Communist Party leaders of the world who stared down at us dourly.

Three flights of steps led down from a promenade in front of the schoolhouse. One, at the western end, led to a gate to the Chinese headquarters, and another in the center led down to a large mud playground which was used for exercise and prisoner formations. The third, on the east end, led to the cook house. This structure, another long, partitioned building, contained primitive ovens and huge cast iron cooking pots. It also had a small room to accommodate the fourteen prisoner cooks and a communal bathhouse which had been built so inefficiently it was never serviceable.

A few yards behind and higher up from the schoolhouse were another promenade and several Korean houses. Originally quarters for the staff of the former school, they now housed overflow prisoners from the schoolhouse. The area was known as Snob Hill. Perhaps one of the most important places on Snob Hill was the barber shop. In this unusually snug little room were a stove, table, two homemade chairs and three homemade barbers— one combat engineer, a marine and one airman. They ran a popular enterprise here which provided a weekly shave with a cut-throat razor, a monthly haircut and unlimited repartee. As in many a small town, the barber shop provided a sounding board for all matters of controversy in the community. The time came when the barbers constituted a self-appointed board of assessment for all rumors relating to the peace talks—rumors which ran rampant and were uniformly taken more seriously than anyone cared to admit.

There were the usual lean-to latrines which afforded little protection from the biting winds of winter. An unavoidable visit here at 2:00 a.m., with temperatures at minus 35 degrees, was a harrowing experience. Down inside the pit, the human waste froze into reverse icicles that would have to be chipped away periodically.

At the edge of the wire inside the compound, seven stately populars graced our habitation. Beyond them and the fence, the life of the Korean hamlet of Ping-chong-ni went on in its traditional, one-clan-family way. The farmers cleared the forest on the hills by burning, and in turn planted crops of coarse grains, such as millet, and potatoes. Their primitive farming techniques were harmful to the woodlands and the soils. Reforestation efforts, if tried at all, were largely unsuccessful. The farmers, when they weren't burning down the forests, were denuding them for fuel, and what they didn't take, we did, especially in the cold months. This combined with soil erosion and insects to devastate the land. Serious gully erosion could be seen everywhere in the hills, and since our camp was situated generally at the bottom of a natural depression, we were swamped with spring thaw. In short order, we would be up to our eyeballs in yellow mud. Superimposed on this pattern of life were the busy comings and goings of the Chinese garrison and prison cadre, most of whom were billeted in the village. Others were in the compound with us.

The winter of 1951-52 was harsh. Our treatment was equally severe and continued to take its toll. Everyone was sick from one thing or another as hepatitus and pneumonia became increasingly common additions to our list of maladies and causes of death. We knew nothing but hunger, disease and sorrow, and would continue in this way for God knew how long. We were at the mercy of our captors with no way out and no end in sight. Some prisoners simply couldn't endure the prospect of continued brutal misery and accordingly chose to escape by the means most readily available—death. The Give-up-itis I had seen at Pak's Palace reemerged as a disturbingly frequent pattern at Ping-chong-ni.

It always followed the same predictable course. From the time a man stopped eating to the time he would die could be forecast with a kind of grim precision. The first symptom would be the lag in appetite, something obviously out of step for men whose primary obsession was food. The individual would give away ever-increasing portions of his meager rations or abruptly refuse to eat. Within days, he would become more and more withdrawn, speaking to his friends less. Shortly thereafter, he would pick out a spot for himself and pull a blanket, coat or whatever else was available over him, curl up into a fetal position and enter a cocoon-like existence. In another day, he would be dead. One night, a lieutenant suffering from Give-up-itis was lying beside another man. He advised him not to bother him in the morning as he'd be dead. Morning came—and he was. The whole process, time after time, man after man, was always the same and required a uniform period—about ten days.

There were basically two ways to treat Give-up-itis. One, which we had used at Pak's Palace, was characterized by cajoling, encouragement to eat, appeals to reason and logic and efforts to bring the man back to reality. We would spoon-feed him, kill his lice, clean up his dysentery and wash him. We would give him an extra coat to keep him warm at the expense of someone else's warmth. In short, overwhelmed by sympathy for his hopelessness and sorrow, we would baby him. Sadly, very few responded.

The second treatment seemed far more effective. While it appeared cold, callous and cruel, it worked and was applied in a variety of ways. We would tell the man he was going to die and that nobody gave a damn. We told him he wasn't worth saving and in front of him would make deals among ourselves dividing his meager belongings. We gloated over the prospect of getting his food ration. A concerted effort was made to insult and humiliate him so badly that he would become angry. He might not feel that he could lash out at anything else in his miserable world but he *could* lash out at friends who were betraying him and burying him before he was dead. The prospect of acting upon something evil and seeking vengence seemed to provide him with a reason to live, and reactivated a dying soul. His anger would jolt him back to reality and out of the deep state of depression that would otherwise be fatal. Perhaps the most dramatic example of this technique involved a seasoned Army infantry officer who had endured combat in World War II and Korea but for whom captivity was proving to be more lethal than any of the battles he had fought.

He was a big man, proud of his German extraction. It angered us to see him voluntarily lying down on the floor and allowing life to ebb away without lifting a finger in defiance of the Grim Reaper's approach. We were angry because we could do nothing but stand by, watch and bet cigarettes on what day he would die. He ignored our pleas to fight back. He had given up.

"It's not worth the effort," he would say. "We're all gonna die here anyway."

The kind treatment wasn't working and the man was going fast. Doc Andy prescribed the other and only remaining option. He consulted on the case with Doctor Sidley, a Jew.

"This guy hates Jews, y'know. Shoots his mouth off about it all the time. Aryan bullshit and all that," said Doc Andy, developing his idea. "I want to put on a disgusted routine, maybe something like 'I'm fed up, can't help you anymore and I'm turning you over to a Jewish doctor' or something along those lines. That should really piss him off."

Esensten got the drift and would take the cue. He could act stereotypically Jewish if he set his mind to it and by adding in some spice, he knew he could provoke this dying, Jew-hating P.O.W. to anger. The two doctors left together to make their housecall. Squatting down to speak to the despondent prisoner, Doc Andy began his performance.

"You're dying. You know that. You won't let me reach you or help you so I'm finished with it." His tone became a little sharper, a little more heated. "You know, I've had a *belly*-full of your chicken-shit attitude and I'm bailing out. You want to croak, you croak on some other doctor, not me. I'm washing my hands of you. Esensten's your doctor now. Maybe *he* can help you but I've *had* it. *Die* if you want to." He got up and left in a huff.

As Doc Andy walked out, one could already see a reaction in the P.O.W.'s face. While springing from the evil of anti-semitism, something good seemed to be happening. The prospect of being treated and tended to by a Jew moved a lethargic psyche. This man who at the brink of despair was concerned with nothing, not even his own life, suddenly cared about something. A tenuous thread had been tossed to him and now bound him to something outside himself that maybe—just maybe—could pull him out of his tailspin. The tenuous thread was not made of the best materials. It was spun from hatred—a deep-seated hatred of Jews. And yet that evil was rekindling the flame of life within this dying man. The thread was tying these two men together, one a Jew, the other man malignantly proud of his German heritage. Perhaps, for once, enmity might ironically work for the good.

Esensten alertly spotted the reaction and moved in. He had a prominent nose, which he adeptly brought into play. Shoving it into the fuehrer's face, Doctor Sidley glared at him hatefully.
"I know you hate Jews. And you know I'm a Jew. Well guess what, *kraut. I'm* in charge of you now—and you're dying." He paused to raise the temperature. "And guess what else. I don't give a shit *what* happens to you. Know why? 'Cause I hate you lousy Germans, every goddamn one of you. This Jew doesn't give a good shit whether you live or die 'cause if you croak, there's gonna be one less kraut in the world to worry about—and that's just *fine* with me," he yelled. Esensten pulled back for a moment to measure his impact and let the words sink in. It was working. The prisoner was livid. He decided to lay on the coup-de-grâce. Pressing even closer than before, he leered at the P.O.W. and said, "Besides, once you kick the bucket, *I'll* get your shoes—*kraut.*" Projecting the deepest venom he could muster, Doctor Sidley's eyes bore into the prisoner's, delivering an undeniable wish for his death and a promise to dance on his grave.

The prisoner was incensed. He tried to raise himself off the floor but his self-imposed starvation made him too weak to move. He slumped back, leaning on his elbows. Furious, he glared up at Esensten, the glassy eyes of death disappearing like morning mist before a rising sun.

"No. *No,* you Jew sonofabitch! You're not gonna bury me, you bastard," the P.O.W. wheezed. "I'm gonna *live,* you lousy kike! And then I'm gonna bust your fuckin' Hebe *nose!*" He shifted to raise his right arm in a threatening, clenched-fist gesture. But the effort failed and he collapsed backward, lying there flat and prostrate on the floor.

"You'll do *shit,* dutchman," said Esensten, scoffing at him. He turned away arrogantly and walked out.

Staring helplessly at the ceiling, the P.O.W. seethed with anger, his heart filled with a determined hatred. He now had the reason and the will to live, simply to punch out his despised Jewish doctor. He began to eat again, regained his strength and soon could stand, feed, wash and dress himself. With time, he began to emerge from his cocoon and the little dark corner that had so nearly been his last resting place. Finally, he was back on his feet and ready to settle the debt.

"Where's Esensten?" he demanded. "Where the hell is Esensten?" He was directed to the doctor's location. He entered the room where Doctor Sidley was tending another patient. Sid turned and looked up at the hulking German-American.

"I'm here, Esensten. You were *wrong.* I'm *alive,*" the prisoner said. His face contorted and he staggered toward the good doctor. He drew near him, his eyes reddening. Then, confronting Esensten, he delivered not a blow but an expression of gratitude and contrition. He wept, and between the tears and sobs, we could hear his words:

"You saved my life, Sid. Thanks for saving my life."

15

Everything human is pathetic. The secret source of Humor itself is not joy, but sorrow.

—Mark Twain

Their stake in the negotiations at Panmunjom had an effect on our captors for now their wholesale slaughter of prisoners had to be curtailed. It was now 1952 and while illness and death were still with us, our prisoner population began to stabilize. We came to suspect, after a time, that our captors' brutal past behavior might be catching up with them, if only a little bit. They started pressing us to write down names of prisoners we had run across at one time or another. Whether they were dead or alive seemed to make little difference. The Communists just wanted names. We figured this might mean that they were being held accountable at the talks, at least numerically, and were having a difficult time proving their contention that all had gone well under the Lenient Policy. If that were so, and if they were foisting off numbers that were padded with the bodies of our dead, we knew they could no longer risk eroding their position further by cold-blooded executions or mass neglect and starvation. Those of us still alive were now worth something more to them, particularly since it was becoming evident that a complete military victory would be denied them by the U.N. We were bargaining chips at the negotiating table. Thus the risk of being killed outright was substantially reduced. It made resisting less a gamble. Accordingly, we engaged in campaigns of harrassment against them and became bolder in our efforts to turn the tables on our tormentors.

Perhaps owing to my own English ancestry, the British in our company stirred a particular fascination within me. Along with their dauntless spirits, their boundless capacity to shift from droll subtlety to brazen horseplay made these Englishmen a durable, steadfast segment of the P.O.W. population. Their manner was such that our Asian captors had great difficulty in anticipating how to deal with them in various situations. The cultural chasm that divided Occidental from Oriental was so great that the British and Americans could make fools of their captors with simple humorous attacks, puns and practical jokes. While mockery would be identified sooner or later and an appropriate punishment meted out, more often than not the Koreans and Chinese would become unwitting victims of jokes with comical results.

In the case of one Englishman, our captors learned that he had been in the Royal Navy. There being few prisoners with naval experience, he was a unique prize and was singled for prompt, early attention. The interrogations had not progressed well, so the interrogator tried a negotiating tack.

"We will make a fair deal with you," he offered. "We will promise you peace and quiet. We will leave you alone and bother you no more."

"In exchange for what, might I ask?" replied the skeptical Briton.

"You may keep all the information you wish to yourself and we will not press you. We ask only that you describe one weapon system that your fleet uses.

We know you have many of these, but we ask you to tell us only of one. Do this and you will be left alone." The Brit thought for a few moments, pondering the offer, although not seriously. He knew that there would be no peace after a single betrayal. One would lead to another as his interrogator tried to expand the commission of one compromise into a habitual pattern through the use of guilt, fear of exposure or force. The patient interrogator waited calmly. The Englishman spoke.

"It's a deal. I'll describe one system I observed on a destroyer once."

"You have made a wise decision," said the interrogator, pleased with his easy success. A description of a heretofore unknown weapon would be highly prized by his superiors. It would be a feather in his cap. A bright future surely lay ahead of him.

"Well. Now then," said the Englishman clearing his throat as if in preparation for the delivery of a momentous scientific paper. "Our experience with the Germans taught us to have a great respect for submarines. Accordingly, we have devoted much research and many resources to finding better ways of countering this threat." The Englishman paused as if he was having second thoughts. The interrogator nodded encouragingly.

"Go on! Go on!" he urged the prisoner.

"Yes, of course. Well. We've developed a new and rather innovative technique. It works like this. When a submarine is thought to be in the area, we . . ." He lowered his voice and gazed at the interrogator. ". . . we spread green paint across the surface of the sea." The interrogator frowned, not understanding. "You see, the reason for the paint is quite simple actually. We knew that sooner or later the submarine would raise its periscope to look for us." The interrogator was still lost. "Well they have to *see* you to fire a torpedo at you, old man," said the Briton condescendingly.

"So the paint would blind them?" asked the interrogator.

"Yes, of course, in a way, but that was hardly the point. As I said, the paint was *green,* you see, the same hue as the ocean itself. So when the submarine's commander looked out, all he saw was the green color which was now smeared all over his periscope. It was then logical for him to assume that he had not reached periscope depth but rather was still too deeply submerged beneath the sea. Are you with me?" The interrogator was listening intently. He began taking notes. The prisoner chattered on enthusiastically. "Now, thinking he was still underwater, the submarine commander would continue to rise, waiting for the periscope to break the surface and the whole of the Royal navy to come into view. But due to the green paint, he would be misled to the extent that he would simply continue to come up and up. Did you get that?" The interrogator nodded, writing furiously. "Good. Let's move along then. Well, eventually the deceived commander rose completely out of the sea. Once he had ascended to an altitude of one thousand feet above us, we would turn our anti-aircraft guns on him and shoot him out of the sky, thus destroying the submarine. Rather ingenious, don't you think?" he asked smugly. The interrogator, who by now was on his second page of copious notes, paused, his head bowed down toward the table. But then he stopped writing. His color began to change as he slowly raised his angry eyes toward the Brit.

"Do you have any questions you'd like to ask me?" queried the Englishman in a friendly way. The interrogator leaped from his desk, roaring epithets in Chinese now that he realized he had just been made to look like an ass. Calling for the guards, the interrogator had the Englishman dragged from the room. The deal was off.

Another Englishman, the Reverend Sam J. Davies, was the chaplain to the Glorious Gloucestershire Regiment in Korea and was captured by the Chinese on April 25, 1951. Padre Davies gave us something rarely to be found—a living example of how solid Christian faith could sustain courage, sanity and hope while at the mercy of a cruel enemy. In this way, he endeared himself to us. Yet despite his usual strict adherence to high standards of personal integrity and proper conduct, there came a time when profanity seemed the most appropriate means of expression, even to the Good Reverend.

It was a cold, snowy, dark winter morning in 1952. All we were interested in was keeping warm in the sub-zero temperatures, and getting some sleep. Into our squad room came Tien, an interpreter who spoke adequate English. With him was a non-English speaking Chinese we called Sloe Gin. Both were our honorable platoon leaders. Tien was pulling a very early reveille on us, the more uncooperative segment of the prisoner population. He was shouting in a shrill, excited manner.

"Everyone upla, upla! Loll call! Loll call!" he demanded. His orders were accompanied by kicking and yanking at the P.O.W.'s as they lay on the floor unmoving.

After fifteen exasperating minutes of no success in arousing the prisoners, Tien called in some additional guard-help. Still the sleep-in continued. Finally he spotted the Padre. He reasoned that if he could rouse up the men's religious leader, they would all follow suit. He strode over to Padre Davies' spot on the floor, reached down and grabbed him by the scruff of his jacket.

"Get *up* and out to loll call!" he shouted in his face. The Padre pulled himself free rebelliously and lay back down. Tien hauled him up again. Davies flopped down again. Up again. The Reverend was getting irritated at the ruckus this was creating. It violated his sense of propriety. One simply did not conduct one's affairs in such a fashion in another man's bedroom. It was shocking behavior. The matter had to be dealt with.

Padre Davies sat down once again and solemnly folded his arms across his chest. He then took stock of the situation and surveyed the room. It was most appalling. The prisoners were quite unhappy and grumbling. Tien was grousing and shouting. Sloe Gin was standing there stupidly. The guards were pondering where to stick their bayonets and it was far too early in the day for such annoyances. He turned his eyes toward Tien. Then, intoning his speech in a manner befitting the finest of Shakespearian actors, this honored graduate of the University of Durham calmly counselled his flock: "Ig-naw-w-w the bahs-tahds," he said and slouched backward to a prone position in keeping with his own edict. We happily followed suit and ignored the bastards.

Needless to say, the sleep-in was eventually broken up and we all made loll call outside in the snow at minus twenty degrees. But with the chaplain's help, we had given it a bloody go. But the Padre's sense of commitment to impeccable personal conduct was in conflict with his rebellious and profane action. Embarrassed and contrite, he publicly apologized to us for his improper choice of words but it wasn't necessary. We well knew that these were the times that tried men's souls and diction. Padre Davies, like his beloved Gloucesters, was truly glorious.

Finding its roots in performances such as these, harrassment of the enemy eventually graduated to pre-planned group efforts. The theory was that if you couldn't kill them, you could drive them crazy and we had plenty of time to figure out creative ways of doing so. One of the earliest attempts was organized at Pyoktong before we left for Ping-chong-ni.

One of the Honshos in charge of us was a rather unstable individual with yellow eyeballs. When he got upset he would quake and get almost irrational. We nicknamed him Tilt, after the malady pinball machines suffer when they're shaken too much. Tilt was the camp quartermaster.

Noticing that the prisoners were spending inordinate amounts of time and energy picking and boiling weeds, grass and anything else for food, Tilt decided he would channel our efforts into more productive agricultural endeavors. Tilt informed us that he would provide us with seed to plant in order to grow better food to supplement our meager diets. He gave us two types of seed, scallion and dikon, the latter of which is a carrot-shaped cross between a radish and a turnip with a leafy green top. We willingly tilled the soil and tended our crop, hungrily envisioning something better to eat than weeds. The work was of considerable difficulty to us, weak as we were, but for food, no effort was too great.

Finally the seeds sprouted, the tender shoots broke through the ground and our crop flourished. We were overjoyed until we noticed that as portions of the crop ripened, Tilt would pluck up the mature plants and carry them to the cook house for use in preparing the Honshos' meals. Our crop was feeding them and flavoring their meat but none was left for us. We were bitter and angry at yet another betrayal. We vowed to get revenge and our fair share— namely everything that was left in the ground.

Retribution began with short, intermittent forays with the raiders pulling up only small quantities at a time. We theorized that within a few days Tilt would notice something minor was amiss. He did, and in a half-tilted state of mind, salted down with reasoned thinking that things aren't too bad, rationalizing that by spreading large quantities of P.O.W. shit all over the garden, he could save his crop from any more scavengers.

Then Tilt made his big mistake. Feeling secure with his shit scarecrow, he left town for a quick overnight trip across the Yalu into China. Late that evening, we raided the patch. We pulled up every scallion, leaving neat little holes as if gophers had come along and pulled the plants down into their burrows. We plucked up the dikons, eating the bottoms off every one and saving only the green tops. These we placed back in their holes and much to our surprise they didn't wilt overnight. The potency of P.O.W. manure was mighty and should not have been overlooked.

The next day, Tilt returned and walked over to the patch to inspect his crop. Noticing that the scallions were completely gone, he went wild. He began cursing, raving and shouting in a shrill voice, fit to be tied. Looking toward the dikons, he calmed down momentarily at the sight of the healthy green tops. Apparently that much had survived. Not all was lost. He went over to look closer and pulled one up. He did a double-take staring at it. No bottom! He pulled another and looked at it horrified. His face was ashen with disbelief. In panic, he began making his way down the rows, pulling up one plant after another, heaving the tops over his shoulder every which way, now shouting and screaming again. He went totally berserk, raising such a din that it attracted the guards' attention.

Tilt was completely unglued by the time he reached the end of the last row. He started swinging at the guards as they arrived and had to be subdued. They carried him off as he shrieked in protest. Tilt dropped out of sight around the compound for awhile.

We came to find out that Tilt had suffered a complete nervous collapse and was being confined under heavy guard somewhere in the camp. Eventually, he reemerged—but under escort. He was being removed, under protective custody, from the compound, back to China. On his way out, he passed through our area, all the while muttering to himself. Our doctors said he looked dopey and speculated that he had been heavily sedated. Poor Tilt. It broke our hearts to have pushed him over the edge—so badly in fact that we vowed to try more attacks like this at every opportunity.

Another guard had a pet rabbit that he kept in a little hutch and cared for meticulously. It was a beautiful little bunny with a slick, satin black coat. He was healthy—and *fat*. Like a gang of crazed Elmer Fudds, we quietly spirited him away one night and made some delicious rabbit stew. As an expression of gratitude and to provide the guard with a lasting memorial to his beloved pet, we surreptitiously returned the ears, tacking them upright to the floor of the guard's room just inside the door. We thought he would appreciate this gesture, but he never showed any thanks whatsoever.

Sometime later, at Ping-chong-ni, we struck on another idea. One morning before dawn and pre-muster bed check, one squad of twenty-five P.O.W's got up extra early. Collecting up their few belongings, they left their little room and hid themselves anywhere in the building they could. Their Honsho, Gee, also known as Gee-string, came in to check his wards, only to find an empty room. Gee-string panicked. It was a mass *bug-out!* This development could have grave consequences for him. However, an alert response and prompt recapture could make him a hero and earn him a commendation.

Gee-string stampeded out the door sounding the alarm, arousing everyone. Whistles were blowing, bugles sounded and the guard company scrambled with flashlights in hand. Gee-string even rousted the camp commandant, Ding, known to us lovingly as the Snake.

During the pandemonium, the twenty-five P.O.W.'s got up from their hiding places, slithered back to their squad room, laid down in their assigned places and feigned sleep.

Gee-string came hustling back into the building with his entourage. The Snake was reluctantly in tow. Dramatically, Gee-string grasped the sliding doors and flung them open wide, to proudly point out the evidence. His jaw dropped at the sight of twenty-five warm bodies all in their places, just as they were supposed to be. Snake turned to Gee-string. Both were highly agitated, one with rage, the other with fear and humiliation.

"What is this?!" asked the Snake angrily in Chinese. "There has been a great mistake! The entire camp, the guard company, the security police in town and I have all been raised at dawn! For what?! Someone will pay for this grave error!" He stormed off, leaving the crushed Honsho remorsefully holding the bag. Snake said someone would pay and someone did—the hapless Gee-string. He was transferred. Rumor had it that he was sent back to China for refresher training and reindoctrination.

A Honsho in another area was very concerned about neatness within the P.O.W. quarters and would impatiently kick away debris that untidy prisoners might leave lying about. In the warmer months, the Honsho and other Chinese walked around in soft, slipper-like shoes. Keying on these two characteristics, the prisoners found a way to retaliate. They nailed a "GI Boondocker" down to the middle of the floor then stuffed it with small rocks from the toe to the heel. The Honsho predictably kicked it with great vigor during an inspection. To the prisoners' delight, he hobbled out of the room shrieking and cursing in pain.

Then there was Dirty Picture Wong who was not exactly the victim of our purposeful humor. Rather his inadvertent victimization by us was humorous and useful. Dirty Picture was another of the exceptionally arrogant Chinese Honshos who lorded his position of superiority over us and constantly reminded us of it. His name was inspired by the occasional peeks we had of his quarters which were inside the wire with us. He had nudie pictures hidden from all but surreptitious P.O.W. scroungers who discovered them during break-ins for soap, tobacco and other goodies we could rob him of.

He, like other Honshos living inside the compound, was always subject to our surveillance as we tried to determine his pattern of comings and goings throughout the day. One day, when we were certain he was out of his room, two room-robbers decided to plunder his belongings in search of food and other potentially useful items. They sneakily made their way to his room, and when they were certain they were unseen, burst in. Three surprised faces met each other in the room—the two robbers' and Dirty Picture's. He was home! They'd been caught breaking and entering—a high crime against a peace fighter. They were in for trouble—or were they? It suddenly dawned on them that Dirty Picture was lying on his cot with his drawers down. The robbers gasped in embarrassed surprise as they realized that the naughty boy was playing with himself. And they had caught him at the zenith of his kinky pursuits. As the initial shock wore off, they began to gloat over the strength of their position and the weakness of Dirty Picture's. They might come away from this no richer than they began, but they would be in no trouble either. Dirty Picture didn't *dare* turn these criminals in. He knew if he did, there would be a terrible stink over his decadent, capitalistic perversions. Playing with oneself in front of nudies was not good Marxist behavior. Neither was getting caught with your pants down by two half-starved prisoners. Without exchanging a word, a mutual understanding was struck and the two intruders left quietly. Dirty Picture avoided those two religiously in the future and ceased to be a major source of trouble to us all.

Isolated events such as these and a growing record of comical successes, prompted us to organize an all-out effort. It was called Crazy Week. For an entire week, each P.O.W. was to go crazy. Everyone had a specific assignment. Air Force F-86 pilots, for example, were jets for a week. Head down with their arms swept back, they made marvelous aircraft swooping around the compound. When a Honsho came by, they would peel out of formation and strafe him complete with sound effects.

Captain Ralph Nardella, who had fashioned the stethoscope for our doctors, already had a somewhat tainted reputation. Suffering from a severe hormonal imbalance owing to disease and malnutrition, he had begun to sprout a rather nice set of feminine breasts. We called him Tits Nardella in recognition of this remarkable feat. But Ralph's claim to fame in Crazy Week was not his physical peculiarities. It was his dog—an imaginary dog.

The animal was a good pet and he and Ralph went

everywhere together. Ralph talked to him endlessly, petted him and played with him. Great pals. The dog didn't have much of an appetite which was just as well since there wasn't enough food to go around anyway. He was well trained and housebroken and was always careful not to soil our quarters or the compound. He did have one problem though. He disliked Communists. It seemed that everytime a Honsho passed by Ralph and his dog, an unsavory incident would occur.

"Mo-mahn-tee! Mo-mahn-tee! (Wait a minute)" Ralph called to the Honsho. "Oh I am so *sorry!* Tsk, tsk. I just don't know what to say about this. I'm so embarrassed. I hope you'll forgive me and my dog," Ralph implored. The puzzled Honsho frowned at Ralph.

"What is *this?!* he demanded impatiently. Ralph didn't answer immediately. He was preoccupied bending over and slapping his ill-behaved canine.

"Bad dog! Bad dog! Stop that! Go on! *Scat!* Get outta here, goddamn *mutt!*" Rising to the Honsho, he apologized again and explained further. "I just can't seem to break him of this habit! There are so few trees, perhaps. He lifted his leg on your trousers. Down there, see?" said Ralph pointing.

The Honsho jerked his head down, bending over to inspect his pantleg. He looked around for the would-be dog and back at his trousers. He wiped at them, then walked off cursing at Ralph, who continued to apologize profusely. After several repetitions with this guard and others, they all began visualizing moisture on their legs and admonished Ralph to keep his damn dog under control.

As for my part, I had the dubious distinction of being history's first helicopter pilot to be shot down and captured in war. This explains Captain William McTaggart's reason for dubbing me Rotorhead and for the name sticking. In recognition of the name, Captain Joseph O'Conner made me some little rotor blades that twirled on a post, and fastened them to a cap, creating a very attractive beanie. It became an essential part of my Crazy Week image which focused on an imaginary motorcycle. It was a fine work of art—a Harley-Davidson covered with shining chrome. I rode it everywhere.

About the third night of Crazy Week, while enduring yet another evening class on communism, I was called upon to give my cognition of Karl Marx's book *The Decay of World Capitalism*. I rose and began my recitation.

"It looked extremely rocky for the Mudville Nine that day. The score stood four to two with one inning left to play. But when Cooney died at first and Burrows did the same, a sickly fear came over the patrons of the game. . ." Stifled laughter rippled throughout the class. "There was ease in Casey's manner as he stepped into his place. There was pride in Casey's bearing and a smile upon his face. And when responding to the thousands, he lightly doffed his hat. No stranger in the crowd could doubt that Casey's at the bat. . ." The indoctrinator began thumbing through his reading material in a desperate but futile attempt to find my source. There was more snickering in the class.

As I continued through the phrases, a favorite Chinese interrogator of ours whom we named Quasimodo after the Hunchback of Notre Dame, dropped in. He was accompanied by another Honsho we called the Friendly Prosecutor. Friendly handled all the disciplinary infractions and never lost a case. Punishment from him usually meant time in the Hole. I dramatically finished my recitation with a flair.

"Oh somewhere in this favored land the sun is shining bright. And somewhere bands are playing and somewhere hearts are light. And somewhere men are laughing and somewhere children shout. But there is no joy in Mudville, for Casey has struck out." Quasimodo was inflamed.

"Thorn-ton, what is this?!"

"Casey at the Bat."

"Karl Marx did not write on this Casey at the Bat! You are inciting a riot and keeping the other students from learning the truth! Come with me to the camp commandant! Now! Kah-quay-lee! (quickly)" ordered Quasimodo.

"Mo-mahn-tee," I replied. I went over to my spot on the floor that I called home, where I slept and kept my beanie and parked my motorcycle. I put on my beanie, kicked out the parking stand, straddled the bike and stomped the starter. It was extremely cold, even inside the building, and it took quite a few jumps and a little priming before she finally sputtered to life. I gunned the engine. "Phoom! Phoom!" I said, mimicking an oversize motor. She vibrated heavily but I was ready now and I flipped my beanie in excited anticipation of a ride to the commandant. Quasimodo opened the door with a rather perplexed expression. Friendly seemed a little befuddled.

"Kah-quay-lee!" shouted Quasimodo. I roared out the door, shifting gears in rapid succession. My Harley was fast and as I sped away from them, I shouted over my shoulder, "Kah-quay-lee! Kah-quay-lee!"

My run was a short one as I quickly reached the wire and a suspicious guard who was pointing his bayoneted rifle at me. I stopped, as any lawful driver would, and waited for Quasi and Friendly to catch up. While I waited, I periodically gunned the engine to keep it from stalling in the cold, and flipped my beanie propeller. The guard stared at me in wary mystification.

Finally, Quasi and Friendly made it to the gate. We went through the wire and out of the compound. The commandant's quarters were about 150 yards beyond. Snake lived with his wife in an attractive, Japanese-built house with a courtyard in front. I knew where it was and roared on ahead across a terraced field, the two Honshos wheezing in pursuit.

"Mo-mahn-tee! Mo-mahn-tee!" they cried from the distance.

"Kah-quay-lee! Kah-quay-lee!" I yelled back, waving them on.

I beat them to the house, pulled into Snake's courtyard noisily and parked my Harley. I was busily polishing the chrome as Quasi and Friendly puffed their way toward me. They immediately called for Snake. As he emerged from his house, I was told to stand at attention. As always, I declined. "Why you will not show the respect and stand at attention?" demanded Quasi.

"You're all volunteers! We were taught that there's no rank in the Chinese Peoples' Volunteer Army. I don't see anybody here with rank superior to mine. However, I will make you a deal. If you will tell me your ranks and these are superior to mine, I'll stand at attention. Waddaya say, huh?" I proposed.

There was some conferring among themselves but no answer was forthcoming. The issue was dropped without further discussion. Meanwhile I slumped around slouching, spitting, blowing my nose and generally trying to be as slovenly as possible. Quasimodo was still speaking to Snake in Chinese, apparently, I surmised, bringing him up to date on motorcycles. They talked for thirty minutes on how to deal with an off-balance P.O.W. who insisted he had a motorcycle that didn't exist and recited

baseball poetry instead of Karl Marx. Given the protracted nature of their discussions, the question was
obviously a difficult one. Marxism-Leninism offered
no guidance on matters such as this. Finally, Quasi
turned to me.

"Thorn-ton. The camp commandant is being very
lenient with you. He is not going to punish you this
time but he wants you to know one thing. You have
broken the camp rules and regulations. Motorcycles
are not allowed in camp! Now you may go back to
your quarters." I nodded back, stupidly repeating
his pronouncement.

"Motorcycles are not allowed in camp, no, and I can
go back now." I went to where my motorcycle was
parked, kicked up the parking stand, stomped the
starter, gunned the engine, flipped my beanie and
sped away toward the compound.

Quasi and Friendly had lost face in front of the
commandant. For such a display of slack discipline,
they would have to self-criticize later. For now, they
would have to catch up with me. I arrived at the wire
again long before they, and once more confronted
the bewildered guard. I requested to be allowed in
the compound. He made an ugly face and refused. It
apparently didn't matter that I was a bona-fide
P.O.W. I marked time, gunning the engine and
twirling my beanie's blades while we waited for my
two pursuing Honshos. They made it eventually and
passed me through the wire. I was ordered to their
quarters.

"Why must I go to your quarters?" I asked, confused.

"Thorn-ton. You have refused to give up your
motorcycle. These are not permitted in the camp so
you will not be allowed back to your squad room.
You have disobeyed." We arrived at their quarters.

"Can I bring my motorcycle inside?" I implored.

"*No!* You must keep this dirty machine outside. You may not bring it in our house!" snapped Quasi. We went inside where he then repeated his lecture on the camp rules forbidding motorcycles. I pleaded.

"But I *must* have my motorcycle! I am a sick man. I have no mail, no medicine, nothing to make me happy and well. I need my motorcycle to get around the compound." It measured seventy by a hundred yards. "I *have* to have wheels!" I cried. Quasi held firm.

"No. It is not allowed. If we allow you to have this motorcycle, you will use it to *bug out!*" he said, using some borrowed American slang. I raised my eyebrows with interest but then sagged.

"That's a very good idea. But you do not have enough *gasoline* here for me to escape. It's hundreds of miles to the front lines and I couldn't get enough gas to make it all the way. You *know* this to be true!" Quasi and Friendly were getting fed up with going around and around with a madman.

"Thorn-ton, it is forbidden for you to have this motorcycle. You will leave here *now* and go back to your squad room!" Balking, I argued back.

"I demand my rights as a *person*, as one of the *peoples!* I must have my motorcycle! I will go through the chain of command!" In a huff, I turned and stalked out of the building toward my squad room.

Back in my own quarters, I approached the three Americans in charge of the three squads in our prisoner platoon. Relating my tale, I got each one of them to go back to the Honshos and obtain the release of my motorcycle. Resolutely and with straight faces, we marched on Quasi's house and demanded an audience. Reluctantly, Quasi agreed to see the squad leaders. They presented their grievance, one man acting as spokesman.

"Thornton must have his motorcycle! We demand

this in his behalf! It is only right that you should do this under the Lenient Policy! You should *allow* motorcycles in this camp!'' Quasi repeated the camp rules and regulations along with his conviction that I would try to use the motorcycle to escape.

"Furthermore," said Quasi, "if we allow Thorn-ton to have his motorcycle, we will have to give one to all the other prisoners! We do not *have* them! He *cannot* have his motorcycle! This is the decision of the commandant and this is the *rule!* Now you come with me.''

Quasi took the four of us out of the building to a ditch nearby that served as a shelter in the event of an air raid. He stood by it solemnly.

"You see there?" Quasi said, pointing into the ditch. "We have broken this motorcycle and thrown it into the ditch. It cannot be used anymore."

I was crestfallen. The squad leaders shook their heads sympathetically. There was nothing they could do. We turned and trudged back to the squad room where we enjoyed a good guffaw at the disruption we had created. Yet, refusing to let the matter rest at that, I played the game a little further.

Regularly, I visited the ditch and my ill-fated Harley. With proper piety, I would remove my beanie, place it over my heart and mutter a benediction over my defunct motor as I imagined her lying there, busted and broken-hearted. In the end, my irksome captors even took away my beanie, fearing perhaps that Rotorhead would rotate up, up and away. And so went Crazy Week.

When we weren't busy scrounging for food, being interrogated, indoctrinated, shanghaied for work details or harrassing our captors, we invented strange but amusing ways to pass the time. The occasion of another sudden shift in camp policy toward us heralded what we called ''Be Kind To Prisoners of

War Week.'' A precipitous reversal of our harsh
treatment and the earnest revival of the Lenient
Policy usually meant a momentous disgorgement of
goodies. Distribution of these items was typically accompanied by copious picture-taking, which made
for good propaganda at home, abroad and of course
at Panmunjom. We knew the party would be over in
time and the policy would shift again, in the hope of
tripping us up in a productively psychological way.

Among the goodies we received on this occasion
were candles. This was not an insignificant prize.
Candles meant light within our cells after dark,
which cheered our confinement a little and brightened the evenings. They would serve as cigarette
lighters, should we be lucky enough to have cigarettes. They would do well as flashlights for the night
blind. The risk of tragic midnight disappearances
into the depths of the latrines fell off remarkably as
long as there were candles to light the way. Of equal
importance was the central role played by the
candles when we pursued a popular P.O.W. sport of
dubious virtue.

''What do you suppose is going on?'' asked one
English prisoner of another. The sound of muffled
laughter, curses and quiet outbursts suggesting the
occasion of good or bad luck drifted down the long
corridor of the schoolhouse to their squad room.

''Sounds like they're playing a game of dice, or cards
perhaps. Do you suppose the chinks passed out a few
decks of cards?'' speculated the other.

''Let's go see, shall we?'' said the first, and off they
went down the hall. Arriving at our squad room,
they slid open the doors and beheld the scene.

''Great God!'' gasped the first Englishman. ''The
wicked sods have gone mad!''

He had stumbled upon one of our most creative
and hotly contested pastimes—the ignition of in-

testinal gas. Crouched before a candle with his bare buttocks exposed, one G.I. awaited the arrival of what he hoped would be some prize-winning flatus. It would ignite upon contact with the burning candle, creating a marvelous blue flame of astonishing length. The contest was an event we had been anticipating for quite some time, not only because of the amusement it afforded but also because it signaled a widespread recovery from our endless bouts with dysentery. Indeed, rather than suffering from the dreaded Trots, many of us had gone to the opposite extreme. I had regained control of my bowels and was quite happily able to relieve myself at will on a more regular basis—every three to four weeks. What little food I consumed was picked over so thoroughly by my digestive tract that very little remained to be expelled—excepting gas, of course, which abounded within my ravaged intestines. To my pleasant surprise, this minor discomfort was offset by a very beneficial side-effect in that I had actually begun to regain my strength and a little body weight, besides. All these developments put me in great shape for the Camp Fart-Lighting Contest.

The squad room was buzzing with activity as the contenders readied themselves for this great test of noxious superiority. At stake was the much coveted title of Champ of the Camp. An elimination contest had already been held. Since our compound was organized by squads, platoons and companies, representatives of each would enter and fart their way up the organizational chain of command to levels of semi-final and final competition. As with any sport of skill, there were a few naturals and many who tried hard, only to drop out in the early heats.

The criteria for advancement, which was subject to review of an accomplished panel of self-appointed judges, covered several categories. Length of flame was of course the primary measure of excellence, although weakness in this area could be offset by other considerations such as quality of color, sound, quantity and aroma. There was some debate on how this latter category should count, given the close confines in which the competition was held. Some maintained that strength of odor should result in penalties while others maintained that pungency demonstrated excellent developmental skills. Fortunately, the races never needed to be decided on this factor alone, so the issue never really came to a head.

The contestant at work when the Brits arrived was in deep concentration.

"You're taking too long, dammit! Hurry up!" said a heckler in the crowd.

"Yeah," echoed another. "We oughta time these things. A quick pace keeps the game lively. Move your bowels for cryin' out loud."

"Gimme a chance! Gimme a chance, will ya?!" cried the contestant.

The pressure was on him now. A silent moment passed. The crowd was expectant, with many eyes turned to the candle. The quiet was broken as a sporadic hiss followed by a baleful squeak emerged from the man. No ignition occurred. A groan of anticlimactic disappointment swept the crowd.

"Disqualified! Get your ass outa here!" ruled the judges. The crowd was in hysterics. The Englishmen recoiled in mortification.

"Next man! Next man!" called the mob. He appeared and prepared himself before the candle.

"Wait a minute!" interjected a spectator. "You still got the Trots, don't you?" Eyebrows raised throughout the crowd. A man who still had the Trots could easily mistake a dysentery contraction as gas. The results could be disastrous for the contestant and the candle, not to mention unfortunate spectators who might be in the line of fire.

"No, I'm better now," asserted the contestant. He looked around sheepishly at the many pairs of wary, skeptical eyes which were now fixed on him. Disbelief hung heavy in the air. People began sliding around to the side walls as a precautionary measure.

"Really, I haven't shit in a *week,* guys. *Really!* I *swear* it!" The crowd was not reassured.

"You shit and you're disqualified." The judges were getting grouchy.

"I know, *I know!*" replied the contestant, waving them off.

"And to think these are American officers," muttered one Englishman to the other.

"They do seem to be having quite a jolly time of it, though. I'm rather beginning to enjoy it myself," said the other, chuckling. The first Englishman cast him a horrified look of disgust.

The contestant readied himself. The crowd grew silent. He opened up. A sickly gurgle ensued as the worst occurred. The prisoner snapped upward, trying to minimize the destruction to his person and the contest arena. The crowd cracked up at his desperate antics, then pounced unsympathetically with harrassing catcalls.

"He shit! He shit himself!" they roared.

"Whatsamatter? Your pucker string break?" bellowed another heckler.

"Out! Out!" booed the judges as the prisoner fumbled with his drawers.

The spectators howled in laughter as he sullenly slunk out of the room, cursing under his breath at his bad luck. Better luck next time, but for the moment, he had to repair the damage done to his clothing and his ego. He had blown his one chance at immortality.

"Somebody remind me before the next contest to define adequately what we mean when we say these are elimination rounds," said one judge to another in a tone of exasperation. The crowd cackled perversely.

It was now my turn. I felt great and hadn't crapped in at least two weeks, maybe more. I had survived the semi's and having reached the finals, the championship was within my easy grasp. The pressure in the contest was as great as that within my digestive tract, but I felt confident that I would win way out in front.

I took my place at the candle. The crowd, whose interest had been dampened by the last two dismal showings, was impatient.

"C'mon, Rotor, get the show on the road," said one itchy on-looker.

"All right, all right, just wait a minute. I'm not gonna let you guys down." Silence again reigned supreme. Then, a strange barking sound suddenly illuminated the crowd as its forebearance was rewarded by my machine-like efficiency. Demonstrating marvelous control, I lit off several beauties in rapid succession, each with four- and five-inch flames. The spectators ooh-ed and aah-ed, and with good cause. The color was an attractive, sulphurous blue-green. There was good tone and volume and a considerable amount of variety. I tastefully mixed in a wide range of squeaks and flutters along with the more conventionally resonant kind. I received high marks from the judges and the crowd applauded with respect and admiration. They liked my style. Stepping away from the candle, I swelled with pride and another attack of gas. Strategy dictated that I hold it in reserve, however. I couldn't afford to be caught short in the face of a challenger.

"Amazing. Truly amazing," said the second Englishman. "I've never seen anything quite like it, actually." The first Englishman, in spite of his distaste, had been rubbernecking trying to get a view. My inspiring performance had piqued his curiosity and taken the edge off his indignation. "Do we have anyone entered?" he asked.

Whereupon a brisk discussion ensued among the British contingent. The Commonwealth *had* to be represented. Hurried inquiries were made as to experience, practice and the ability to perform on the spur of the moment. Finally it was settled. England would indeed participate. The British champion would enter as a wildcard contestant.

The new entrant strode forward confidently and assumed the proper posture. This was critically important, and his obvious, in-depth knowledge of the sport put my nerves on edge. Sitting in a half laid back sort of hunched position, firmly grasping his knees, while keeping them slightly spread the Englishman was ready. This was no pantywaist, I thought, but an accomplished professional.

Tense silence gripped the squad room. Then, with a loud report, the pride of the Glorious Gloucesters, the finest of Jolly Olde England, fired away in one monstrous fusillade.

The crowd was electrified. The sound was solid, the flame of the candle was blown horizontal and the gas ignited out to a distance of six to eight inches. It was an incredible display of fire power. The color of the burning gas spanned the full range of the sulphur spectrum. Then, as if for an encore, the candle made a sputtering, crackling sound, flared and abruptly went out. It was the dramatic finale of a truly outstanding and memorable performance—the *best* anyone had ever seen!

The decision of the judges and crowd was

unanimous. The Brit had taken the sweepstakes. Amid laughter and applause, he was rightfully dubbed the Champ of the Camp. I had met my match.

Humble in victory as they are gracious in defeat, the Englishmen came over, their champion offering his praise to me for an excellent number-two showing. I told him he had the wrong man, that it was the one before me who shit himself. He laughed and said he quite understood. Concluding his complimentary remarks, he couldn't conceal his elation at winning, and in a heavy Cockney accent revealed his secret for success.

"Rotor," he said, "you've got the quantity, but *I've* got the *quality!*"

Hear, hear.

16

The reports of my death are greatly exaggerated.

—Mark Twain

In time, the reality of my absence and uncertain fate settled into a kind of abnormal normalcy for Jinny. She was in limbo, knowing little of the present, be it hers or mine, and even less of the future. She was on her own without the promise of reunion or even, bad as it may have been, the certain knowledge of how, when or where she became widowed. How long would it go on like this? How long could she endure it? What could she do or where could she go to find answers? So many questions, so many imponderables and nothing ever seemed to come along to change that—just the same anxieties and fears day in and day out. There were, on top of that, the usual problems which plague every household, but which had been shouldered by two before. Now they were hers alone. There were house problems, car problems, money problems, balancing-the-checkbook problems, illness, skinned knees and broken dishes. There were good days and then there were bad days. Very, very bad days. Every evening at dinner time, she would see other women's husbands arrive home from work on time, every day. Their families were intact, while hers was in such a shambles.

The blues would cascade over her some days and

sweep her away down a fast-moving river of grief. Gasping for air between her sobs, she was sure sometimes she would drown in it. During these deepest fits of depression, it seemed that our child was her greatest comfort. Young as he was, Jay seemed more able than anyone to retrieve his mother from the sorrow that was dragging her under. He seemed able to understand the abyss into which she had plunged and, rather than dive into his own, he sought to pull his mother out of hers. It was his job to do that, he thought. His father had told him to help his mother whenever he could, and cheering her up seemed like the most important and most necessary way he could do so. She had wiped his eyes and blown his nose when he had fallen and been hurt. Now she was hurt and weeping. It was only right to return the favor to someone who had cared for you so often. And so he did. He knew that words would help her, for her words had helped him, and he offered them freely, always knowing what it was she needed to hear. There was only one thing that could make her cry and that was Daddy. He knew he couldn't change anything. He'd have given anything if he could. Mommy was so very sad. But all he could give was sympathy, encouragement and a kleenex.

In his own way, his child's way, he had grieved my loss. A chair stood by the front door where I had always entered every night after work. He ate raisins from a little red box and now, in my absence, put handfuls by the door. "Put some for Daddy," he would say. "Daddy eat some when he come home." Jinny would find broken toys lying on the chair. "Daddy fix," was the reason.

Because this sort of thing was lingering with Jay, many people suggested putting his dad's picture away—to help him forget. This Jinny would not and could not do! This little boy *must* remember who his

Daddy was, dead or alive. Besides, even at so young an age it would teach him further how to cope with life's harsh realities now and in later life.

Gradually, with time and growth, he came to understand that Daddy might not come home for awhile. And although he always believed that sooner or later I would come home, it was his mother's doubts and the way those doubts shattered her that was his own greatest sorrow.

During this time, Jinny went to church more often and took confirmation lessons to become, formally, a member of her adopted Episcopal Church. She was confirmed on February 10, 1952. The rector of All Saints Church in Rhawnhurst was, as the communicants called him, Padre Arthur Worthy. In Jinny's Book of Common Prayer he wrote 'May the arms of Lord Jesus Christ always uphold you.' The confirming bishop, J. Gillespie Armstrong, wrote 'Trust in the Lord.' Padre Worthy stopped by to visit Jinny often and they would talk. She described her deep depressions and the overwhelming sense of desperation that would inundate her at times. He, like I, believed that love and deep emotions traversed the miles. "Perhaps," he would say, "when you feel bad he does too or is enduring some terrible ordeal. Help him," he said, "by keeping your spirits up." He believed I would feel it, and I think he was right.

At church, Jay showed no interest in attending Sunday school with the other children. It was his job to stay near his mother, and he was insistent. Besides, it seemed to him that there must be something of greater value going on in the church services. After all, that's where all the grown-ups stayed. And he liked the church. It was pretty inside, peaceful, quiet and ordered. It was a refuge from a world that seemed all too hostile. Padre Worthy was a nice man too and his mother liked him. This was the proper place to be and Jay would sit quietly through the entire service. Jinny asked Padre Worthy about this as she was concerned that her son wouldn't learn as he should, but the priest reassured her. "He's in God's Church. He'll learn." And again it seemed he was right.

It was after midnight and Jinny was asleep. She was aroused by murmurs. The sound was coming from Jay's room. Rising, she went to check on him thinking he might have been coming down with another asthma attack which afflicted him from time to time. Quietly, she opened the door and peered into the darkened room.

"You O.K., honey?"

"Yeah."

"You're not getting sick, are you?"

"Uh-uh."

"Did you have a dream? It sounded like you were talking in your sleep or something."

"No. I was awake."

"It's awfully late to be awake. Were you playing or pretending?"

"No. Jesus was in here." She didn't quite know how to take that one. She sat down beside him on the bed. "He was?"

"Yeah. I talked to him. He's pretty." Jinny was a little uneasy about this dream or fantasy or whatever it was but decided to let him talk it out.

"What did he say?"

"He said Daddy's all right. He said not to worry about him."

"What else?"

"That's all. He just said he'll be all right."

"You sure it was Jesus?"

"Yeah. He looks just like the pictures. He's real pretty." She kissed her son and told him she loved him.

"You better go to sleep now. It's late."

"O.K. Nighty-night."

"Nighty-night, sweetheart."

About a year after I was shot down, Jinny got my first letter. I had written it in September, 1951 on our anniversary. She received it in March, 1952. I had scribbled over the return address on the stationery the Communists had supplied us but Jinny could still make it out: 'Chinese Peoples' Committee for World Peace and Against American Aggression.' A peace dove was also emblazoned on the envelope. The letter was the first tangible evidence she had that I was alive or that I was alive six months ago. She knew all of that could have changed for the worse after the brutal North Korean winter. For many wives' husbands it had indeed gone for the worse. The letter was a thin shred of hope. But it was a shred, nonetheless. From my belligerent scribbling over the return address, she could deduce my hostility toward my captors. The letter was short, only two pages, and in parts cryptic. I said I was all right but I could sure use some Red Heart. What did he mean by that, she wondered. He sure wasn't saying he was hoping to see the communist light in the depths of his spirit. Then it dawned on her. Red Heart was a brand of dog food. The meaning was clear. I was eating badly or not at all. In other masked phrases I related that I was feeling pretty sick. I asked for Jay and what my growing son was doing these days. I gave her my love and told her I missed her and then signed off. We weren't allowed enough paper for more than a few fleeting sentences.

As my captivity progressed, I would write again whenever it was permitted. I wrote on Christmas and on Jinny's birthday. But a total of only four letters made it to her in almost three years. The fastest arrived four months after I had written it. Accordingly, the letters she received, encouraging as they might have been, were never enough to substantiate my whereabouts satisfactorily, or my current status, or even who was holding me. In the absence of concrete lists naming the captured, lists which the Communists steadfastly refused to provide the Red Cross, I continued to be carried by the Navy as missing.

The first letter sparked some interest within the news media, although by and large the plight of prisoners and their families was generally overlooked. It resulted in a short article in a newspaper, along with a picture of Jinny and Jay. The brief flurry of notoriety did not go unnoticed by other less supportive parties. One evening, around 8:30 p.m., there came a knock at the door. It was getting a little late for visitors and Jinny was just about to get Jay, who was playing on the living room floor, settled in for the night. She opened the door. A lone man was standing there in the darkness.

"Yes?" she asked guardedly.

"Are you Mrs. Thornton?"

"Yes, I am." He gave his name. It didn't ring a bell. He didn't ask to be invited in and she didn't make the offer.

"I saw your coverage in the paper not long ago and wanted to get in touch with you. I have a relative who's a prisoner in Korea too. I've had a good deal of contact with him and he's spoken quite well of the treatment he's been given." An alarm went off in Jinny's head. Good treatment? A lot of contact? The stranger went on.

"I think the Koreans and Chinese have really been quite maligned in the press here in the States," he asserted. Her guard was up. This was some kind of pitch from a highly suspicious source. She was getting uneasy and fearful.

"Well, that's not my understanding of it," she

responded. "I'm told the treatment is pretty bad. No food, no medicine, no mail, nothing."

"I'm not so sure, I'm really not. My relative tells me he's been cared for in just about every important way. And we *have* been corresponding fairly often. There doesn't seem to be a problem in that respect. I'm wondering if you'd be interested in pursuing this further. I have some literature on the subject, even some pictures of the prisoners."

"No, I really don't think I'd be interested," she said, wanting to terminate the discussion as quickly as possible.

"You could help us try to build some bridges and set the record straight. It would certainly help your husband, I'm sure. He and everyone over there would be very pleased to have your support on the home front." Jinny was getting anxious and impatient. She was bracing herself against the door jamb and clutching the knob, ready to slam the door in his face if he tried to force himself in on her.

"No. No, I honestly don't think I can help you. I'm really not interested and I don't think you're right about this at all. I hope you'll excuse me. It *is* getting late and I have to put my child to bed."

"Certainly. Cute little boy you have. Looked great in the paper. Well, I hope you'll give it some thought. We'll stay in touch."

She closed the door and took a deep breath. It looked like some of the war had just reached Philadelphia. Who was that bastard? Maybe she could get a look at his car or license-plate number. Cautiously opening the door, Jinny peered out into the dark street. There was no car to be seen. She stuck her head out farther and then stepped out a short distance. She looked up and down the street again. There was nothing. Not a car was in sight and there wasn't a soul to be seen anywhere in the hushed night. He had vanished as quickly and mysteriously as he had appeared.

Sometime later, and periodically thereafter, she began receiving copies of communist publications in the mail. Some covered a wide variety of topics coming, of course, from one special viewpoint, while others dealt more specifically with the war and the prisoners. They were poorly done and too glowing to be even slightly convincing. Their appearance in her mail box every now and then was a disconcerting annoyance. Worse than that, it was intimidating—a very personal threat that made her feel vulnerable and wary. It would go on for years, long after the war ended. She was on their mailing list.

As time dragged by and little word was forthcoming on my status, Jinny tried her best to find out what she could from whoever would listen and respond. Over the course of my captivity, she made incessant inquiries of the Navy. She wrote her senators and congressman. She wrote to two presidents and the American ambassador to the U.N. As a matter of routine, the Mayor of Philadelphia in 1952 wrote to the Navy requesting a list of their personnel killed in Korea. While never inquiring specifically in her behalf, the Mayor thoughtlessly provided Jinny with a copy of the response they had received from the Navy. It was devastating!

DEPARTMENT OF THE NAVY
Bureau of Naval Personnel
Washington 25, D.C.

In reply refer to
Pers-G231-EMK
7 July 1952

Executive Secretary
Office of the Mayor
Philadelphia, Pennsylvania

Dear sir:
Further reference is made to your letter of 7 May 1951 wherein you requested a list of Naval Personnel killed in the Korean campaign from the City of Philadelphia in order that the Mayor might write letters of condolence to the next of kin. You are advised that the following person has died in the Korean campaign. He is John William THORNTON whose next of kin is his wife, Mrs. Virginia R. Thornton, 1026 Van Kirk Street, Philadelphia, Pennsylvania. Any future names will be forwarded to you.
By direction of the Chief of Naval Personnel:

Sincerely yours,

Assistant Head
Casualty Branch

Killed? How, when I was believed to be alive? Getting no help from her home town, confused and puzzled, she appealed to Mayor Fred Chapman of the City of Somers Point, N.J., for help. He, in company with Senator H. Alexander Smith (N.J.), persistently queried the Navy, asking "who reported Lt. (JG) Thornton dead? Who saw his remains? Confirm or correct."

At length, the error was corrected.

17

I know why the caged bird sings, ah me,
When his wing is bruised and his bosom sore,
When he beats his bars and would be free;
It is not a carol of joy or glee,
But a prayer he sends from his heart's deep core,
But a plea, that upward to Heaven he flings —
I know why the caged bird sings!

—Paul Laurence Dunbar
Sympathy

The year 1952 slowly expired in another brutal winter. Time dragged by. No news, no mail, tired jokes and the same filth, sickness and scant, rotten subsistence rations plagued us. In the frigid winter weather, we could mark the passage of time in growing mounds of frozen urine and crap back at the latrines—one layer per day, like the yearly rings of a tree. Come spring, our excremental timepiece would melt away, much of it trickling into our compound, but with it or without it, time and captivity remained heavy on us. It was as if nothing existed beyond the wire. There was only us, our captors and a never ending struggle to survive.

We would set our hatreds, anxieties, hopes and fears to music to pass the time and generate a much-needed laugh or two. Maybe it was Christmas and the German carol "O Tannenbaum" that inspired one. It was about disaffected students of Communist theory such as us:

The Peoples' Flag is bright and pink,
It hangs behind the kitchen sink.
The Working Class can kiss my ass,
I've got the foreman's job at last.

Now up the rich and down the poor,
Make every working girl a whore.

With the periodic arrival of new prisoners, we had
some means of keeping up with the outside world.
They were our only link with what had happened at
home since our own descent into oblivion. After
contending with interrogations by the Communists,
they would be required to face still more with us.
What was happening in politics, sports or popular
music? How about new comedians and some fresh
jokes? How was the war going? What was happening
in the States? Did the people care? Was the economy
suffering or prospering? How about the peace talks?

Word about the peace talks was generally depressing. They ran hot and cold, on again, off again, with
impasse after impasse miring them down. The boys
at Panmunjom/Kaesong were mostly spinning their
wheels. Inspired by this, our talented lyricists found
themselves moved to song. They used the tune made
popular by the late and great Eddie Cantor,
"Makin' Whooppee." It went like this:

We hear they're meeting down in Kaesong,
But they've been meeting too doggone long.
While they're debating, we sit here waiting
To make some whooppee.

We thought way back in last July
That we'd be leaving here by and by.
With lots of money, we'd find a honey
And make some whooppee.

The agenda was finally settled.
We thought we had it knocked.
Then both the sides got nettled.
We found we'd gone off half-cocked.

For many months there was no news.
The Daily Worker, the *Shanghai Blues*
Were kept in hiding; we quit deciding
To make some whooppee.

Point Two was settled and that was fine.
We thought we'd soon be below the line.
Point Three caused friction, more contradiction.
We ain't got whooppee.

They accused us of spreading rumors,
Saying what harm we'd done.
But who wants to spread a rumor?
That ain't our kind of fun.

Now we're not selfish. A little peace
Is all we ask for, so let this cease,
Cause satisfaction, don't come from batchin'
But makin' whooppee.

Point Four is our point and Good Lord please,
We pledge to you on bended knees,
No more will we roam. We want to go home,
And make some whooppee.

Home. It was so far away, a distant dream with
about as much tangible substance as a dream. As
time went by, there was always the knowledge that
you were missing so much that was so important. It
wasn't just the journalistic news items that were
accumulating and leaving us farther and farther
behind the real world. It was much more than that.
Without any mail, we could know nothing about the
growth of our children, what they looked like, what
happened on birthdays, holidays and important
events in their lives, like first days at school, first
communions, graduations and all the other things
that normal folks could enjoy at will. There were
anniversaries, the deaths of loved ones and close

friends, illnesses. A long and ever growing list of personal histories that help define your own was denied us. And in its absence, a certain vitality was also missing within us and set our souls adrift on an empty sea. Yet occasionally, some scrap of information, perhaps not even directly related to our own families or homes, would find its way to us. Like a life preserver thrown to a foundering man, it would hold us up above troubled waters just a little longer.

It was that way when an Air Force jet jockey named Don Dishon joined our company. We called him Dikon after the turnip-y radish vegetable we ate now and then. While dikon the vegetable was rather dull and tasteless, Dikon the man was quite the opposite. He had a good head and excellent recall, a boon to us as well as him since new P.O.W.'s who couldn't remember much news were coldly ostracized. So great was our hunger for an infusion of "home" that anyone who could have provided us this nutrition for the soul but didn't because of a bad memory was looked upon with much resentment. Dikon was not that way and he helped me at a particularly bad time when my spirits were way down. "Who's singing these days, Dikon? What are the songs?" I asked hungrily.

"Oh there's Johnny Ray, Eddie Fisher, Julius La Rosa. Was Mario Lanza out when you left? He's gotten pretty popular lately," answered Don. My mind ran back to the day before I left for Korea, riding home from Lakehurst, New Jersey through the pine woods listening to my car radio. Mario Lanza was on.

"Yeah! Yeah! He was up and coming then. Hadn't really made it yet. I always told my wife he'd be a big hit someday. What songs does he have out?"

"Oh hell, a bunch of 'em, really. He made a movie

recently. The biggest hit from it was 'Be My Love.' "

"Geez, Don, I listened to him sing that on the radio, last day home. I knew it'd be a winner. I told Jinny that too. It reminded me of us. What was the movie?"

"Well, it was about a singer, naturally, back in the early part of the century. Famous Italian guy, you know, just like Mario Lanza is now. The movie's called 'The . . .,' uh, um, 'The Great. . .,' ah shit. . ."

"Caruso! The Great Caruso! Is that it?"

"Yeah, *that's* the one," said Dikon, slapping his forehead.

"Damn! Did I call that one! I *told* her Mario Lanza was that good—another Caruso. I *knew* it! And now he made a movie on that very guy. I'll be damned. Hey Don, can you remember the words to the song? 'Be My Love'?"

"I think I can get them straight in my head. Let me try to collect 'em up. If I get it right, I might even sing it for all you guys."

By and by he did, and endeared himself to us for his precious gift of a little piece of home. Dikon made us feel good with the delicious morsels of lyrics he offered from a beautiful song. It especially made *me* feel good to remember, to hear and to make a connection in the present with a little part of my past no matter how tenuous it really might have been. I even found pleasure in thinking that I might have had some kind of critical musical acumen. In these small but important ways, the contents of Dikon's memory, which he willingly shared with us, had a value that compounded itself as we savored each little scrap in our hungry minds. In this case, a seemingly insignificant and unrelated series of events and recollections served to pull me out of a deep depression and cheered me.

Later I wondered what it was that brought events like this together—my memories of a distant time when my mind dwelled on a not-yet-great singer and his song; the memory of my wife; Dikon's memories of the same singer and the same song now turned famous. And then all of it converged from distant points here at Ping-chong-ni at a time when I needed a lift. Was it just chance or was something else at work here? Maybe it was that same Gentle Hand that always seemed to send help when it was needed most. It was something I pondered often in the lonely, slow-moving hours of countless nights on the long road home.

Our compulsive pursuit of new information about home was as broad as it was determined. At times, it, like everything else we did on our own initiative, led to trouble of one kind or another. It was so in mid-winter when Gerry Fink and I were alone in the Communist Peoples' P.O.W. Library. Starving for news from the homefront, we were perusing copies of The *Daily Worker,* printed in New York City and The *Peoples' Daily World,* published in San Francisco. While both were American communist tabloids whose pages were stuffed with propaganda, we had learned how to sift through the baloney and ferret out some real and useful news. We were deeply immersed in this activity late one evening long after bedtime. All prisoners were supposed to be in their squad rooms for the night and the library should have been closed. But we lingered on.

Gerry Fink was from Cicero, Illinois and was well familiar with the Chicago mob, the Dillinger types, Baby Face Nelson and the rest. He had the tough Chicago accent and readily slipped into the gangster role when he felt the urge. Not long after we had met each other, I began playing along with him in mobster routines just for fun. But Fink-o was always the best at it. Naturally, he became The Boss of our two-man Mob.

An annoyed, English-speaking Honsho approached to chase us out. He was among our best interrogators and looked the part, sharply dressed, with his Russian machine pistol dangling by his side. Without even discussing the matter, Fink and I decided to give him a hard time and launched into our mobster routine, complete with heavy Chicago accent.

"Hey, Ger. Here comes one uh duh mob from duh otha side uh duh tracks. He don't look friendly."

Fink-o frowned. "Yeah. We bettah check 'im out real good. See if he's got a gat on 'im and find out what gang duh punk belongs to."

We pretended we had weapons of our own. Mine was a shoulder-holstered pistol under my coat. Fink's was concealed in his right coat pocket. His index finger made a convincing barrel. We glared at the approaching Honsho. I menacingly slipped my hand into my coat. Fink's went into his pocket. We closed quickly and aggressively on the Honsho and before he knew what was going on, The Boss had his finger pointing at him threateningly and backed him against a wall. He pushed his face toward the Honsho and waved his pocket at him.

"Dis ain't no ham sandwich I got heah," he said in an ugly voice. The Honsho's eyes widened and his jaw began to drop. "Frisk 'im, Rotor. See if he's got a *gat*. I got 'im *covahed!*"

"Hands up, goon!" I said twitching my hand inside my coat. The Honsho's hands leaped skyward. "Spread 'em!" I spat out, kicking at his feet. The Honsho complied. He was ashen, unable even to cry out in fright. I pointed to his machine pistol. "Hey,

Ger! He's got a *gat* all right! Look!'' The Boss frowned meanly as he looked down, and then raised his eyes from the gun to the Honsho.

''O.K. Louie, drop duh gun. You ain't foolin' *any*one,'' he said, in the tempo of a rhyme. But being a cautious hoodlum, Fink-o quickly rescinded this order. ''Nah! Faw-get dat! Rotor! Grab duh gat!'' Jerking around my concealed pistol, I reached for the Honsho's weapon. He didn't budge or even attempt to resist. I snatched it from the holster and examined it closely. The Honsho was now in shock. ''Dis gat is loaded and ready for *bear!* Heah, Boss,'' I said, handing it over to Fink. The Boss was unhappy as he eyed the evil-looking gun.

''Dis ain't nice,'' he hissed through gritted teeth. He turned his eyes back to the Honsho. ''What mob ah you from? What ah you doin' in our territory?'' asked Fink-o. The Honsho was silent and speechless. He was trembling with fright. ''Dis ain't nuttin' but a lousy *punk*. Unload duh gun,'' said The Boss. He handed the machine pistol back to me.

I took the gun and pulled the bolt back. A round popped out and thunked on the floor. I did it again and again, the bullets clattering down at the Honsho's feet until the whole magazine was empty. I picked up all the bullets and put them in my pocket. ''Get rid of 'im,'' ordered The Boss. I returned the empty machine pistol to the Honsho and made an ugly face.

''Scram, *punk!* Don't come back in our territory no maw,'' I growled.

Dumbstruck, the Honsho reclaimed his useless weapon and backed away, terrified. Fumbling with the door, he beat a hasty retreat into the darkness of the cold winter night. We also beat a hasty retreat, expecting full retribution for this threatening assault. We scurried back to our squad room and burrowed into our alloted floor space, squeezed between our fellow prisoners. Feigning sleep, we awaited the retaliation that had to be forthcoming. We had caused an Honorable Peace Fighter to lose face. We and the whole P.O.W. company would pay for this one. The silence was deafening, but by the time dawn finally arrived many hours later, nothing had happened.

Days went by. The hatchet never fell. Eventually we figured that the humiliation the Honsho would face before his superiors by admitting he had been cornered, frisked and disarmed by two sick, weak, unarmed P.O.W.'s was not worth the value of reporting a serious security violation. Besides, we had released him unharmed, had given him back his weapon, and hadn't tried to escape. And after all, what was wrong with reading The *Daily Worker* late at night?

18

He began to eat. He started with the watery stuff on top and drank it right down. The warmth went through his body, and his insides were sort of quivering waiting for that gruel to come down. It was great! This is what a prisoner lived for, this one little moment.

—Alexander Solzhenitsyn
One Day In The Life of Ivan Denisovich

The cook house at Ping-chong-ni was a separate building, with a stove constructed of stone and mud. Standing about four feet high by four feet wide, the stove accommodated up to three large cast iron, bowl-shaped pots about three feet in diameter and two feet deep. The front of the stove opened up at about floor level for firewood, with the flue running back along the rear. It was moderately effective but only as long as the wind was right. Ill winds blew the smoke back into the cook house.

There were other problems as well. One happened to be particularly acute at another camp. The latrines were located near the kitchen and in the summer, this caused a terrible fly infestation. After many complaints, the Chinese came up with a solution. They suggested that the prisoners build a rock fence around the kitchen high enough so that the flies would not bother them. Understandably, the prisoners discarded this questionable advice on the assumption that the flies were probably smarter than the Chinese anyway.

Wood for the stove was provided by the infamous wood runs we made frequently into the mountains to collect deadfall. As time went by, axes and hatchets materialized, but we were allowed to cut dead trees only. Come autumn, any tree that had brown leaves on it or no leaves at all was dead as far as we were concerned and would be promptly chopped down.

Almost everything we ate was boiled, including the water, which was drawn from wells perilously close to the latrines. Scant servings of mush and gruel made from millet, kaoliang (sorghum heads), dicons or beans were standard fare. Potatoes and cabbage would also appear from time to time, although in the early days these were uncommon. The diet was a starvation one and many prisoners succumbed to numerous diseases triggered by malnutrition. Interestingly, the negotiations at Kaesong and later Panmunjom would influence the menu, depending on how well the talks happened to be going at any given time. At Christmas, 1951, they must have been going fairly well, as we received a huge disgorgement of meats ranging from pork to chicken to beef. But then it fell off again, back to the old stand-bys of millet, mush, or thin gruel.

Given the bankruptcy of our diet, it was imperative that we supplement it by extralegal means. This was extremely risky business since pilfering the Peoples' food was a high crime bearing severe penalties. We generally felt that starving to death was a worse penalty, and accordingly took the gamble. Outside the wire, the Koreans always allowed their chickens to roam freely, and often they would wander our way, hopping through the fence into our compound. The challenge was to acquire them, surreptitiously of course, without undue fanfare, cackling or scrabbling about. An efficient snare had to be devised.

For six months, 1 gathered and saved bits of string and old shoelaces which I pieced together into a snare twenty feet long. The snare was actually a noose at one end which I would lay on the ground in a six-inch diameter loop. I would then let out about twelve feet of string to my hiding place which could be anything from a latrine to a ditch. I baited the noose with whatever grain I could obtain and, if possible, laid a trail of it toward the prospective victim. Having completed this, I would then conceal myself and start clucking to the chickens quietly, hoping that they rather than the guards would hear. Happily, my efforts paid off frequently and I gained a great reputation among the P.O.W. populace as a chicken thief par excellence. My labors were not without hazard, though, as I repeatedly strived to fill our cookpots.

One day, I observed a large rooster and several hens near the fence and set to work. For my hiding place, I chose a small ditch which ran toward a water-filled fifty-five gallon drum we had sunk in the ground. The part of the ditch under the drum contained wood which we burned to heat the water. At this particular time, the wood was only smoldering, so the ditch made a fine hiding place. After laying out my snare and some bait, I crawled in and began clucking with the confidence that neither guards, prisoners nor chickens could see me. Patiently I waited and clucked on. After a fair amount of time had elapsed, my forebearance was rewarded by nothing less than the approach of the big red rooster himself. He was a delightful bird—somewhat scrawny, fut fleshy enough. He and his compatriots were in good shape, so good that they could readily fly. They even roosted in the trees for the night.

Pecking along the trail of grain I had laid out, he drew closer. Then he eyed the little pile I put in the center of the loop and went for it eagerly. One more step, I thought, watching him hungrily. As he stepped forward, a single foot went into the noose. That was all I needed. I yanked on the string and it tightened securely. What a prize! We would eat like kings tonight. I began hauling in the line forgetting in my glee that I had recently broken the middle finger of my right hand. It was painful and was messing up my grip and speed.

After being dragged half the distance toward me, the dim-witted bird finally realized he was in trouble and rebelled. Wildly flapping into the air, he began to squawk hysterically. To my criminal ears it sounded like a burglar alarm going off. I had to move fast and struggled to reel the bird in. After a protracted effort, I got him into the ditch and lunged for him. He fought back like a demon, smacking me in the face, feathers flying everywhere as he flailed about angrily. I couldn't get a decent grip on him and he refused to shut up. Too much of a din was being raised and I wondered if retreat might not be the wisest move to make. Of far greater value than the rooster was my precious string. I could always go for another chicken, but if I was caught in this uproar, my string would be confiscated. Collecting enough for a new snare would take months. The hell with the bird, I decided, and struggled to remove the noose as he continued to bellow and beat me in the head with his wings. My dexterity was wrecked from the broken finger and I couldn't get the tangled string untied.

Suddenly the bird broke loose. He shot into the air like a rocket, shrieking like a banshee. My string played out as if I had hooked a ten-foot marlin and I grabbed the end just before it ran out and away with the bird. It was like flying a kite in a hurricane. The chicken seemed to be flying in reverse rather than forward as I tugged on him in panic. Finally, I reeled him in again. I was getting exhausted from the struggle and couldn't grab him well enough to snap his neck, so, for the moment, I decided to forget the string and sought to ruin his ability to fly. Holding him by the neck and legs, I shoved him into the smoldering wood, hoping to burn off his feathers. He was an incredibly powerful bird and thrashed about with immense strength, kicking up ashes, smoke and sparks. My eyes began burning and I started to choke. His continued squawking was making my position untenable but I pressed my attack. Satisfied that I had now burnt him up well enough so that he could no longer fly, and I hoped not struggle as fiercely, I pulled him out of the growing cloud of smoke and attempted to break his neck. I was in the process of twisting his head one way and his torso the other when I heard my lookout's voice.

"Pss-s-st! Guard!" Oh shit, I thought. Dumping the bird and the string, I barreled away from the scene of the crime toward the far end of the ditch, hoping to leap out in time to avoid detection. Some things just aren't meant to be, though. The guard was already there, waiting and pointing his rifle at me. My heart sank. I'd been caught. But then the guard became distracted and turned his eyes away from me. I followed his gaze and beheld a strange sight.

Half dead, the charred rooster hopped out of the trench, his burned feathers smoldering and his leg trailing twenty feet of string. He walked haltingly past the guard with his head and body pointing in opposite directions. He was still clucking, but in a choked, rasping manner. The guard looked at me with disdain and, still aiming his rifle at me, said in a disparaging manner, "Nee dee boo how (you are very bad)." He then lowered his weapon, turned away and followed the bedraggled bird who was now meandering in a somewhat drunken fashion. The guard shook his head in sympathy as they both walked off. The chicken was never seen again and neither was my precious string. I wound have to start saving all over again. Win some, lose some.

Happily, not every chicken dish in my prisoner diet was dependent on my own sometimes errant trapping skills. Other good thieves who specialized in chickens would succeed when others failed and would share their bounty with the rest. Generosity was commonplace, and in view of our constant hunger and the selfishness one would expect it to engender, sharing was a particularly admirable characteristic of most P.O.W.'s. Depending on each other, helping each other and respecting each other were important, indeed, pivotal, factors in our survival. It was an unwritten code we observed, a code which needed little if any overt preaching or publication to be reenforced in our minds. It was just done as a matter of course with the knowledge that the efforts of one would be repaid by the group. Those who didn't do so, and there were plenty of them, had to commit their infractions secretly or earn the intense scorn of their excluded compatriots—or worse.

Fitting in to the category of the incredibly generous, at least so far as I was concerned, were the Turks. Ever since their courageous show of unity and fearlessness at Pyoktong, they had earned the respect of all P.O.W.'s, including me. I had sought to learn their language and their customs to gain a deeper insight into what made these men so uniquely intrepid and, in turn, so feared by their captors.

It was a year after their show of strength that I was invited by Yuzbashim Hamid Yuksel to dine in his meager prisoner quarters. I already knew something of the customs and manners the Turks followed in treating guests. I also knew that these Turks were as badly off as the rest of us and could hardly afford to entertain. But more important, I knew that to refuse the invitation would be considered a grave insult. And so I went.

When I entered and sat down, I was given some tea and a handrolled cigarette. Then came the food—half a chicken. I waited for it to be divided but was informed that the entire half-chicken was for me. I was stunned. Even though the Chinese had eased off the Turks and given them rations of chicken—no pork—in deference to their Moslem faith, it by no means meant that they had fallen heir to the Horn of Plenty. They received a very paltry issue of one chicken for twenty-four Turks. If I ate this half-chicken, it would mean that twelve Turks would have to go without. I couldn't countenance this and attempted to decline Hamid's offer as graciously as possible. Hamid insisted—graciously of course—that I eat it. I felt guilty, but quickly realized that to refuse this gesture of friendship and respect would be a heinous insult to their hospitality and their pride. I knew that once a person had won the respect of the Turks, as I apparently had, they would give you their all, including the food from their mouths. As I reconsidered the situation, I began to feel proud that these brave and determined prisoners—these Turks—thought that much of me as an individual. I still felt very uneasy about it, but I ate the entire half-chicken anyway and honored their offer of a generous gift. It was an unprecedented feast for me. When I was finished, they astounded me with an offering of seconds. I knew I could take it with no questions asked and make a pig of myself. It was tempting enough in my starving condition, and my concern for them could easily have been thrown aside in favor of my own stomach. I would probably be praised by the other Americans for gouging these Turks out of their chicken ration by taking advantage of their customs. But I couldn't do it. Good friends lasted longer than food, and the Turks were good and powerful friends. In hard times, it would be they rather than a chunk of dead chicken that would bear me up and even bail me out of grave difficulty. I flatly refused any seconds from Hamid and told him I would never return if food was involved. While I respected his custom and was honored by my treatment, I told him, it was not *my* custom to take twleve men's food ration. He accepted this without insult and our friendship was sealed.

As time went on, I learned more and more of their language and their characteristics. I knew from past experience that these Turkish soldiers were some of the fiercest fighters in Korea. Having seen the devoted care and help they offered each other and their friends, such as that they had offered me, I knew their commitment, once made, was without qualification. They would absolutely die if necessary for those whom they cared for and respected.

Eventually, they accepted me as one of their own and even gave me a Turkish name.

"Your American friends," said Hamid to me, "they call you Rotor Head."

"Yes. Since I'm the only helicopter pilot here. A rotorhead is the hub of the blade assembly."

"I see," he said nodding. "This name," Hamid continued, pondering the matter, "Do you like it?"

"Sure. It fits, I guess."

"Good. Then your Turkish friends will know you by this name as well. But we will say it in Turkish."

"Fine," I said smiling. "What is it?"

"*Paravena Kafa*. Propeller Head. We do not have a word for rotor."

"That's close enough."

19

*Go home to thy friends, and tell them how
great things the Lord hath done for thee,
and hath had compassion on thee.*

—Mark 5:19

Negotiations had been dragging on at Panmunjom
and then at Kaesong since July, 1951. Finally in
April, 1953 an agreement was reached to exchange
sick and wounded prisoners. Coincidently perhaps,
the agreement, known as Operation Little Switch,
was struck a month after Soviet dictator Joe Stalin
died and four months after General Dwight
Eisenhower took office as President. We were elated
at seeing some of our friends going home, or at least
beginning the process of doing so. But as it turned
out, only about six hundred sick and wounded
departed. The U.N. handed over nearly ten times
that number.

Many among us who would have legitimately fit
into the category of sick and wounded did not leave
in Operation Little Switch. Lieutenant Colonel
Harrison, whose leg had been torn off while bailing
out of his plane and was replaced by Gerry Fink's
homemade limb, was purposely overlooked. We had
been using his hollow, artificial leg as a filing cabinet
for storing documented evidence against the
traitorous collaborators in our midst. We planned to
use this material against them in court-martial
proceedings once we got home. Unfortunately, the
word leaked out and Harrison was nailed when a

stool pigeon blew the whistle on him. His leg and its contents were confiscated. As further punishment, Harrison, who was already branded a reactionary (uncooperative) P.O.W., was subsequently classified as neither sick nor wounded and was held back. Worse, there were threats that he might not go home at all.

As galling as this was to the rest of us, what really made us choke was the inclusion of the healthy "progressive" P.O.W.'s in Operation Little Switch. These were the prisoners who had sold out long ago to our enemy and subsequently enjoyed a captivity of relative ease, comfort and good health. Their early release was in further payment of services rendered during their imprisonment—services that were at the expense of their country and their fellow P.O.W.'s who resisted. We vowed, should we be lucky enough to get out, to have our day in court with these traitors, even if it was without the benefit of Harrison's lost documents. Eventually, we, did, although with mixed results.

Those of us who stayed beind continued to sweat it out. Things looked up in June, but then trouble bogged down the negotiations. Finally, on July 27, 1953, a cease-fire truce was signed. The war hadn't actually ended, though. It was just a time out, of sorts, that we hoped would endure. The cease-fire was to go into effect at 10:00 p.m. on the 27th, and at 8:00 p.m. a B-26 night bomber came over the camp very low, dropping leaflets to let us know that the truce had been signed. This was in the event our captors might overlook our interest in being informed of the latest happenings. Operation Big Switch, the full repatriation of all prisoners, was about to commence. Under the terms of the armistice, the Red Cross was to be permitted entry into the camps to assist in the repatriation effort.

About four days after the cease-fire was signed, we saw a jeep go by the compound flying a Red Cross flag. They were not allowed in to see us that day, or any other day for that matter. Our captors had no intention of letting them see the squalor in which we lived. They had good reason to be fearful that their minimal face-lift efforts would be too unconvincing. We weren't looking too great either.

Immediately, there was a sudden and abrupt change in our treatment. The Communists began feasting us and presenting us with gifts, hoping to fatten us up before we got home. They also apparently hoped we would have short memories and forget the past, honoring the dictum 'time heals all wounds.' They broke out canned meats, fruit, eggs—the works—food which had been stored for an untold period of time, probably in anticipation of a future truce. While we ate it with relish, we couldn't help condemning our born-again captors. Where was all this food when we needed it, when men were dying of starvation or when others' bodies were being rotted from within by dysentery and a host of other diseases spawned by malnutrition?

The Communists hustled trying to distribute ditty bags to each of us. The bags contained sweet-smelling soap, nail clippers, razors, combs and a carton of the best Chinese cigarettes. They knew the Red Cross would be bearing similar gifts and they wanted to beat them to the punch. While it was transparent to us, we knew they would represent to others that these ditty bags were proof that they afforded us treatment under the Lenient Policy every bit as good as the Red Cross's. While the Red Cross was never permitted to return, we eventually did get their ditty bags. When we opened them and saw real honest-to-goodness American cigarettes, soap, razors and so on, we went wild. These seemingly trivial items represented our first tangible contact with home and we rejoiced at simply touching them. After we recovered from our ecstasy and settled down, we decided we didn't want the Marx Brothers' inferior and hollow gifts. We dumped them in an ignominious heap and told our on-looking captors where they could stick them.

As the days passed, truckloads of P.O.W.'s began rolling by, but our compound of malcontents was never invited to join the exodus. We were getting increasingly uneasy about this until finally, in August, it appeared we would be moved. Prior to that, however, exit interviews were held.

"Thorn-ton. You have been a reactionary. You have not been cooperative. You should not be allowed to go home."

"You *have* to send me home. Your government has agreed to it."

"We are not bound to anything that is not in the interests of the people! But under the peoples' Lenient Policy, you will be permitted to leave."

"Thanks." The interrogator shifted his tone and gazed at me intently.

"Thorn-ton. Do not be so foolish to think that just because you are going home we cannot get in touch with you. When we want you, we will come for you."

On that threatening note, my interview was concluded. At this point, I decided I wouldn't believe in my own release until I was absolutely out and in American hands. The journey home had been a long one already, spanning years, and for all I knew it could take years more, at least in my case. I knew I was on their blacklist along with many other long-term P.O.W.'s. We had been segregated for most of our captivity from other, newer prisoners because of our exceptionally poor behavior and because of the uniquely bad experiences we had suffered in the early part of the war. They didn't want us polluting the minds of the new guys and would have preferred that we not do so back in the States either.

One person I had heard of who seemed a likely candidate to be held up or back entirely from release was always shadowy at best. Around Christmas of 1951, I had run into a man whom I eventually learned had been involved in many behind-the-lines activities of a paramilitary or guerrilla nature. He had spent considerable effort concealing this from his interrogators to protect himself and others in stir, not to mention the valuable information he possessed. He told me of a mysterious man who had earned the profound hate of our captors. He was an incorrigible, just a mean, hard-bitten P.O.W. known only by his mispronounced American surname. Wootsahn, the chinks called him. There was considerable doubt as to whether this guy would ever get out. His behavior had been so outrageously rebellious, it was speculated that he might just be quietly held back, and with no way for our side to verify his status with the Communists, carried indefinitely as missing. Finally, he would be presumed dead and forgotten, consigned to fade away with the memory of a forgotten war. Many of us were pondering and fearing this very real possibility for ourselves as our much-hoped-for repatriation drew closer.

Our contingent was told to move out. Finally we were heading south. We were loaded into trucks, brand new vehicles of Czech and Soviet manufacture. Then, after keeping us waiting an hour, our captors told us to get out. We weren't leaving. The excuse was that the road ahead had washed out. Begrudgingly, we gave them the benefit of the doubt. The rains had been tumultuous that year, with water cascading down the mountain slopes. In our own compound, the mud and rock carried down from the stripped hillsides was a foot deep. To our relief, though, the next day we were again ordered to move and this time we got underway with no false starts.

We went to Mampo-gin which I, and some of the others, had passed through two years earlier. Here we would catch trains south. All along our route to the town, the North Korean citizenry turned out for one last look at their American guests. We thought we would try to spread a little goodwill among the natives by tossing out some of our goodies as we rolled by. We thought they would be delighted to receive scarce items such as soap and cigarettes and it turned out they were. They scrambled about, snatching up our offerings. They also snatched up rocks which they angrily hurled back at us. They had been well propagandized by their government to hate us even though it was that very government which had initiated the war and brought such great loss to their families and their country. They were incensed that we were being permitted to leave. So much for building bridges of goodwill. We kept the rest of the goodies to ourselves.

At Mampo-gin, we boarded our next means of conveyance—cattle cars. They stank of cattle but at this point, nobody cared. We were happy to be moving and didn't smell that great ourselves. About this time, a song was composed by two P.O.W.'s which the rest of us learned and sang often. Adapted to the tune of an old Second World War ditty called "Bless 'em All," the song expressed our feelings well. Several terms of prisoner jargon used in the tune are: six-by (an Army truck), C.P.V. (Chinese Peoples' Volunteers), sol (solitary confinement), and kimchee (fermented Korean cabbage). It went like this:

Oh they say there's a six-by a-leaving
     Pyoktong,
Bound for old Panmunjom,
Heavily laden with prisoners of war,
Speeding back home to the land they adore.

So we're saying farewell to that fat Mao
     Tse-tung
And to his C.P.V.
We're leaving behind us, that Communist
     kindness.
We're bound for the land of the free.

Oh the treatment they gave us was so lenient.
Of that there is no doubt.
They pushed us and kicked us and laughed at
     our sickness
And said that we'd never get out.

Bless 'em all, bless 'em all,
And all of the days spent in sol.
Bless all of the letters that we didn't get,
And all of the treatment we'll never forget.

So we're saying good-bye to them all,
The kimchee, the lice and mud walls.
There's no more explosions on Old Frozen
     Chosen,
So cheer up my lads.
Bless 'em All!

After three days' travel by cattle car, we arrived at
Kaesong grimy and tired, but getting happier as we
neared freedom. On the first day there we each
received a peach. I sucked on the stone for two days.
Then the food got rotten and sparce again. As we
were taken out toward the lines to be repatriated, we
asked our captors to let the Red Cross over with
food. It was not allowed. We later heard that there
were even two boxcars full of chocolate candy for us

over there. It would probably have made us violently ill, but nobody cared. No matter. We didn't get it anyway. But cigarettes did make it through and as the days continued to drag on, they were my salvation. For better or worse, that was where I picked up the habit. It was a wondrous and precious luxury that helped pass the time and take the edge off my continuing hunger pangs.

We sat there waiting for days on end. I was beginning to go stir crazy with impatience. We were only a mile or two from Americans, good food, medicine, kindness and decency. We could hear our helicopters, and sometimes even caught a glimpse of one as it appeared over the hilltops transporting freed men on the first leg of their journey home. Names were being called and men were leaving, everybody and every name except mine. I knew they hated me and I knew they'd keep me if they felt like it. I also knew that I'd never go back with them. I'd break out or be shot down, but one way or another, I'd be free of them. Finally, on September 6, 1953, the Communists yielded up their "Bonus" repatriation group—one hundred and five of us held to the bitter end. We were the last group to be released. Yet there were 944 men still behind us. They never made it out. Sadly, these forgotten men joined the faceless ranks of thousands of German and Japanese P.O.W.'s from World War II that Soviet and Asian Communists buried in slave-labor camps after years of untold anguish. Our joy at being repatriated was badly dampened knowing that other Americans would be denied that same joy and would rot in the God-forsaken north until they mercifully died.

I climbed into a truck and was taken to Freedom Village. As we rode along, I had my eye on one of our indoctrinators, a Chinese named Sun, who was coming along for the ride. Not only had he been a major source of trouble for us but his presence on this happy occasion was irritating me immensely. I resolved to choke the bastard the minute we got to Freedom Village.

The truck ground to a halt and we prepared to disembark. I was almost wringing my hands together in bloodthirsty anticipation, waiting for my target and me to hit the ground. We're on *my* side of the lines now, you rotten little shit, I said to Sun in my mind. Sun hopped out and, right on his heels, so did I, ready to rip his throat out. Landing on the ground, I almost fell over, then righting myself, looked one way and then the other. Where the hell did he get to that quick? I couldn't see him anywhere. Where are you, you little sonofabitch, I growled aloud, straining my eyes to spot him in the crowd. It was no use. He was gone. Later I found out that the Americans in Freedom Village had anticipated the possible outbreak of spontaneous slugfests between the Communists and their former captives. There were a lot of scores to be settled. An M.P. had grabbed Sun, apparently in mid-air, and told him to go back where he came from on the double. In a somewhat threatening manner, he had asked Sun if he needed any help in this matter. Sun apparently didn't and promptly evaporated.

The hell with him, I figured. I'm out now. As I walked down Freedom Way to Freedom Village, I was jubilant. The sensation was indescribable. The first G.I. I saw was an M.P., his steel helmet shining brightly. He and everyone that I subsequently passed snapped a salute and gave a "welcome back" smile that brought tears to my eyes.

Headed northward, in the opposite direction from mine, were repatriated Communists. Shouting slogans, they pulled off the G.I. clothing, underwear and boots that had been issued them. Clothing was strewn all along Freedom Way. Good riddance, I thought. The ingrates had been clothed, fed and medically treated as well as any American G.I. on the front lines. The U.N. had even imported two types of rice so they could have a choice between occidental high-protein rice or oriental high-carbohydrate rice so their diets could adjust. We starved at the hands of their countrymen while they got fat on our side. It was a fundamental comparison of the virtues and values that lay on either side of the lines as I looked at these healthy Communists crossing paths with us emaciated Americans. I fumed as I watched them and wished I could run over to plant the toe of my boot up their asses to help them move north a little quicker. But I relented and decided I had more important things to think about now.

Freedom Village was a magnificent sight to our weary eyes. The U.N. flag flapped overhead, and representatives from every service of every government that had fought under the flag were present. There were tearful embraces, hysterical outbursts of laughter, cheering, sporadic applause and back slapping all around as we had little tags hung on us that showed our names, services, ranks and so on. Some Marines were there and they gave me a cap with a Marine insignia on it. Then came my greatest source of pride, my Navy Wings of Gold. I choked up as a Navy pilot pinned them on my shabby clothing where they glittered brightly. I was taking the first wonderful steps back to the life of a free man. I felt like the resurrected dead and rejoiced.

There were chapels set up for every denomination if anyone desired to pray, and there were precious few who didn't. Four other ex-P.O.W.'s and I entered one with a chaplain, and on our knees thanked Almighty God for our deliverance. We also prayed for our buddies who would never return. We were indeed blessed by God, for of over ten thousand captured troops, only 3,508 came home. I wondered about Woot-sahn and what his fate would be.

After praying, I asked for a cup of vanilla ice cream and a cigar. No questions asked, I was given both. We were living high on the hog again. We discarded our prison garb, were deloused, and received delightful hot-water showers with lots of soap. It was magnificent. We were then given thorough physical check-ups. The very sick were immediately airlifted to hospitals in Japan while the rest of us were issued fresh fatigues.

It was then that I ran into Woot-sahn. It was as I had suspected. The incorrigible, hard-bitten P.O.W. was none other than Watson himself. He had been captured the same day I was near the village we both had sought so desperately to reach—the ill-fated town of Yang-gu that had fallen to the Communists only one day before we arrived. It was good to see him after all these years of ordeal in which we had endured separate but parallel miseries. Watson had survived his second captivity in two wars. He was a formidable man, and in my mind he seemed almost a legend of sorts. Between us was something of a mutual pride in that we both knew now that our independent efforts to resist and reveal nothing of value to our captors had paid off. After inflicting on us nearly three years of captivity, beatings and interrogations, they had never tied us or our shared past together. It was good seeing Watson alive. Hell, it was great just *being* alive.

Woot-sahn and the rest of us who didn't need intensive hospital care were flown out of Freedom Village to Inchon. Here we were loaded aboard ship for the long-awaited trip home. The voyage would take more than two weeks.

* * *

Jinny had been spending the summer in New Jersey with her parents, and anxiously monitored the progress of the prisoner exchanges. Day after day, a new list of names of the released would appear. I hadn't been among the sick and wounded, and as the exchanges went on later in the summer, the lists seemed to get shorter and shorter. My name was never showing up, and her hopes were beginning to dim. The mayor of the little South Jersey town of Somers Point, Fred W. Chapman, had interceded time and again to get some indication, any shred of evidence, of my status or whereabouts. Now, as always, there was nothing new to be unearthed. Jinny doubted I would get out at all but she figured if I did, it would be at the bitter end, the very last day.

It was September 6th, late in the evening as the last edition of the television news was going off. The anchorman had read one more time the latest names that had been received. It was the last day of Operation Big Switch. After this, there would be no more names. Concluding his reading, the newsman began his sign-off for the evening. Jinny was feeling glum. Suddenly an arm was thrust in from the edge of the TV screen, waving a paper. Startled, the newscaster took the sheet, not quite knowing what to say about it. Inaudible voices were muttering something to him off camera. He understood now.

"Ladies and gentlemen, I've just been given the name of another prisoner released in Korea today." Jinny was breathless. The announcer paused and then turned his eyes to the paper. "He is Lieutenant John William Thornton of Philadelphia. . ." She heard it! She *had* heard it, hadn't she?

"*Yes!*" came the roaring response of her father and

mother. "Johnny *made* it! He's alive! He's *out!*" they shouted.

It was pandemonium. Jinny had put Jay to bed only a little while ago and she careened into his room. Sleepy eyed, but awake, he inquired as to what had happened. What was all the noise?

"Daddy's O.K.! He's coming *home*, Jay! I just heard it on the news!" came his mother's incredible answer. Jay was flabbergasted, almost unable to perceive what she was saying to him. The thought of his father being at home was almost inconceivable. He could hardly remember what it was like to *have* his father at home. He was five and a half now, and living alone with his mother had become a kind of abnormal but accepted way of life. But this is what they had been waiting for all these years. It was finally happening, now, tonight, for real. He could see it in his mother's face and her soaring ecstasy was like a contagion. He became excited beyond anything he had ever felt before. Outside the whole town seemed to erupt around him as he heard neighbors clamoring at the door, laughing and shouting. His mother pulled him out of bed and with trembling hands, she took off his pajamas and dressed him. This was incredible in itself. Something big *had* to be going on, he thought. He *never* got to stay up *this* late before. When he and his mother entered the living room, Mayor Chapman was standing there ready to go. Go where? Chappie had said, at the beginning of the P.O.W. release, "If and when John comes out we'll ride on a fire engine." "Like I said, it's right outside," he proclaimed now. "C'mon Jay, c'mon Honey—we're gonna take a fire engine ride!"

It was incredible! The Mayor had pulled a beautiful, shiny fire engine out of the station. He then took his two cherished friends from

Philadelphia who couldn't even vote for him on a riotous, roaring joy ride through the streets of the town. It was jammed with mystified Labor Day tourists who looked on wondering where the fire was. The three of them were piled into the front seat of the cab with the driver and raced through traffic, sirens blaring and lights flashing. A huge bell hung on the front of the cab. An inviting rope hung down and the Mayor handed it to Jay.

"Ring the hell out of that bell, Jay!" shouted His Honor over the din. And ring it he did. It was a night of redemption, rejoicing and reunion.

* * *

I arrived in San Francisco on September 23, 1953. I had taken advantage of the long voyage across the Pacific to fatten myself up. I now weighed all of 119 pounds. The next day, I boarded a big T.W.A. Constellation and flew east brimming with excitement. Hours later, we began our descent, and after almost three years of absence, I prepared to set down in Philadelphia. As the plane circled the airport, my heart started racing with anticipation. My head was overflowing with questions. What would it be like? Who would be there to meet me? Will Jinny look the same? How big has Jay gotten? Will *he* recognize me? He's going on six almost. How do *I* look?

The plane touched down and taxied along the runway to the passenger ramp. I was craning my neck at the tiny window trying to get a full view of what was awaiting me, to spot Jinny, my in-laws, any familiar face. I could see a crowd of people as the plane turned in toward the apron. I strained my eyes, scouring the mass of faces. Then I saw them! What a moment. What an indescribable thrill. For two and a half years I had wondered what it would be like. It was this vision, this fantasy of reunion now come true that had helped keep me going. Jinny looked beautiful, tanned from her summer in New Jersey, dressed sharp and not aged one bit from the last time I had laid eyes on her. My son was greatly changed, having grown from a baby into a young boy.

The plane parked and cut its engines. Passengers began to disembark. I kept peeking out the window as my heart pounded fast as a kitten's. I looked out again. They were waving! They could see me! Let me outa this plane, I thought, knowing now what a racehorse must feel standing in the starting gate. Another ex-P.O.W. was with me, going through the same torture of ecstatic anticipation. The flight crew, wisely expecting a mob scene to occur, asked if we could let the other passengers out first. We both agreed. After all this time, what difference would another minute or two make? Waiting there, I still could hardly believe it all. But it was no dream. It was real. I could finally touch my loved ones again.

We got the signal to go and I emerged from the plane. Standing below me at the bottom of the steps was my beloved wife. Clambering down the stairs, I finally reached her after a journey of years and thousands of miles. It was as if the world had become one again, whole and alive once more. A verse from the Psalm I had struggled to remember at Pak's Palace flashed through my mind: my cup runneth over. Almost hidden amid a mass of feet and legs was my little son. He came over to me and I picked him up, overwhelmed with emotion. The three of us clung together in a tight little knot, laughing and weeping at the same time. He put his arms around my neck and, hugging me closely, said, "I'll bet you're happy to be back in America." He had said a mouthful. My joy at that moment defied description and does even to this day. I was surrounded by family, friends and neighbors, all of them visible testimony to the fact that I was *home.*

I was driven home in a long procession of neighborhood and family cars led up Philadelphia's main drag, Broad Street, by a motorcycle policeman. Horns blared like a high school homecoming parade and we waved to the people on the streets who looked back with puzzled expressions. As we pulled into the street where I lived, I could hardly recognize my house. The neighbors had draped and festooned it in red, white and blue bunting. American flags, many of which had been lent by the widows and parents of American war dead, hung everywhere. This was one of the greatest honors bestowed upon me at my homecoming. Lights were strung across the street for its entire length, and huge signs were hung here and there proclaiming "Welcome Home Johnny" and "Hi Ya Johnny." Later, a huge block party would be held in my honor.

We pulled up in front of my house and as I got out of the car, I was assailed, grabbed, hugged and kissed by men and women alike. My heart soared with gratitude and again I was overwhelmed with emotion. But the most touching moment was yet to come. Great men in history, both military and civilian, have had guards of honor lining the routes of their triumphant marches homeward but none have ever been as great as the honor guard that lined the steps to my front door. On both sides of the walk were all the neighborhood children. Some had been babes-in-arms when I left. Now, they stood before me, each with a little American flag in hand, waving it and saying softly, shyly, "Welcome Home Johnny." Heaven's angels couldn't have offered a more sincere, gentle and sweet welcome.

At last, I was home.

EPILOGUE

Say not the struggle naught availeth,
The labor and the wounds are vain,
The enemy faints not, nor faileth,
And as things have been they remain.

—Arthur Clough
Say Not the Struggle Naught Availeth

The role played by faith in our captivity cannot be understated by those who survived. For the faithful who did not survive, it was a solace, a promise of something better awaiting men whose sufferings were insurmountable. Watching men such as these die would, at first glance, seem ample reason to abandon faith, condemn God and scramble to stay alive at any cost. In fact, there were those who did so. But for most, the realization that those closer to death than any, those who were actually about to "cross the bar," continued to cling to their faith to the end, was evidence of its durability and its value. If a man found strength in his faith even though he was dying, how could those of us still walking feel anything less? Faith, then, helped the living to live and fight on as it helped the dying to die and move on.

Faith was thus a powerful, versatile weapon that was very soberly recognized as such by captive and captor alike. It was why so many of the arguments, debates and great pressures were focused by the Communists in this particular area of the prisoner psyche. Those P.O.W.'s who insisted on answering to, relying upon and having trust in a higher authority could obviously not sublimate themselves to another lesser authority. The Communists could not tolerate this and sought to stamp it out by every possible means. But most of the time, their efforts would backfire. Reenforced by the horrors of captivity perpetrated by avowed atheists, prisoner resistance was only hardened. For those of the deepest faith who looked beyond this world to an eternal peace, death itself became no kind of effective threat. If prolonged agony at the edge of death was then counter-prescribed by our captors, the confidence that God would bear us along through it all made the torture endurable. Either way, faith was an impenetrable bulwark for those who clung to it. In death, we would be spiritually unbeaten. For the living, there would be yet another reason, another example of why and how we should fight back.

Obviously, none of the faithful were willing to die. Faith was not a license to perish with a whimper and a prayer. We were simply *able* to die if we had no other choice. And the choice was God's. It was His judgment to make.

Perhaps the most inspiring aspect of faith was its universal presence within a group as diverse as our prisoner population. It could be found among the white, Anglo Saxon, Protestant Americans and Englishmen. It could be found among the Catholics. It could be found among the Black and Jewish Americans. It could be found burning fiercely in the hearts of Moslem Turks. It, like the cross of the Mampo-gin Church, was there for all to behold and it refused to be destroyed.

This universal nature of faith was personified by one man who could never be forgotten by any prisoner who ever knew or had merely heard of him. He was a young Army chaplain, a Catholic priest named Father Emil J. Kapaun. Captured early in the war, Father Kapaun ministered to his flock with a selfless, loving dedication. In the vicious winter of 1950-51, he would go out in the sub-zero, pre-dawn blackness searching for twigs and pieces of scrap wood. He would build a fire and carry water to fill pans he had made out of old pieces of sheet metal. Then, removing the trousers of men who could no longer control their natural functions, he would wash, boil and dry these ragged clothes. Finally, he dressed the pathetic hulks of skin and bones that were the sick and dying. Their faintly beating hearts would become a little stronger. The spark of life would flicker a bit brighter in their hollow eyes. The vacant stare of death would be erased as the corners of their mouths turned up and smiles appeared on their tortured faces. They would swallow hard, choked with emotion and gratitude and with tears in their eyes weakly whisper, "Thanks, Father."

He was a counselor, nurse, leader, provider, defender of his fellow prisoners and his faith. He was even a thief, one of the best in the camp, and so fed the starving. He credited his successes to frequent prayers to the Good Thief, Saint Dismas. He was an inspiration to men of all races, nationalities and creeds.

One prisoner, Air Force Captain Robert E. Burke, knew of Father Kapaun's example. Himself almost blind from vitamin deficiency and malnutrition, Burke remembers it this way:

By February and March 1951, the majority of us had turned into animals, fighting for food, irritable, selfish, miserable. The good priest continued to conduct himself as a human being. When the chips were down, Father proved to be the greatest example of manhood I've ever seen in my life. Although not every man slipped into primitive and savage existence, our good priest stood head and shoulders above everyone.

Another P.O.W., Air Force Lieutenant Colonel David MacGhee, a Unitarian, described it like this:

He was by the far the greatest man I ever met. He came close to saintliness. Father gave himself unsparingly to his fellow men; carrying a wounded man on a stretcher for more than one hundred miles; holding religious services despite dire threats; giving of his own meager food allowances; assisting the dying of all denominations.

Father Kapaun took great risks and suffered abysmally for his humaneness. In the end, he fell victim to the same savagery that slowly whittled away his flock. Frank Noel, a captured Associated Press correspondent, observed that, "Father Kapaun's death could have been prevented with fundamental medical care. He had two strikes against him. Of all P.O.W.'s, he was treated worst." Captain Sid Esensten, our beloved Jewish doctor was there during Father Kapaun's final days and recalls:

He forced himself to walk on a swollen leg with much pain and came to me two weeks after the onset. He had phlebitis, a blood clot. After I insisted he rest, the swelling went down in about two or three weeks. About ten days before he died, he could take a few steps. Four or five days later, he got dysentery. This subsided, but then he got a pain in his chest, and fever. It was pneumonia. The Chinese insisted on moving him to the hospital, away from our care. He died there.

The Bishop of Wichita, Mark K. Carroll, memorialized Father Kapaun with these words:

In fierce, bloody encounters, they called him "Christ on the Battlefield." In grim P.O.W. compounds, they called him more than a man—a saint. Sick, emaciated, in extreme pain— waiting in the very vestibule of death, this young priest smiled to his comrades as he was removed to a hospital which the P.O.W.'s knew was a morgue. Like our Lord in His agony on the cross, he whispered, "Father, forgive them for they know not what they do." Father Kapaun died as did his Master on Calvary, amid human filth and awful blasphemy. Of such gigantic stature do "little souls" become through the Grace of God."

Perhaps the warmest and kindest words and gestures came not from other Christians but from two Jews who said it all. Sid Esensten summed it up best when he said, "I am a Jew, but I felt the greatness of the man regardless of religion. The closest thing to a saint on this Earth was Father Kapaun."

Gerry Fink, also a Jew, produced the most moving physical tribute to Father Kapaun even though he never met the man. He did it while we were still in captivity. Fink had to fashion his tools first. He made a knife from the steel arch support of an old boot, a chisel from a drain-pipe bracket. He used these with a little mallet to sculpture firewood. The wood was carefully selected after a search of many days' duration. Finally his work of art emerged after an effort of nearly three months under the noses of the guards.

It was a crucifix. The cross was over three feet high, made of scrub oak. The frail and slender Corpus was about two feet long and was carved from cherry wood. Radio wire served as the crown of thorns and resembled barbed wire—so much so that we called it "Christ in Barbed Wire." The expression of His face was perhaps most touching of all, for it captured the common sorrow that both Christ and Father Kapaun shared, a sorrow which all prisoners understood and showed in the lines of their faces.

Padre Sam Davies blessed it when it was completed in mid-1952, and we were able to use the crucifix for the remainder of our imprisonment in open religious services. Miraculously, it was never confiscated, and we eventually brought it out with us when we were repatriated. It was later placed in the Father Emil J. Kapaun Memorial High School in Wichita, Kansas, a lasting memorial to the Good Father and the men who, like him, never came home.

Years later, Fink tried to produce a comparable likeness but failed. The problem was in the face. It seemed that as a free man, Fink was now unable to capture the emotions, the sorrows, the despair that is known only to the persecuted at the depths of their trials. The Christ in Barbed Wire, then, was a one-of-a-kind tribute to a one-of-a-kind man—Father Kapaun.

He embodied and illustrated the power of faith and inspired everyone around him. He inspired me, though he had already performed his wonderful deeds—and had died—at Pyoktong, by the time I arrived there. I never met him, which is my loss. But just the same, I felt I knew him. By profiting from his legacy, I was helped to live. Such is the power of faith and God that the living can be saved by the dead.

Fraternity, caring for each other as brothers, was one of Father Kapaun's hallmarks. He, like others, showed the way to live by the Golden Rule in an environment where one's first inclination is to throw all rules out the window. Fraternal caring was there in the camps and I am in the debt of many who extended that care to me but whom I was never able to repay. It was afforded me in the earliest days of captivity by the South Korean who had no reason to care for me and every reason to avoid it. Yet he fed me, cleansed me, gave me the little brass spoon and was killed for it. Father Kapaun did the same for others, and also lost his life. Men such as these gave their lives so that men like me might be the beneficiaries. If man has no greater love than to give his life for another, then there was much love to be found beneath the angry veneer of hatred and violence that gave our captivity its most obvious outward appearance. We cared for each other through the duration of our illnesses of body and mind. We stole food and fed each other. When some of us might be up, we tried to bring cheer to others that were feeling very down. In the freezing winters, we gave each other the heat of our bodies and slept in each others' arms to ward off the cold. Nick Leamon was my frequent sleeping mate and we carried one another through the numbing cold of endless nights. A bit of meat from a friend, spoon-feeding a sick man, making a terribly saddened prisoner laugh or just stopping to pass the time of day with another sitting alone and by himself—this was fraternal love. Perhaps it was more than that. Perhaps it was the love of God funneled through a gaggle of wretched, filthy beggars for whom He cared. If that was so, then by being His instruments, we could not fail in being our brothers' keepers. Had we failed, many more of us would have died, including me.

Reasons for being, for going on day by day through life's difficulties, can be as varied as the personalities to be found within the human race. Some live for the sole purpose of gathering wealth or power to themselves. Others live to serve their fellow man or to achieve some great or even modest goal. Still others go on driven by hate, ego or only inertia.

Perhaps all of these particular incentives can be found in each of us in varying degrees. In my case, my greatest and *only* real reason for being, and in turn surviving Korea, was my wife and my family. They were on my minds constantly. There were times I would look up at the night sky and give messages to the Man in the Moon to deliver to my loved ones as he traveled around the world. Unknown to me, my wife and son were doing the same thing. It was a simple illustration of how we were bound together in our hearts.

It was the loss of my wedding ring to the two North Korean officers that drew my attention to the fact that a marriage—a *good* marriage—is built upon something intangible: the souls of two people who truly love and who in turn are welded together by the greater love of God. It was the certainty of that love and the knowledge that it would always be there waiting for me that gave me the will to live and a reason for being. Without that, dying would have been easy, a quick release from the unendurable. It was the vision of my wife that pulled me out of a sinking airplane, flooded with water and submerged beneath the sea for two minutes in World War II. It was the memory of her and then a son that drove me to fight my way out of Korea. They gave me something personal to defend beyond my own self-interest or the larger, yet impersonal interests of two hundred twenty million people who call themselves Americans. In 1960, I was a passenger in a helicopter that crashed and burned, killing the pilot and almost killing the co-pilot. As I dragged the co-pilot out of the wreckage, my fuel-soaked flight suit burst into flame. I received second- and third-degree burns over forty percent of my body. Again, dying would have been easy. Indeed, it would have been a welcome relief from an agony that even surpassed the pains I felt in Korea. But again, I was drawn back to life by my wife, my son and a third little person who brightened my world and gave me a reason to stay in it just a little longer. I now had a four-year-old daughter, Joy, who needed me and who added another compelling purpose to my being. Her innocent presence, her unqualified child's love and a concern for my survival that I could see extended to the depths of her young soul, all called out to me, saying, "Live!" And so I did, through another crisis in my life.

I believe that to the sum of the three elements—faith, fraternity and family—should be added one last one—fortitude. It is supported by the first three, and if they are strong, fortitude is the natural consequence and product. And it seems to me that this holds true for nations as well as men, and that it is the weakening of one or more of those first three supports that erodes and ultimately destroys the fourth, in turn causing individuals and civilizations to collapse. Faith, family, fraternity and fortitude—these for me are the demonstrated key to survival.